Electronic Negotiation Support Systems and their Role in Business Communication

Frank Köhne

Electronic Negotiation Support Systems and their Role in Business Communication

An Exploratory Evaluation of Auction Use

VDM Verlag Dr. Müller

Imprint

Bibliographic information by the German National Library: The German National Library lists this publication at the German National Bibliography; detailed bibliographic information is available on the Internet at http://dnb.d-nb.de.
Any brand names and product names mentioned in this book are subject to trademark, brand or patent protection and are trademarks or registered trademarks of their respective holders. The use of brand names, product names, common names, trade names, product descriptions etc. even without a particular marking in this works is in no way to be construed to mean that such names may be regarded as unrestricted in respect of trademark and brand protection legislation and could thus be used by anyone.

Cover image: www.purestockx.com

Publisher:
VDM Verlag Dr. Müller Aktiengesellschaft & Co. KG , Dudweiler Landstr. 125 a, 66123 Saarbrücken, Germany,
Phone +49 681 9100-698, Fax +49 681 9100-988,
Email: info@vdm-verlag.de

Zugl.: Stuttgart, Universität Hohenheim, Diss., 2007

Produced in USA and UK by:
Lightning Source Inc., La Vergne, Tennessee, USA
Lightning Source UK Ltd., Milton Keynes, UK
BookSurge LLC, 5341 Dorchester Road, Suite 16, North Charleston, SC 29418, USA

ISBN: 978-3-639-02022-9

Dissertational Thesis, accepted by the University of Hohenheim on 17 October 2007
Faculty of Business, Economics and Social Sciences, Dean Prof. Dr. Müller
Prof. Dr. Schoop, Chair of Information Systems I
Prof. Dr. Voeth, Chair of Marketing
Prof. Dr. Pfetsch, Chair of Communication Science and Media Politics

Acknowledgements

First of all I want to express my gratitude to Prof. Mareike Schoop for her support, her commitment and her openness to my ideas. Unfortunately, the persons to whom I am indebted the most need to remain anonymous: I would like to thank my interview partners for taking the time to share their perceptions and views with me, since these represent the core of the study.

Further, I want to thank Prof. Markus Voeth and Prof. Barbara Pfetsch for their contributions as well as Prof. Stefan Klein and Dr. Bernd Schneider who raised my curiosity in Information Systems research and motivated me to pursue a PhD in the first place.

I am also deeply indebted to my colleagues, to my friends and, of course, to Yvonne for providing sufficient room for an academic maneuver such as this one in many different ways.

Through the unplanned sociocultural consequences of technological progress, the human species has challenged itself [..]. This challenge can not be met with technology alone. It is rather a question of [..] discussion.

Jürgen Habermas (1970), Toward a Rational Society, Beacon Press, Boston, p. 61.

Contents

1. Introduction

Negotiation is an omnipresent process across societies. Especially in high value transactions among business organisations, ordering from catalogues with fixed prices without some kind of negotiation is highly exceptional. The nature of business negotiation processes has changed fundamentally in recent years through the diffusion of electronic commerce.

1.1 The Need for E-Negotiation Field Research

As the differentiation of products and services progresses while electronic communication media and electronic commerce mature, buyers are more intensively involved in processes of specification and value creation. Examples are product and service customisation and integrated supply chains. Companies concentrate on core competencies while other product or service components are acquired through procurement processes or other forms of collaboration. Yet these processes take substantially less time than ever before. This is a consequence of the coordinating effect of Information Systems (IS), i.e. inter-organisational information technology and their social environment of business processes and organisational change. It is illustrated through transaction cost reasoning in the seminal *move to the middle* hypothesis (Clemons et al. 1993, Bakos, Brynjolfsson 1993). This hypothesis predicts a move towards long-term outsourcing relationships with smaller sets of suppliers in reply to the *move to the market* hypothesis (Malone et al. 1987), which also predicts increased outsourcing in response to decreasing coordination costs, but under increasing market competition.

A study by BME[1] and Siemens (2006, p. 11) draws an interesting picture regarding electronic sourcing and supplier relationship management systems in Germany: Only 17 percent of the respondents neither use Supplier Relationship Management (SRM) systems or

---

[1] Bundesverband Materialwirtschaft, Einkauf und Logistik e. V., a German association dedicated to knowledge exchange, training and the development of standards in the field of business procurement and logistics.

e-procurement systems nor plan to do so. In other words, electronic Business-to-Business (B2B) transactions have become a matter of course. Only lately electronic commerce began to extend beyond the shopping-cart metaphor. As the futurist Toffler (1980) sketched, the borders among numerous producers and consumers are partly blurring: More and more complex market transactions are conducted electronically and fast in dispersed, inter-organisational networks that transcend traditional buyer-seller relationships in the sense of catalogue based buying and selling in many ways. More intensive, more frequent interaction and more flexibility in prices and service delivery are observed.

All of the developments sketched above require extensive negotiations rather than catalogue based procurement processes. Contracts are changed more often, negotiation becomes even more frequent (Toffler 1980, p. 238).

Many transactions are conducted in re-negotiation settings (Salacuse 2001), where an existing contract is evaluated, re-discussed and possibly renewed, often through (e-) auction protocols (including requests for quotations, RfQs). On the background of these developments, the electronically mediated conduct of negotiations is a field that needs special attention both in research and in practice for a number of reasons:

1) First of all, it has long been documented that, from a rational point of view, people are ineffective negotiators and decision makers in general (see e.g. Bazerman et al. 2000, Kahneman, Tversky 1984, Simon 1957). They often fail to discover mutually beneficial solutions in a process that often tends to be complex, time-consuming and emotionally laden. Given the omnipresence and increasing importance of negotiation processes, any opportunity to diminish negotiation inefficiencies is highly valuable.

2) This brings up the issue of information technology impacts and organisational changes – an issue whose importance few researchers in the Information Systems field would question. However, the body of knowledge accumulated so far does not support reliable generalisations (Markus, Robey 1988). Hence, technology clusters need to be investigated individually.

3) Through the recent developments in SRM, processes such as supplier selection and price negotiations are supposed to be streamlined in a way similar to what we have

seen in operational fixed-price procurement processes based on catalogue solutions. However, these processes are traditionally of a more strategic nature. There are critical statements regarding for example the ethics of e-auctions or the fact that the *low hanging fruits* regarding savings are harvested already, making e-auctions appear less suitable as a long-term strategy (e. g. Hannon 2003, Jap 2003, Emptoris Inc. 2005). Both points indicate the strategic relevance of knowledge on E-Negotiation impacts.

4) Existing research on electronic negotiations deals with automation and quantitative efficiency measures (i.e. prices or utility values) mainly, while more fundamental questions have been neglected so far (Ströbel 2000a), such as the actual use of negotiation support technologies, the determinants of successful use of such technologies and what successful use of such systems means. It will be argued that present negotiation support research is limited both in terms of theoretical perspectives (see 2.2) and in terms of methods (see 2.3).

5) Further, negotiation support technologies can be applied and understood in different ways and have not yet lost their interpretative flexibility. They possibly yield organisational and inter-organisational effects on transactions and relationships beyond the often claimed reduction of prices or transaction costs. Thus, they offer a rich area for inquiry.

An exploratory survey study on business practices in trade negotiation processes, electronic as well as non-electronic, was conducted in 2005 (Schoop et al. 2006b, Schoop et al. 2007a). It indicates interesting inter-organisational effects: The rules of conduct in a procurement process such as a priori commitments to award business and hard deadlines for offers, both constituting properties of electronic auctions, appear to systematically increase the likelihood of unplanned re-negotiations. Thereby hidden, ex-post transaction costs seem to be introduced through a qualitative component of E-Negotiation outcomes that is not quite understood taking a traditional negotiation theory point of view.

Interestingly, a media richness argumentation, namely the idea that for example product specifications are deterministically oversimplified if communicated through inappropriately poor communication media, can not explain this effect (see also p. 27 on media effects).

This area of business communication has a long tradition of exchanging textual offers, i.e. to communicate complex or ambiguous information through narrow channels. The causalities at work after the introduction of electronic negotiation technologies seem to be more multi-faceted and contextually embedded than expected.

The following example case, which we will revisit in the course of the thesis, illustrates some problems of auction-based inter-organisational coordination. As the case was publicly discussed in the media, it can be used here to illustrate the relevance and the context of the phenomenon under study.

☐ **Example Case: HypoVereinsbank 's Wealth Management customer magazine**

On September 20, 2006 from 10:00 to 10:20 a German bank, the HypoVereinsbank, auctioned a service contract on the I-Faber electronic procurement platform. The contract covered the handling of a planned biannual customer magazine to be labelled Wealth Management through an advertising agency. However the (reverse) auction specification did mainly reveal that a customer magazine was to be produced. A detailed briefing, a common business practice in corporate publishing projects, or a set of strategic goals were not included. It was speculated that some bidders did receive a personal briefing.

While details on the content of the specification package are not available, it is evident that the services to be provided were specified only vaguely, while the process of interaction was specified in detail: All participants were invited via electronic mail. It further contained about 30 pages of auction principles and general terms and conditions. Bidding was to be carried out via the platform exclusively. While the auctioneer specified a set of communication channels through which participants were meant to be available if needed, the auctioneer on the other hand would accept messages via certified (physical) mail exclusively. Participants were required to sign a general non-disclosure agreement covering all documents exchanged in the process. It should further be noted that the I-Faber platform, a subsidiary company of the Italy-based Unicredit group, which in turn held a majority of shares of HypoVereinsbank at that time, is open only to registered suppliers, to whom a registration fee applies. Technical training for the platform was not provided but is available commercially. The winning bidder of I-Faber procurement auctions is charged a transaction fee based on transaction volume.

In this case a winning bidder was determined by the system. Shortly after, disregarding the decision rules established beforehand, the bank invited a group of bidders for further, open ended negotiations.

The case generated a lot of publicity. Especially advertising agencies and spokespersons of the marketing community criticised both this particular procurement process as well as the general idea of reverse-auctioning such services online, because that would imply a similar strategic value of their work as for example office supplies or other indirect goods. It further disregards *existing business relationships and the specific, creative role of marketing agencies and custom-er's interaction with such agencies.[2]*

While some flaws of this case are evident, it is unclear what the general effects of elec-tronic negotiation in practice really are and which model of negotiation is appropriate for which business scenario.

There is currently a general lack of empirical field work in the area of negotiation sup-port, mainly for two reasons: Firstly, negotiation data and negotiation skills are valuable strategic assets. Therefore, non-disclosure agreements are often in place and it is thus dif-ficult for researchers to gain access to field data. This is even more problematic in cases that were not successful for obvious reasons, although these are especially interesting from a researcher's point of view.

Secondly, companies began only recently to conduct complex negotiations electronically in terms of regular business practice – the use of reverse auctions et cetera is no longer experimental or driven by a hype. Hence, these technologies can now be meaningfully investigated in use. Further, companies begin to use more sophisticated multi-attribute Internet based procurement auctions, or a dedicated negotiation support system (NSS) such as SmartSettle[3] (Thiessen, Soberg 2003) or collaborative functionality in electronic marketplaces (e.g. SupplyOn) in order to overcome the limitations of fixed price elec-tronic commerce with homogeneous goods and services.

---

2   This summary was collected and translated from the corporate publishing press by the author using the
    following sources:
    Hermes 2006,
    http://www.onetoone.de/index.php?we_objectID=12177
    http://www.forum-corporate-publishing.de/showNewsInhalt.php?id=911
    http://werbewoche.ch/newsmail060917_hypoverein.werbewoche?ActiveID=2007
    http://www.cp-wissen.de/news/auktion.html, each last accessed 2007-07-29.
3   Trademark of ICAN Systems Inc.

1.2 Research Goals

The situation sketched clearly shows the need for empirical field research on the use and effects of electronic negotiation support technologies. Since the electronic reverse auction paradigm is the dominant type of electronic negotiation in practice, this study will empirically investigate the appropriation of electronic reverse auction technologies in complex B2B negotiations, and identify the qualitative consequences of such electronic negotiation implementations on the processes and organisations involved. Acknowledging the interpretative flexibility of such new technologies, their effects especially regarding changes in communication quality and (inter-) organisational communication structures will be investigated. These have been largely disregarded hitherto, but represent a vital part of each negotiation process. There are first indications for the existence and relevance of communicative impacts (Schoop et al. 2007a, Weigand et al. 2003), which need explanation and contextuality to be useful both in a practical and in a theoretical sense.

The pragmatic goal of this thesis is to inform the choice and design of auction-type electronic negotiation systems in a socio-technical sense by generating an understanding of their desired and undesired effects on business processes. Due to the contextuality of this goal and a general lack in existing research, which has led scholars to speak of a gap between Electronic Negotiation Support (ENS) research and practice, this will be accomplished by drawing on interview data from the field. Thus, a secondary goal of the thesis is to better ground the academic discussion in the lifeworlds of business negotiators and to point out the limits of generalisation from experimental work in ENS impacts. Further, the thesis contributes to establish the communication perspective in electronic negotiation research. In line with these goals, detailed research questions for the thesis are motivated through a thorough literature review (see p. 55).

1.3 Structure of the Thesis

The thesis continues with an introduction of negotiation support as a research discipline (see Chapter 2). The basic concepts of negotiation support are described primarily regarding the Business-to-Business scenario – its main field of application. As these technologies are often part of larger, more complex frameworks such as eProcurement and Supplier Relationship Management in practice, a review of different technologies and precise definitions is provided, in order to clarify what constitutes the subject of research.

In a second step, it is reviewed which theoretical perspectives are of relevance, what we already know about electronically conducted negotiations and how this knowledge has been gathered. The result of the literature review is twofold: the identification of the persisting research opportunities, which lead to the formulation of a set of detailed research questions later on, and the introduction of key constructs. As a lack of communication dedicated empirical research is identified, the use of Habermas' ideas on communicative action both as a structure and as a theoretical reference point of ideal communication is proposed.

Further, regarding the empirical part of the thesis, methods of data collection and data analysis for the empirical study are discussed (see Chapter 3); the Grounded Theory method is argued to be most suitable and is then introduced.

Consequently, a Grounded Theory is derived from the qualitative data collected in a series of interviews with domain experts from the industry and from secondary data (see Chapter 4), i.e. core concepts of a communicative perspective on negotiation support systems impact are presented, grounded in interview data and linked with existing theory. This basic pattern repeats for antecedents and consequences of ENS technologies in different roles, namely as process tools, communication barriers and business relationship threats.

Finally, an integrated contingency model of the three roles and their interdependencies is proposed (see Chapter 5). Limitations of the present study as well as future research opportunities attached to the findings made are discussed.

Drawing on the results, implications for electronic negotiation research and practice, both on the buyer and on the supplier side, are presented (see Chapter 7). Here the correspondence of relational strategies and electronic auctions are evaluated, the idea of a Dialogue Sourcing strategy is proposed and sketched.

2. A Review of Electronic Negotiation Support Research

While introducing the basic concepts of the research project,[4] different theoretical per-spectives on electronic negotiation systems will be presented and the state-of-the-art in electronic negotiation research and methodology will be reviewed in the following sec-tions. Approaches and perspectives form a matrix structure, which we will use to identify research opportunities.

2.1 Subject of the Study – What is an Electronic Negotiation?

Before introducing the main streams of ENS research and their differences, we need to clarify the definition of negotiation in general and that of electronic negotiation in particu-lar, before it can be decided which kinds of applied supporting systems are within the scope of the study and which are not. Therefore, the following definition based on Bichler et al. (2003) will be used:[5]

"[Negotiation is] an iterative communication and decision making process between two or more agents (parties or their representatives) who: (1.) Cannot achieve their objectives through unilateral actions; (2.) Exchange communicative acts comprising offers, counter-offers and arguments; (3.) Deal with interdependent tasks; and (4.) Search for a consensus which is a compromise decision."

---

4 This chapter serves a dual purpose. It not only provides an introduction to the research subject and its theoretical borders, but also explicates the researcher's pre-understanding, i.e. the starting point for an inductive analysis, as described in the methodology section below (see p. 60 for the epistemological justifications).

5 The definition has been adapted to the Language Action Perspective of communication (see p. 24) by replacing the exchange of 'information' with an exchange of 'communicative acts.' We thus take into ac-count that, especially in negotiations, not only information (i.e. propositional content) is exchanged, but also for example commitments or threats. On the pragmatic level, actions are performed by commu-nicating (cf. Habermas 1981, Schoop 2001).

A thorough discussion of alternative views in the literature is carried out in the course of the following literature review. Further, Ströbel and Weinhardt (2003) give the following, widely accepted set of criteria to identify electronic negotiations in a narrow sense.

"An electronic negotiation conforms to this notion if it is restricted by at least one rule that affects the decision-making or communication process, if this rule is enforced by the electronic medium supporting the negotiation, and if this support covers the execution of at least one decision-making or communication task."

The reason for the choice of the above definition is that it can easily be applied to identify actual software systems as parts of the electronic negotiation domain. The fact that ENSs not only provide a medium for interaction, but rather take an active role by constraining or reacting to human behaviour[6] (possibly taking the role of an auctioneer or a mediator) is the main difference to e. g. negotiations carried out via electronic mail or video conferencing – both are not considered to be electronic negotiations in the strict sense.

The instances of rules in electronic negotiations can take various forms: Rules are a form of representation for agent strategies and define resource allocation mechanisms (e.g. the lowest bid wins) as well as interaction protocols in more open negotiation support systems such as Negoisst[7] (e.g. if a message of the accept type is sent, the current contract is fixed and can no longer be changed).

It should be noted that the enforcing of rules through an electronic system is not only a restriction of one's behaviour, but has to be interpreted as a guarantee regarding other negotiators' behaviour as well.

Features implementing rules that would qualify an electronic negotiation in practice typically include (but are not limited to) the following:

---

6 Habermas (1970) pointed out that 'Not only the application of but technology itself is domination [..] in it is projected what a society and its ruling interests intend to do with men and things.' Hence, the introduction of a technology can be seen as an act of communication.

7 See p. 34 for an introduction of the Negoisst system.

- *Predefined, fixed negotiation protocols* such as requests for quotations, reverse E-Auctions or the Negoisst message exchange rules. Here, not only a communication medium is provided. In contrast to a mere change of the transport channel for interactions, the communication protocol, including i.e. anonymity or allocation rules, is enforced through software systems (as sketched in the process on p. 32).

- *Communication structuring* is the attempt to structure the content and illocutionary force of negotiation moves beyond negotiation protocols. A practical example, similar to the Negoisst approach, is the GAEB[8] standard used in the German construction industry. Here semi-structured XML messages are described and typed, i.e. as an offer, in order to explicate the pragmatic meaning of a message. This is a prerequisite for the integration of additional software systems such as planning or calculation systems into negotiation processes.

- *Revision safe document management* is also a feature that qualifies electronic negotiations in practice. Since January 2002 German companies are required[9] to provide access to their IT systems (and those hosted by application service providers, ASPs) for revisions through public authorities. This includes the requirement that all documents exchanged e.g. through eProcurement systems are archived and can be reproduced in all former versions. This is a rule that, through its enforcement in IT technologies, distinguishes E-Negotiation technologies from e.g. electronic mail systems and can be expected to impact the way negotiators communicate. Revision safety is explicitly mentioned for example in the service descriptions of www.allocation.net, a German eProcurement service provider. Transaction systems, which are tailored to satisfy the internal and external transparency requirements of the US Sarbane Oxley Act (SOX)[10], may also qualify for similar reasons.

---

8 Gemeinsamer Ausschuss Elektronik im Bauwesen, see www.gaeb.de.

9 Grundsätze zum Datenzugriff und zur Prüfbarkeit digitaler Unterlagen, GDPdU. German standards of data access and verifyability of digital documents.

10 Available at http://www.legalarchiver.org/soa.htm, last accessed 2007-07-29.

- The so-called *shared memory* is a basic concept of group support systems (Nuna-maker et al. 1991) and closely related to document management, but of a strictly collaborative nature. Negotiation support systems are often implemented as web based applications that can be remotely accessed by all negotiators. As a rule it implies that all negotiators have access to a similar and consistent information repository, which is meant to prevent misunderstandings and the use of outdated information, to facilitate understanding and commitment regarding a negotiation. Such a concept is, for example, implemented in the SupplyOn (www.supplyon.de) electronic business transaction process.
- *Anonymity* in RfQs, such as on the ChemConnect platform, allows companies to source raw materials with individual conditions, yet without revealing their identity and thus their potential plans.

There are, however, dedicated negotiation technologies that, if applied, do not constitute an electronic negotiation in the strict sense. Negotiation specific business relationship management technologies as well as unilateral analytical tools would be examples of this category.

2.2 Relevant Perspectives and Constructs

Research on electronic negotiation is highly interdisciplinary and a number of theoretical perspectives are needed to characterise holistically the effects electronic negotiation systems may have. Selected perspectives are introduced. It will further be argued that negotiation technologies are no *artefacts* with a deterministic effect on efficiency. They are rather subject to interpretation and allow for different patterns of utilisation. In order to study the technologies' effects, its interpretations must be made explicit. The adaptive structuration theory (AST) will serve as a lens to achieve that.

In the following sections, central perspectives will be introduced and reviewed. There are other noteworthy perspectives on negotiation and negotiation support, such as a strictly technical (Computer Science) one or an international (diplomatic) one. Both are out of the scope of this work: namely to investigate ENS application in a business setting.

With the selected perspectives in mind, existing empirical ENS research will be classified and research needs will be identified.

2.2.1 Decision and Game Theory View

As already mentioned, decision and game theory are the main roots of present (e-) negotiation research; its relevance here is thus evident. A broad topic on its own, it can not be presented in a complete way. Normative, descriptive and prescriptive approaches will be briefly introduced followed by an overview of the idea of computer support in business negotiations. The chapter closes with a critical evaluation.

Normative Negotiation Analysis

Founded on the idea of a rational decision maker, researchers have analysed how (interdependent) decisions should be made ideally (von Neumann, Morgenstern 1944). The core of pre-1980s research is probably the model driven, mathematical analysis of economic rationality, including assumptions such as total information and operations on utility or preference functions, which rational negotiators are supposed to use. The models derived from the ideal are illustrative and often have some explanatory value for actual behaviour observed in practice.

The negotiation task can be clearly distinguished from other forms of joint decision making. The distribution of knowledge, preferences and goals as well as its inter-organisational character, where individual parties may or may not become part of an agreement in an iterative, communicative process characterise it. It is further guided by special norms and expectations. With this in mind, the emergence of a dedicated decision theoretical perspective on the negotiation problem appears to be justified.

Nash introduced the seminal idea of an equilibrium as a fair (and to be expected) outcome into discussion of bargaining as a non-cooperative game (Nash 1950), under the regular game theoretical premises. Nash considers a solution fair, if it is Pareto optimal, independent of the scales used, symmetric (i.e. having equal outcomes if the solution set is symmetric) and independent of irrelevant alternatives. Hence, given two parties' rational preferences and the above axioms, a fair solution to a bargaining problem can be derived deductively. Alternative conceptions of fairness exist however (see e.g. Kalai, Smorodinsky 1975).

Descriptive Negotiation Analysis

The main stream of behavioural, descriptive research on decision making is tailored to find out in what systematic ways negotiators deviate from the path of rationality. Simon (1957) introduced the construct of bounded rationality, which intuitively extends the traditional economic view by defining rationality as a scarce resource. Simon assumes that decision makers struggle to make rational decisions within certain boundaries of for example available time and information.

The core argument of behavioural decision research is that different cognitive heuristics and simplification strategies are applied. While these allow decision making with impressive speed, ease and often accuracy, they may also fail systematically under certain circumstances. Kahneman and Tversky (1984) investigate the systematics of these failures such as the anchoring effect – the first offer made in a negotiation is used as an anchor and massively influences the evaluation of all further offers - or the fact that negotiators evaluate losses differently than gains and act accordingly. Face saving is an aspect that plays into this as well: Negotiators may avoid actions that would be considered as rational, if their identities (as strong, fair persons etc.) are called into question (Wilson 1992).

Prescriptive Negotiation Analysis

The major contributions in negotiation analysis in the sense of a prescriptive analysis have been made by Raiffa (1982, Raiffa et al. 2002). By taking this perspective, he acknowledges that negotiators themselves do not intuitively follow purely rational strategies (Bazerman et al. 2000).

Descriptive, behavioural decision research was increasingly integrated into such a prescriptive, advice giving perspective on negotiations, building on the works of Raiffa and others. Using the words of Bazerman, the set of goals is:

"[..] to use description to prescribe strategies that would help the focal negotiator increase the likelihood that the parties would grow a larger pie, while simultaneously giving the focal negotiator the needed understanding to maximize how much of the pie they obtained, subject to concerns for fairness and the ongoing relationship." (Bazerman et al. 2000, p. 282)

Inherent in this description are two ideas and fundamental observations for prescriptive research: first, many negotiation situations have integrative but also distributive elements and second, negotiators can not easily recognise and distinguish these elements in all but the obvious cases. Prescriptive approaches as well as the management literature (Fisher et al. 2004 and others) therefore emphasise the preparation phase of negotiations and especially the estimation of preference models, which are then used as tools to shed light on the above problems.

The ideas of Raiffa and other scholars with a prescriptive perspective are the foundation for group decision support systems (GDSS) or group support systems (GSS). In this earlier stream of research, a more general problem solving process is the topic of research. The B2B negotiation setting can be considered as a specific form of a problem solving process. GDSS research has a long tradition. Dennis et al. (2001) reviewed 250 experimental GSS studies that compared GSS and non-GSS groups in a meta-analysis and found decision outcomes improved if task technology fit and adequate appropriation support are given. By introducing these factors, findings from prior GSS studies appear to be far more consistent. This kind of research in game theory as well as in experimental GSS research, is valuable but still lacks contextuality (e.g. by ignoring social relationships between negotiators or between negotiators and constituents), which leads to further streams of research (see Bazerman et al. 2000) to be addressed later.

Lim and Benbasat (1993) stress that the insights from GDSS research can not be used to deduce a theory of negotiation support systems directly, i.e. by understanding negotiation as joint decision making. Group decision research has shown that the type of decision task under consideration can drastically change behaviour in a decision process as well as change the outcome of such a process (Dennis et al. 2001).

Bichler (1999) considers decision analysis a critical enabler for multi-attribute auctions[11] and agent-based approaches, as both rely on abstract utility- or preference functions. Game theoretical studies of electronically conducted negotiations are focused on quantitative efficiency measures and take multiple parties' points of view into account in order to evaluate joint performance, using preference models elicited by decision theoretical means.

The popular Inspire system (Kersten, Noronha 1997) and more traditional group decision support systems offer this kind of support. In line with this understanding and for the purpose of understanding analytical support in ENSs, Kersten et al. (1991) define negotiation as:

> "a form of decision-making with two or more actively involved agents who cannot make decisions independently, and therefore must make concessions to achieve a compromise."

Similar frames are the base for different ENS research activities and, thereby, most studies rooted in this paradigm emphasize and explain the explicit results of a negotiation: the formal contract reached (or not reached) and its evaluation regarding Pareto efficiency, fairness etc. The negotiation process is described in terms of e. g. concession making strategies such as logrolling or satisficing – in terms of actions defined on negotiator's preferences (such as in Filzmoser, Vetschera 2006). The dataset collected in repeated rounds with the Inspire system proved to be valuable and has been analysed with various theoretical lenses.

Critical Evaluation

In field applications, eliciting multiple parties' preferences, as it is necessary for providing decision support in the sense of Raiffa or Inspire, is usually not an option if no trusted third parties can be employed.

Further, decision and game theory based negotiation support depend on a certain level of structuredness and stability of negotiation problems to be useful, but as we learn from Simon, rationality is bounded and negotiators are thereby likely to learn during negotiations, to employ heuristics or to change their preferences (Köhne et al. 2004a). They

---

11 See also Strecker, Seifert (2004) on multidimensional auctions in electronic procurement.

creatively improvise and make use of rhetoric and argumentation in a way that decision theory and game theory do not adequately reflect (Müller 2007).

2.2.2 Social Science Perspective

Relationship and Networking Aspects of Business Negotiations

Major markets experience a paradigm shift: Market trends and environmental conditions drive business into cooperation, both in the form of bilateral agreements and in the form of larger networks with different degrees of stability. In their summary on behavioural research of industrial buying behaviour, Sheth and Sharma (2004) recall that the importance of developing Business-to-Business relationships was realised especially towards the late 1980s and early 1990s:

> "Scholarly opinion seemed to converge on the fact of a paradigm shift from a transaction-based marketing perspective to a relationship-based perspective." (p. 149)

Since then, relationship based strategies such as Customer Relationship Management (CRM), Supplier Relationship Management (SRM), Supply Chain Management (SCM) and Partner Relationship Management (PRM, Riemer 2004) have emerged (see e.g. Meffert 1998, p. 24). All of them stress the importance of the relationship view in practice. These strategies and their according technologies have often been found successful, yet also have been criticised, partly due to the fact that the implicit balance of the giving and getting idea that underlies a good relationship seems to have been ignored (Sheth, Sharma 2004) – an inherent negotiation problem.

An investigation of social aspects of technology appropriation must include aspects of social relationships between negotiators, in order to achieve a more holistic view of the business networks embedding the technology and transactions of interest. Social relationships are a vital part of a negotiations' and they are obviously a result of as well as an influencing factor for electronic negotiations, such as in the interpretation of ethically correct and incorrect behaviour in electronic auctions (Carter et al. 2004).

Operationalisation - The Social Capital Concept

One particular theoretical concept has gained a lot of attention all over the social sciences: the *social capital* concept (based on the works of Coleman 1984, Granovetter 1973, Putnam 1993 and others).

Social capital is the goodwill available to individuals or groups. Its source lies in the structure and content of the actor's social relations. Its effects flow from the information, influence, and solidarity it makes available to the owner (Adler, Kwon 2002), or a group of owners. It takes such actors seriously as causes of behaviour and collective social action and thereby helps to explain the differential economic performance that could not be explained satisfactorily before – it is an empirically driven concept and draws attention to the complexity and inter-connectedness of the real world, which complements more traditional economic approaches.

Social capital is appropriable, similar to financial capital it can be used for different purposes and can to some extent be converted to other types of capital, such as human resources. Social capital, unlike other forms of capital, is not actually owned by a person or institution, but a relationship (and hence interactive) construct and economic ideas like investments and profits are stretching the metaphor to its limits. Thus, it is rooted at the level of individuals and their relationships, which in turn may use it for the purposes of institutions, for themselves or for subgroups. Ostrom and Ahn (2003) describe this to be the dark side of social capital: Collusion and cartels of all kinds rely heavily on social capital. The authors identify three forms of social capital, namely trustworthiness, networks, and formal and informal rules and institutions.[12] The existence of trust can regularly be explained as a consequence of these social capital forms, while accounting for the influence of contextual variables (Ostrom, Ahn 2003) – some scholars use the terms interchangeably. Others focus on particular aspects of the construct, such as differences between network configurations (Granovetter 1973, Burt 1992).

---

12 Subsequently the term is used in the positive sense of networks and trust between dyads along a supply chain. The negative sense of social capital is referred to as *collusion*.

Social capital is relevant due to its prominent role and explanatory power in buyer-supplier relationships (e. g. Nahapiet, Goshal 1998, Riemer 2004, Uzzi 1997) and inter-organisational learning (Kraatz 1998). Because of its wideness and intuitive applicability and its obvious appeal for negotiation settings, it is considered to be a good starting point for further exploration. Further, the interplay of social- organisational issues and information technology (IT) needs to be evaluated.

Information Technology and Organisations

From an organisational theory view, the introduction of ENSs can be seen as an act of (inter-) organisation: They constrain the space of actions to be expected from participants in order to increase transparency and decrease complexity (Kubicek 1975, p. 44). This is true for many different Information Systems, but for ENS, this is a constituting property (see 2.1).

Considering the effects of IT on organisations, there are different models of impact: The technology determinism model assumes that information technology unidirectionally determines certain social effects. In contrast, the emergent process perspective allows for unintended social effects, even though people might try to actively compensate such effects. It is commonly accepted that often there is not a clear *impact*, which can be attributed to the technology in the sense of direct causality, but a complex interplay with the social and organisational context of dyads or groups. Negotiation research, traditional as well as electronic, has been criticised for disregarding this essentially relational aspect of negotiations (Gelfand et al. 2006, Turel 2006).

An attempt to explain (or at least to focus) the interplay of IT and organisations of individuals is the structuration theory, which is based on the works of Giddens (1984), who tried to bridge between societal research and theories of individuals' social behaviour with this approach. Bijker and Law (1992) and Orlikowski (1992, 2000) iteratively applied Giddens' social constructivist ideas into the field of technology and Information Systems. Structuration is a label for the process of production and reproduction of the social systems and structures (such as relationships, behaviour in meetings, the hierarchical structure of an organisation etc.) through members' use of rules and resources in interaction

(Giddens 1984). Thereby the explanatory gap between theories of individual behaviour and organisational structures is bridged. Intersubjective interactions are offered as a level of analysis in between the individual and the organisational level. Unlike other organisational theories, Giddens' argues that members of organisations actively reflect on the structure imposed on them – this is closely related to the Habermasian understanding of communicative action described (see p. 26).

ENS technologies represent structures, rules and resources, which trigger and recursively interplay with, but do not determine structure in organisations (Orlikowski 1992, DeSanctis, Poole 1994). A technology is perceived and causes effects only as it is utilised, while technology utilisation is determined by individuals' interpretations, goals and expectations. Here, technology and the organisational implications, which go hand in hand with its employment, are recursively shaping during interactions through a process of structuration and framing. A frame is one of potentially more than one interpretation of a technology, which is often shared in groups such as managers, technologists etc. (Orlikowski, Gash 1994).

This view is immanent in studies such as Fulk's (1993) on communication technology and constitutes Bijker's illustrative notion of socio-technology (Bijker, Law 1992). Although this view has become one of the basic assumptions in the Information Systems (IS) discipline, empirical research considering this construct is not wide spread.

DeSanctis and Poole (1994) bring the idea to an operational, empirical level with their adaptive structuration theory (AST) for computer supported group decision making. Here the technology appropriation process is illustrated to represent the dynamics of technology interpretation and utilisation. The construct was further operationalised by Chin et al. (1997) and has been successfully used by Dennis and Garfield in the eHealth domain (2003).

Critical Evaluation

The capital metaphor makes the Social Capital construct easy to understand and apply, which both appears as a strength and as a weakness. Social Capital has been criticised to be an elastic "umbrella-concept" (Hirsch, Levin 1999). Its multi-faceted nature implies problems of measurement. Dasgupta (2000, p. 327) claims that the different facets can not be amalgamated. Through its explanatory value in empirical studies, it has overcome the critique of being a buzz-word without originality and inherent value. It links between micro and macro levels, like structuration theory. However, it thereby abstracts from important aspects of social networks, such as the content of specific relationships (for example negative ties (Granovetter 1973). In general, its positive connotation needs to be scrutinised, because it may actually yield negative effects (Gambetta 2003, Ostrom, Ahn 2003).

Similarly, structuration theory is criticised for using an unclear terminology and for being too abstract for empirical research.[13] The latter point is however easily resolved. Giddens proposes structuration as a very general – abstract – social theory and leaves its application to the different social science disciplines (Kieser, Walgenbach 2003). AST is such a less abstract application from the Information Systems and Group Research domains. It has been criticised for that it applies only if technologies have already had some impact and because it offers only an incomplete explanation of the mechanisms that produce actual situations (Contractor, Seibold 1993). However, a more complete and more operative explanatory framework of the dynamics of technology appropriation and use in groups has not yet been established. Therefore and despite criticism, the structuration perspective is a meaningful "lens" (Orlikowski 2000) for field research of ENS impacts, because the appropriation of such systems, whether completely understood or not, must be made explicit before causal relationships between ENS features and negotiation efficiency may be claimed.

2.2.3 Communication and Media Theory View

The Communication Aspect of Business Negotiations

A different stream of negotiation research stresses the interactive process character of negotiations and thus their communicative character. Buyers and sellers are regarded as

---

13 See e.g. (Kießling 1988) for a critical analysis of structuration theory.

boundary spanners that link communications between companies (Clopton 1984) and thereby not only shape the transaction, but also the company's business relationships.

The basic model of communication underlying communication centric research has changed dramatically since the ideas of Shannon and Weaver (1949), who proposed that communication is the process of transferring information (as an object) from a sender to a receiver through a channel. Riva and Galimberti (1998) make the following point:

"The information-transfer model of communication does not take into account the cooperative component, which stipulates reciprocal responsibility for successful interaction [...]."

The current understanding of (computer-mediated) communication is more complete and includes the joint construction of meaning in a discourse and the interdependencies of language and actions (Searle 1969, Habermas 1981).

An utterance may be descriptive, i.e. carry information about aspects of the world or the speaker, but can also change aspects of the worlds (performative). In negotiations, utterances frequently change the deontic state of a negotiation through commissives (commitments or offers), directives (requests) or declaratives (such as accepting an offer and thereby closing a negotiation). The idea that communicating and performing actions are intertwined activities, which must be addressed from an integrated point view, is the basis of the so called language action perspective (LAP, see Flores et al. 1988, Schoop 2001). LAP is largely based on the works of Habermas.

In his theory of communicative action (Habermas 1981), he proposes that everyone seeking communication implicitly claims the comprehensibility, truth, truthfulness and appropriateness of her communicative actions – and that the speaker thereby makes references to either her subjective world (preferences, associations, emotions etc.), the objective world (facts, contract elements etc.) or the social world of norms and values (e.g. fairness or confidentiality in negotiations). Figure 1 illustrates this idea. While claims for truth reference the objective world, claims for truthfulness reference the subjective and claims for appropriateness reference the social world of norms. Each of these claims is evaluated by the hearer and may be rejected, which would lead to further discussion in order to resolve the rejection or a breakdown of communication: a discourse.

It should be noted that all communicative actions can be rejected due to each of the three references. Assertions may be rejected, because they are considered to be false (reference to objective world) or violate social norms in a negotiation such as confidentiality or reciprocity (reference to norms).

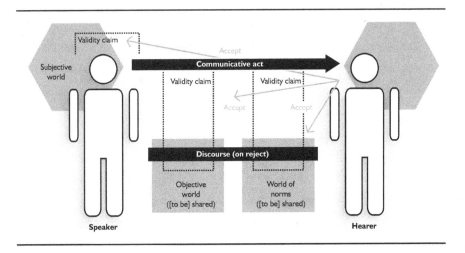

Figure 1: Habermas' concept of validity claims and references in communicative action (based on Habermas 1981, vol. 2, p. 193).

The acceptance of these claims is necessary to actually achieve communication and thereby to accomplish any kind of coordination of actions. One might object that this was untrue in the case of business negotiations. Strategic actions in negotiations, e.g. the attempt of influencing others through bluffs and the success of such attempts, are not evaluated on this level of communication. Habermas points out the following:

> "If the hearer would not understand, what the speaker says, a speaker acting teleologically would be unable to influence the hearer [...] An attempt of communication succeeds, if a speaker reaches her illocutionary goal in the sense of Austin." (Habermas 1981, p. 394).[14]

---

14 Statement translated from German. We will revisit Habermas' notion of ideal speech in greater detail, in order to contrast it with the perceptions of business negotiators in electronic negotiation settings.

Unlike the Shannon & Weaver model, the addressee of the communicative act has an active role. He/she actively interprets what was communicated and reflects on the validity claims made.

The communication perspective of negotiations has been used in non-electronic (face-to-face) negotiation settings (Putnam, Roloff 1992). The need for a communication perspective in electronic negotiation support that takes the communicative action understanding into account has been stressed only recently (e.g. Schoop et al. 2003, Weigand et al. 2003, Köhne et al. 2004a).

Media Effects in Negotiations

Further, ENSs take the role of (active) communication media. They are therefore associated with a certain media richness (Daft, Lengel 1986, Ngwenyama, Lee 1997) and a set of media effects. Most ENSs to date do not employ explicit communication support and ENSs are usually poor communication media in the media richness view (Daft, Lengel 1986). Media richness theory is a theory of rational media choice. It proposes that communication media can be assigned a certain richness and that communicators in business settings choose media based on the fit of richness and the equivocality of the task at hand. Most ENSs therefore appear not well suited for intense, highly ambiguous negotiation tasks. On the other hand poor and asynchronous media allow negotiators to better reflect their actions and to access additional information sources as needed (Robert, Dennis 2005). Research findings on media effects in negotiations are currently mixed, which generally may indicate the importance of contextual variables or the need for additional dependent variables (Johns 2006).

The rules constituting the negotiation support in this view can take the form of (semi-) structured communication, for example in the Negoisst system (Schoop et al. 2003, see Figure 4, p. 40).

Successful or efficient communication leading to a shared understanding between the negotiators is critical for a successful negotiation process, as for conversation in general (Clark 1996). Mutual *understanding* between negotiators is crucial as contracts should not only be fulfilled by the letter, but in line with the intentions of the contractors (Fortgang et

al. 2003). There is a 'social contract' in every negotiation that transcends the terms negotiated and agreed upon in textual form. If the negotiating parties have different interpretations according to an agreement, this indicates a poor quality of the negotiation process
and poor individual performance. Neither can be measured with the means of decision
theory. Therefore, it is necessary to additionally use a communication centric, interpretative measure of efficiency in ENS field research to compensate the weaknesses of the
decision theoretical approaches (Köhne et al. 2004a).

Hirschheim et al. (Hirschheim et al. 1995) and O'Donnell & Henriksen (O'Donnell, Henriksen 2002) consider the philosophical and communication theoretical works of Jürgen
Habermas a solid ground for IS research. This is a non-consensual position and his ideas
regarding communication theory are still subject to ongoing discussions. Major problems
are the simplification of the pluralism and idiosyncrasy of communicative acts and their
grounding in communicative rationality (e.g. Lyotard 1989). However, Habermas' perspective is sensitive to the life worlds of actors and their organisational contexts – consistent with the current understanding of communication – and open to different methods of
data collection (Ngwenyama, Lee 1997). An intuitive way of evaluating negotiations is to
analyse the speech acts in a negotiation transcript, in order to see whether the validity
claims that Habermas (1981) proposes hold.

Auramäki and Lyytinen (1996) reflect on the success of speech acts and validity claims in
Information Systems. Raulet (1987) proposes that the choice of an (electronic) communication medium influences the frequency of rejected validity claims regarding truthfulness
and appropriateness. He claims that with the codification of communication into a technological medium meta-messages get lost and thereby validity claims no longer hold. In the
more general computer mediated communication research outside the language action
perspective this is framed and discussed as the so called cues filtered out hypothesis (for
example Culnan, Markus 1987) that underlies the media richness theory. In practice such a
decrease of communicative efficiency may mean that re-negotiations become more common while the degree of cooperative behaviour (i.e. social capital, Adler, Kwon 2002)
decreases as well, as long as communicators do not adapt their behaviour to the situation.

The idea of communicators who adapt their behaviour to media properties is discussed as the theory of social information processing (Walther 1992) – empirical evidence shows that for example electronic mail is richer then could rationally be expected, because people consciously compensate weaknesses of the medium, e.g. through the use of emoticons in chats and electronic mails (see Döring 2003, p. 151). Both media richness and social information processing are theories of individual, rational choice making. On the other hand, there are theories of norm guided media choice and use (see Fulk et al. 1990) – here media are socially constructed and embedded into a social environment, which offers norms in the form of experiences and expectations. These structure an individual's interaction with an electronic medium (see p. 22 on structuration). Regarding compensation strategies and choice norms regarding business-to-business negotiation support technology, there is little to no empirical evidence.

This yields a range of research opportunities. In contrast to existing research on computer mediated communication, the negotiation context needs to be taken into account – the language action perspective is introduced here for this very purpose, because it considers important pragmatic aspects of negotiations such as commitments and trust. Habermas' norms, which depict an ideal communication situation of *communicative rationality*, can be used as an *abstract reference point*. They can be understood as a communication centric analogy of the decision theoretical notion of efficiency in negotiations, namely Pareto efficiency, which is rooted in the assumption of economic rationality.

Ngwenyama and Lee (1997) and Heng and De Moor (2003) follow this idea for the evaluation of more general electronic communication systems and Dennis and Garfield (2003) claim that often the spirit of group support systems is to promote what Habermas terms ideal speech or communicative rationality. Raiffa's illustrative concept of Full (Partial) Open Truthful Exchange (FOTE, POTE) is similar, but not identical to this idea, as Raiffa regards the decision theoretical (perlocutionary) consequences of FOTE / POTE, but disregards the communication and mutual understanding required in any complex negotiation process. He does not distinguish different layers of communication in negotiation interactions.

Critical Evaluation

One of the main criticism of Habermas' conception, and the same could be said about Raiffa's conception, is that of being utopian and non-empirical.[15] This critique is inadequate, as both theories claim a position as abstract reference points and not as observations. One part of this critique is nevertheless relevant, i.e. the problem of disregarding the possible positive effects that efficient power relationships may have in coordination processes, the problem of dropping useful variety in favour of reason and consensus (Lyotard 1984). Habermas' concept of strategic action and the examples he uses seem not only to describe goal-oriented behaviour in situations of interdependency, but appear to be more closely related to opportunistic behaviour, as defined in the New Institutional Economics (NIE).

Similarly, one can criticise Habermas' conception as being too much rooted in Western culture and ideals or to be gender-blind. These arguments do not reduce the usefulness of the communicative action theory as one relative reference point for comparison for an exploratory study within a western society. While the shortcomings of human (electronic) negotiation behaviour in relation to traditional economic rationality are well documented, e.g. in prospect theory, we know little regarding possible shortcomings in relation to communicative rationality.

2.3 Electronic Negotiation Support

Negotiation is a crucial activity in numerous economic and social settings. Any improvement in the efficiency of negotiation processes or of outcomes would, therefore, have strong effects. Electronic negotiation support research has worked towards this goal with two distinct approaches: the automation of negotiation processes (Sandholm 1999, Peters 2000) and the provision of tools to support human negotiators. These ideas have led to a

---

15 Habermas' concepts are often used to describe the Internet or computer mediated communication in general as enabling improvements of the public sphere in a society by fostering the democratic and fair discussion among large numbers of citizens (see Poster 1995). On the other hand his call for rationalism in the society is criticised by post-modernists like Lyotard as, despite his intentions, leading to efficient and consensual but totalitarian regimes. These discussions are mainly of political and ethical nature and will not be covered in greater detail here.

stream of research on negotiation agents rooted in Computer Science and Artificial Intelligence on the one hand and to a stream of research summarised as negotiation support systems (NSS), including aspects of group decision support (GDSS) and computer supported cooperative work (CSCW) on the other hand.

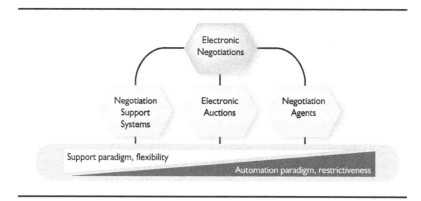

Figure 2: Electronic negotiation typology.

The predominant electronic auction research can be seen as an intermediate stream (see Figure 2), because auctions automatise negotiation activities by means of mechanisms, but retain decisions in human hands. However, the threefold classification is not strictly disjoint as hybrid systems are developed and allow an ad hoc engineering of electronic negotiation systems (Bichler et al. 2003) on a case by case basis. The three classes of negotiation software systems will be introduced and reviewed in the next paragraphs.

2.3.1 Electronic Auction Research

Electronic auctions and RfQs (request for quotation) have become very popular in business-to-business commerce in recent years (Ströbel 2000b) and a plethora of concepts and special auction models has been introduced to a number of markets. It can be argued that electronic auctions have by now (i.e. after the dot.com hype) reached a status of considerable adoption rates as well as a healthy scepticism, which enables a structured empirical analysis of technology effects.

The Electronic Auction Concept

The electronic auction (E-Auction) term in a business environment most often refers to the case of a procurement auction, also known as a reverse auction, electronic reverse auction (E-RA, Emiliani 2004), online auction, or online bidding event, due to the prevalence of buyer markets. It is subsequently used here with this meaning.

The general process schema of electronic (reverse) auctions (for a detailed analysis see e.g. Bichler 2001b, Dani et al. 2005) is often a variation of the following process:

1. Demand is identified in an organisation; the sourcing department takes the initiative.
2. A specification of the goods or services is prepared and coordinated internally. Decisions regarding scheduling, lotting and pooling need to be made.
3. The sourcing process is planned, e.g. auction rules are defined. This may include the selection of and interaction with an intermediary or auction technology provider.
4. Potential suppliers are selected and invited to participate (often via electronic mail), auction rules as well as terms and conditions are provided to suppliers.
5. Potential suppliers are selected if they can be expected to satisfy basic quality requirements
6. Selected suppliers are notified and provided with detailed specifications
7. The auction or RfQ runs for a limited time – during this time suppliers have the opportunity to make offers i.e. bids. In the RfQ-case they are limited to a single bid, which is kept confidential. In the reverse auction case, information about the bids is communicated to all parties and multiple competitive bids can be made consequentially.
8. The winner[16] is determined and awarded a contract, transaction fees might apply.

In this view, an RfQ can be considered to be a single-round, sealed bid reverse auction. Here, in line with Kersten and Bichler, auctions are seen as a special, distributive kind of negotiation. This understanding is subject to discussion, and new auctioning mechanisms such as electronic multi-attributive auctions further blur the border between these concepts and allow e. g. logrolling during auctions (Kersten et al. 2000, Bichler 2001b).

---

16 There are auction mechanisms, such as combinatorial auctions, where multiple winners can be expected. See (Bichler 2001b).

The auction paradigm is characterised by the understanding of negotiation tasks as distributive, decentralised resource allocation problems, to be addressed with a resource allocation mechanism. McAfee and McMillan (1996) define this special form of a negotiation as follows.

"An auction is a market institution with an explicit set of rules determining resource allocation and prices on the basis of bids from the market participants."

Online bid mechanisms work according to the known auction principles (such as open vs. sealed and ascending vs. descending) and the best (possibly multi-attribute) bid (or set of bids) is computed according to a fixed algorithm (Peters 2000, Bichler 2001b). Roughly speaking, game theory claims that competitive market mechanisms such as auctions in general work better than bargaining (McAfee, McMillan 1996), i.e. they yield better results due to their competitive nature and are independent of negotiator skills. In theory, they can thus be considered fairer than multilateral bargaining as all bidders are treated equally. Therefore, they are often applied in public procurement.

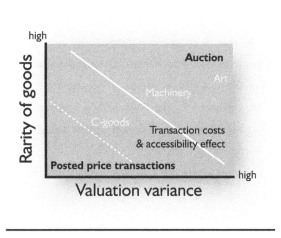

Figure 3: Internet impact on the application of auctions (based on Pinker et al. 2003).

The popularity of online auctions and online RfQs has two main reasons according to Pinker et al. (2003), namely reduced transaction costs and increased accessibility of transaction related information through the interconnected Information Systems available (see Figure 3).

The focus of transaction cost theory, which is based on the works of Coase (1937) and Williamson (1975, 1985), is a single exchange relationship between two or more agents. Regarding the exchange relationship it is not the (physical) exchange of goods that is covered by transaction cost theory but the logically separate 'logistics' of property rights (Picot et al. 2005). According to Picot et al. (2005), transaction costs are all disadvantages which agents have in order to implement an exchange relationship. They are not limited to quantified components but include disadvantages such as the need for contract monitoring. Since the original understanding of the term as given by Coase (1937) was too vague for empirical analysis, Williamson (1975, 1985) introduced a more detailed framework with the analysis of contracts in its centre.

According to Williamson (1985, p. 52) the critical dimensions that favour one form of contracting over another are asset specifity, uncertainty and frequency (based on Picot et al. 2005):

- Specifity can be found, for example, in machinery dedicated to certain customers. Specifity is, however, not constant, but can change over time, e.g. through growing know-how dependencies. There is an increased potential for opportunistic behaviour in the presence of relationship specific investments.

- Uncertainty is a measure for the likeliness and frequency of changes of a service specification. Controlling the execution of contracts also causes uncertainty driven transaction costs.

- Frequency influences transaction costs because different coordination forms call for different a priori investments. This is mainly the case in combination with specifity.

Consequently, economists agree that auctions traditionally are methods of price discovery and price discrimination. Therefore, auctions are traditionally applied for goods whose valuation is either uncertain or variable across market participants. Auctions are traditionally applied when goods are rare, such as art objects or, more generally, when market demand exceeds market offer. This is certainly correlated with the value of goods – for low value transactions, the high transaction costs associated with traditional auctions, involving the co-located synchronous communication of numerous persons, prevents their use. For high value transactions, numerous auctions or auction-like activities (Subramanian, Zeckhauser 2005) are conducted. Internet technologies can be argued to increase the variety of goods for which auction style transactions are suitable (Klein, O'Keefe 1999, Pinker et al. 2003). Low-value goods can be auctioned with acceptable transactions costs and auctioneers can benefit from smaller valuation variances, drawn from larger samples.

Multi-attribute, multi-unit or combinatorial auctions further extend the auction portfolio (Bichler 2001b). They can be understood as enabled by information technologies, because they depend on complex calculations or immediate feedback. Agent negotiation systems often use auction protocols and the effect of their use can be argued to be similar.

Electronic Auction Applications

Business sectors with scientifically documented applications of online auctions include for example the automotive industry (Jap 2003), the Dutch flower industry (Van Heck, Ribbers 1999), the tourist industry (Bichler 2001a), and the financial market (Bichler 2003). The automotive industry had the role of early adopters using online reverse auctions for a large share of their total sourcing volume in the famous Covisint consortium in February 2000 (see e.g. Henke 2000), which failed in its role as a marketplace due to the heterogeneity of requirements from the consortium and lacking acceptance on the supplier side among other problems finally. After the dot.com hype, a phase of consolidation among marketplaces and auction technology providers cut down their number.

Since then, post-hype electronic commerce matured and a reduced set of auction platforms operate profitably. Further, auction technologies are applied both as buy-side procurement platforms and as outsourced, application service-provider settings that keep investments to a minimum. Examples of major software and service providers for commercial procurement negotiation processes in the auction paradigm are shown in Table 1.

URL	Short description
www.click2procure.com	Siemens' procurement marketplace, based on game theoretical principles and Commerce One technologies
www.ariba.com	Solution provider for e-auction and RFQ technologies
www.covisint.com	Automotive e-procurement marketplace lead by a consortium of OEM's; early adopter which moved away from the auction marketplace paradigm and is mainly a technology provider now
www.supplyon.com	First tier supplier lead marketplace in the automotive industry, which includes e-auctions and RfQs.
www.emptoris.com	Solution provider for e-auction and RFQ / negotiation technologies, winner of the 2004 Franz Edelman Award for Achievement in Operations Research and the Management Sciences. The sourcing module is applied by other parties such as www.ibxeurope.com.
www.meet2trade.com	Academic auction suite for market engineering and auction experiments developed at Karlsruhe University.
www.chemconnect.com	An online marketplace for chemical goods including both auction and RFQ functionality as well as more open message exchange facilities while controlling e.g. for buyer anonymity.

Table 1: Examples of auction-based E-Negotiation products, services, and applications.

Strict application of (reverse) e-auctions as a long-term sourcing strategy and the relationship implications of the approach have raised a number of concerns (Henke 2000, Daly, Nath 2005, Emiliani, Stec 2005, Daly, Nath 2005b), because it is perceived as being unethical in existing business relationships or because it may drive suppliers out of the market and thereby may lead to a shift in bargaining power in the long run (Jap 2003). Most platforms are therefore not limited to the provision of a competitive allocation mechanism, but increasingly move towards more collaborative services.[17]

Empirical Research

Empirical research on online auctions from an economics / electronic commerce point of view is, although scarce, the most common among ENSs researched and often utilises price reductions as measures and game theoretical arguments (e.g. Güth et al. 2002, Strecker, Seifert 2004, Pearcy et al. 2007). Emiliani and Stec (2002) fall into this category as well as Reyes-Moro et al. (2003), Schwab (2003), Stein et al. (2003) and Carter et al.

---

17 This increases their importance in the role of communication media which will be discussed in detail in the results section.

(2004). The click2procure platform is explicitly based on game theoretical considerations (Müller-Lankenau, Klein 2003).

Kaufmann and Carter (2004, 2007), Schwab and Stein also address communication and social science issues. Carter et al. as well as Jap (2003) focus on the perception of ethical and unethical behaviour in reverse auctions. These works can currently be considered as exceptional in their openness and theoretical point of view.

2.3.2 Negotiation Support Systems Research

The Negotiation Support System Approach

In a further stream of research, a shift to more complex negotiations and the recognition of the need for computer support of human activity instead of automation can be observed. The negotiation support paradigm has been first researched by Kersten (1985), Jarke et al. (1986, 1987) as well as Jelassi and Fouroughi (1989) and it is rooted in earlier group decision support research. Negotiations here are metaphorically described as a human activity, namely

> "an art and a science, based on interpersonal skills, the ability to employ a basketful of bargaining ploys, and the wisdom to know when and how to use them." (Raiffa 1982)

Since then, there has been a tradition of building and researching NSS prototypes in experiments. While the first wave of research was rooted in the decision support (i.e. science) view, there is a second wave of NSS research grounded in the wider electronic commerce view, i.e. the provision of efficient negotiation media (Yuan et al. 1998, Kersten, Noronha 1997, Schoop et al. 2002, Schoop et al. 2003, Rebstock, Thun 2002) with sufficient room for the execution of negotiation art. The procurement platforms mentioned in the electronic auction section can be argued to gradually approach the NSS paradigm and the conceptual borders between open bargaining and auctions are blurred (Subramanian, Zeckhauser 2005).

Negotiation Support System Applications

The following table gives an overview of examples of these technologies. Another stream of research activity analyses similar technologies for dispute resolution purposes – an application that will not be considered any further in this study nor will the technologies dedicated to this purpose.

URL / System	Short description
www.smartsettle.com	A platform for bilateral negotiation, mediation and dispute resolution, which makes extensive use of utility models.
www.negoisst.de	Academic system rooted in open interaction processes of SMEs, based on semi-structured communication support as well as decision analytical support and document management.
CBSS	Academic, web-based system with real-time communication and preference analysis tools.
PERSUADER	A system that facilitates argumentation by constructing and adapting arguments with a case-based reasoning process.
www.interneg.org	Home of two academic ENS systems, Inspire and INVITE, used mainly for teaching, training and experimentation on a large scale with a focus on decision analysis and optimisation.

Table 2: Examples of negotiation support systems.

The Inspire system (Kersten, Noronha 1997), the most popular NSS, has been used in various experimental studies with different objectives (e.g. Vetschera et al. 2003, Filzmoser, Vetschera 2006). Inspire is a teaching and training system, which offers a set of decision support and communication functionalities. Negotiators explicate preferences for all negotiated issues and these preferences are used to evaluate each (counter-) offer and to analyse agreements for (Pareto-) optimality. Yuan et al. (1998) distinguish two categories of NSSs, which correspond with Raiffa's twofold understanding of negotiations.

Due to its optimisation feature, the Inspire system can be considered to be an example of the solution driven NSS category. The commercial SmartSettle system (www.smartsettle.com) falls into this category as well. On the other hand, process driven NSSs are tailored to provide enriched communication channels and facilitate cooperative work. Examples of process driven NSSs are CBSS (Yuan et al. 1998), PERSUADER (Sycara 1990) and Negoisst (Schoop et al. 2003), while the latter is positioned to bridge between process and solution driven NSSs.

To illustrate the idea of process driven NSS we will focus on the Negoisst system (see Figure 4). The foundations that underlie the web-based Negoisst system are twofold.

First, it guides and clarifies asynchronous text message communication in negotiation processes through explication, i.e. annotation of semantics[18] and pragmatics.[19] Messages contain semantically tagged elements, such as the word *price* in a sentence, and an according value. On demand, the reader is referred to an ontological definition of the term and its relationships to other concepts (e.g. such as *excludes VAT* in this case). If appropriate, OWL-ontologies (Web Ontology Language) exist in a community of practice (or can be agreed upon if necessary). This technique greatly reduces the likelihood of costly misunderstandings on the semantic level.

---

18 See www.semanticweb.org
19 See www.pragmaticweb.info

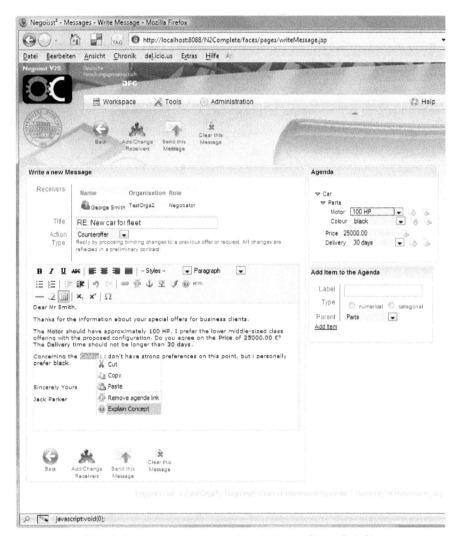

Figure 4 : Semi-structured message exchange in Negoisst (Version 2, draft).

On the pragmatic level, a similar approach is employed. Each message in the system is annotated with a message type that indicates the illocutionary point, i.e. the intention of the sender, such as request, offer, question or accept. The set of types offered is derived from experiments and from empirical field research (Schoop 2002). Given a particular message, the system ensures the consistency of follow-up replies. For example, each question can only be answered with a message of the clarification type and after an accept- (or reject-) typed message is sent, no more offers can be exchanged. Again, misunderstandings are prevented through explication.

Second, drawing on such annotations of requests, offers and the meaning of key issues negotiated, the system is able to integrate the contract document perspective (DOC.-COM, Schoop, Quix 2001) and a utility model (such as in Inspire, Kersten, Noronha 1997) with the exchange of messages. Practically, this means that the utility value or the desirability of each offer is estimated in order to visualise the pattern of the negotiation dance. Further, the system ensures that questions are answered with clarifications and that the process of interaction is fair and permanently documented, i.e. that commitments are credible and can not be withdrawn. For each formal message sent, the system derives the potential contract which would result, if the claims made were accepted.

Empirical Research

There is a considerable diversity of experimental empirical research conducted and documented throughout the NSS community. The majority of published papers uses outcome related variables such as joint and individual utility values, Pareto efficiency, agreement rates (e.g. Foroughi et al. 1995, Delaney et al. 1997, Kersten, Noronha 1997, Rangaswamy, Shell 1997, Goh et al. 2000, Schoop et al. 2007b) or satisfaction (e.g. Yuan et al. 1998, Vetschera et al. 2003, Chen, Weber 2006).

On the other hand, a dynamic process analysis perspective is currently emerging. Studies of this type either take the iterative exchange of offers into focus (e.g. Köhne et al. 2005, Filzmoser, Vetschera 2006, Reiser, Schoop 2007), or employ content analysis on a more detailed level, in order to take further parameter such as emotional behaviour into account (e.g. Köszegi et al. 2004, Graf et al. 2006, Köszegi et al. 2007).

NSSs are not yet widely adopted in industry and hence field research on NSS is scarce (e.g. Lim et al. 2002). Dedicated field studies on NSS impact do not yet exist.

2.3.3 Negotiation Agent Research

The Negotiation Agent Approach

During the 1980s Artificial Intelligence (AI) euphoria, negotiation was identified as a promising field for the application of AI methods (Davis, Smith 1983) and research on agent based negotiation is ongoing (see e.g. Macredie 1998, Maes et al. 1999, Sandholm 1999, Peters 2000, Dignum, Cortés 2001, Kersten, Lo 2003, Oliver 2005, Kakas, Moraitis 2006). There are different motivations for the development of computational negotiation agents: Virtual enterprises or alliances may require ad hoc coordination with high frequency or time pressure. Both situations call for an automated solution. The low variable transaction costs of such interactions may enable dynamic coordination in settings, which relied on less flexible forms of contracting hitherto, such as in case of the allocation of computation capacity or networking resources.

The AI approach to problem solving is to represent problems as a solution space (for example a tree). Solving the problem is then reduced to a question of efficient (joint) search in that space. Consequently, in agent centric ENS research, negotiation is defined along the lines of the following wording:

"The essence of negotiation is two or more parties trying to arrive at a single agreement from a set – often large – of potential agreements." (Oliver 2005)

If the joint search in such a solution space is performed by goal-driven software entities, we speak of agent-based negotiations. Depending on the goals, which the agents have, they can be categorised as self-interested (i.e. they maximize individual utility) or cooperative (i.e. they maximize overall social utility) in an approach of distributed problem solving (Zhang et al. 2006). The main motivation of the agent negotiation idea is that maximising overall social utility is inherently difficult and requires a global view. Acquiring a global view is regularly costly in terms of communication and computation or impossible to achieve. A community of self-interested agents or multi-agent system (MAS) can constitute a market, which performs reasonably efficient without any global view.

Negotiation Agent Applications

The following table lists a set of selected negotiation agent approaches, which can serve as a starting point to the technology.

URL / System	Short description
Kasbah (inactive) Tête-à-tête (inactive)	Both by MIT Media Labs. Kasbah is a centralised agent marketplace where agents pro-actively search transaction partners and negotiate with them on bilaterally on a single attribute for mutually acceptable deals. Tête-à-tête is similar to Kasbah, but multi-attribute negotiation tasks relying on utility theory.
http://tac.eecs.umich.edu/	The Trading Agent Competition, a competition designed as a benchmark for market design and automated trading in supply chain scenarios.
http://jade.tilab.com/	Java toolset for multi-agent development and application.

Table 3: Examples of negotiation agent technologies.

The basic two problems, which agent developers face in negotiations, are the ontology problem, i.e. how to make artificial agents understand each other's perception of the search space at hand, and the strategy problem, i.e. how should they try to reach a given goal in cooperation with other agents and how to brief an agent with such a strategy (see e.g. Dumas et al. 2002, Rahwan et al. 2007). Multiple agent based ENS prototypes (Jennings, Wooldridge 1998) have been positioned between the extremes of oversimplified assumptions and the complexity of the real world. Negotiation agent systems frequently apply communication protocols rooted in speech act theory and simple auction-based negotiation protocols.

Although the search paradigm and subsequent solutions based on it are one of the most successful contributions of AI research yet, it makes strong assumptions according to the structuredness of the problem space and the protocol used for jointly searching within it. Regularly, proposals made by the negotiation agents denote single points in the solution space, the only feedback available is a counter-proposal, an acceptance or a withdrawal; the set of issues is assumed not to change (Kakas, Moraitis 2006).

There are argumentation-based approaches to agent negotiations that go beyond the iterating exchange of positions in an offer space. According protocols have been proposed (e.g. Kakas, Moraitis 2006), but little practical experience with such approaches exists.

Empirical Research

The very size of the solution space or the fact that it may be ambiguously defined, dynamically growing or changing, may also limit the applicability of the idea for many settings in the real world. Consequently, the predominant methods of empirical evaluation for negotiation agent approaches are the scenario technique and the simulation experiment (e.g. in Zhang et al. 2006). This implies an evaluation in a technical sense and not in the sociotechnical sense of Information Systems.

2.3.5 Methods of Electronic Negotiation Research

In electronic negotiation research, we find both model driven methods, which e.g. discuss strategic options in negotiation games and argue on equilibria in markets, as well as empirical methods being used.

By analysing contributions to, for example, the Group Decision and Negotiation conference or the Journal of Group Decision and Negotiation, it is evident that empirical negotiation support research is largely experimentally driven (see also Voeth, Rabe 2004), while only a minority of contributions uses field data. Furthermore, different measures of negotiation performance are applied, which apparently leads to inconclusive results (Thompson 1990). The shortcomings of the experimental approaches applied, as far as these can be evaluated generally, are often as follows:

1. Negotiations are guided by multiple individual's preferences. In order to allow comparative statistical inferences on dependent variables such as Pareto efficiency these preferences need to be controlled and are thus externally provided to the participants as part of a role-playing exercise, while assumed to be stable. Clyman and Tripp (2000) point out the limitations of this approach. The values (preferences) that negotiators bring to the table may differ substantially from those implicit in the measures used to evaluate negotiator performance in an experiment, and they may change dynamically (Köhne et al. 2004b, Müller 2004). Curhan and colleagues make an important point regarding subjective values, such as relationships and face-saving, which they consider to be intriguingly understated compared to

the rationalist components of negotiation performance measures usually applied (Curhan et al. 2006, p. 507).

2. Negotiation data is often at least dyadic. This is a general problem of negotiation experiments and statistical negotiation analysis. Experiments generate data from at least two points of view, which are pairwise interdependent, i.e. in a dynamic multi-faceted relation (Gelfand et al. 2006). Hence scholars speak of a negotiation dance. This needs to be taken into account before statistical inferences on a dataset containing dyadic data can reasonably be made (Kenny 1995, Turel 2006).

3. Regularly, student based samples are used for experiments. The well known Inspire dataset also mainly contains data collected from negotiation classes. This raises concerns regarding a possible student bias. While sampling from students is convenient and may not introduce a bias into all kinds of studies, students generally differ from business negotiators in various ways that need to be recognised. Sears (1986) discusses the specifics of student based samples in Social Psychology research, which also heavily relies on this kind of data source. For example, he points out that compared with average older adults, students are more ready to change their attitudes and thus often behave in an inconsistent manner. There are additional differences in emotional and norm-guided behaviour that may be relevant to E-Negotiation research.

In studies conducted in the E-Negotiation group in Hohenheim, positive feedback is regularly received from students, who participated in electronic negotiation experiments for providing a valuable learning experience, because most of the students never conducted a formal negotiation through electronic channels before. Through such experiences, business negotiators can be expected to develop dedicated practices in order to manage specific problems, i.e. they restructure their work environment in the sense of a technology appropriation, which can not be addressed in student based experiments.

4. Finally, simulated negotiation results re different from actual ones in numerous ways, i.e. they ignore real-world aspects of commercial negotiations (Turel, Yuan

2006). For example, they lack contingencies beyond a signed contract such as the ongoing social or business relationship after the deal and possible communication problems that raise problems in the fulfilment phase. Negotiation is a relational activity (Gelfand et al. 2006). For example, negotiators frequently (and rationally) take risk or the value of ongoing social or business relationships into account when they evaluate their negotiation efficiency. The mixed results in media effects research in negotiations (see Poole et al. 1992) and decision theory driven research indicate a need for a certain contextualisation (Johns 2006).

In an analysis of 234 journal articles on group support systems (Pervan 1998), interpretivist methods are found to be "almost ignored" – the majority of papers are of positivist or conceptual nature. The situation, regarding negotiation support systems, does not seem to be substantially different as of today. Presently, structural equation modelling methods are gaining importance in ENS research (see e.g. Carter, Kaufmann 2007). This deductive, theory testing approach allows for a statistical analysis of latent, i.e. not directly observable variables in complex causal models. Behavioural concepts such as trust are introduced into ENS effect studies (e.g. Chen, Weber 2006). However the methodology leaves little room for contextuality or interpretative flexibility and depends on comparatively large data samples, which need to be collected using complex, established instruments – data that is costly to obtain from the field.

On the other hand, there is a culture of highly illustrative single case studies in negotiation research, such as on the Cuban missile crisis (Allison 1971), with little analogous examples in the field of electronic negotiation. While these approaches are illustrative and richly described, their generalisability is unclear. Studies that bridge between these two methodological clusters in the domain of electronic negotiation, such as the works of Carter and Kaufmann (2004, 2007) are exceptional.

2.4 Literature Review Conclusions

In general, ENSs aim to improve or (partly) automate the process of bargaining and inter-organisational coordination. They address common restrictions such as dislocation and bounded rationality. They provide techniques for decision analysis and strive to systematically orchestrate the pattern of interaction (DeSanctis, Gallupe 1987). If they take such an active role in negotiation processes, we speak of electronic negotiations and electronic negotiation systems.

Subsequently, having introduced theoretical perspectives and methods as well as ENS system categories, their interrelations will be evaluated, in order to point out research opportunities. These are then taken up and formalised into a set of research questions.

2.4.1 Juxtaposition of Theoretical Perspectives

In Figure 5, the perspectives on electronic negotiation processes, which are described in detail above, are summarised. The figure further contains a number of relevant key constructs introduced in these perspectives and theories.

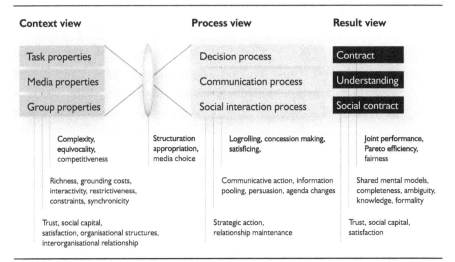

Figure 5: Relevant theoretical perspectives and their key concepts.

The choice of these theories is tailored to cover aspects of negotiation contexts (for example constituents), complete processes (including the time after an agreement), and different facets of negotiation results. Existing research primarily emphasises the analysis of results in a traditional economic sense.

All of the above concepts address the interaction level of analysis between individual and organisational levels. As presented, they form a coherent whole, because they either share the epistemological ground of Symbolic Interactionism (Mead 1934, Blumer 1969) and actors ability of reflection[20] (communication i.e. communicative action and social interaction / structuration views) or the idea of an abstract reference point that eases the interpretation and comparison of observed behaviour in actual negotiations (ideal speech situations in the Habermasian communication view and rationality / Pareto efficiency in the economic decision view).

The concern of the main drivers of the symbolic interactionist point of view, namely Mead, Cooley, Blumer and later also Habermas was to bridge between polarities of Psy-

---

20 Reflective actors are also one of the basic ideas underlying the Grounded Theory method to be introduced later.

chology and Sociology by focusing on interaction of people and their lifeworlds. Strauss (1959) introduced the Symbolic Interactionism theory as a position that stresses the key role of language for human behaviour. The symbolic interactionist position claims that events of social interaction are open and unpredictable: Social interaction is a process guided by rules, norms and order, but its results are uncertain. This uncertainty is not necessarily an obstacle for research, but it needs to be included in scientific reasoning in the field of social science research (Hesse 2001, p. 123). The basic propositions of Symbolic Interactionism, as it was coined by Blumer (1969),[21] are:

(1) that people act with things (i.e. objects, other persons, institutions or technologies) based on the meaning they attribute to these things,

(2) that these meanings are based on social interaction with other people and

(3) that these meanings are evolved and reflected upon through interaction in an interpretative process. Interaction and negotiation of meaning obviously requires the use of symbols (such as language).

Repetition of interactions may establish behavioural patterns, which Blumer named "social institutions" (Hesse 2001, 1994). With respect to negotiation analysis, it should be pointed out that the evolution of meaning and social institutions through social interaction does not assume a socialisation process in the meaning of an inherent tendency towards consensus building. Social interaction may also raise meanings through dissent, through opportunities of differentiation and identity finding. The dynamics of meanings reminds of the structuration view with its recursive nature (see also Hesse 2001, p. 76). In the words of Blumer it is the social process of interaction that yields and maintains (social) rules and not the rules that yield and maintain social life (Blumer 1969).

There are differences between the basic assumptions underlying the economic bargaining view of negotiation, also present in game theory, and the arguing view of negotiation

---

21 The borders of Symbolic Interactionism are not clearly cut. Here the term is used in the sense of Blumer, who established and advanced the ideas of Mead in sociological theory. Mead himself, for reasons unknown, seldom published his works. Thus, these works that were published after Mead's death are open to a number of interpretations (see Hesse 2001, pp. 64, 93). Blumer considers Strauss one of the most competent interpreters of Meads work (Hesse 2001, p. 98).

inherent in the communicative action view. Hence, we will investigate these in particular. As already stated (see p. 26), understanding is a necessary precondition even for purely teleological action. Beyond this simple relationship between these apparent extremes the field of international policy research has investigated the issue in more detail:[22] If the arguing paradigm is associated with communicative action and ideal speech, bargaining is intuitively related to strategic action and thus incompatible with the former. Following Müller (2004), both are speech acts where arguing contains claims of factual truth or normative validity and intends to convince. Bargaining contains promises and threats and intends to change behaviour – rooted in rational economic utility maximisation. Communicative action aims at producing consensus with the presumption that both, speaker and listener enter the communication with a readiness to submit to the better argument. From a game theoretical stance communication can not help in capturing gains beyond a strategic equilibrium without communication. Economists thus speak of *cheap talk* in bargaining games.

But these archetypes of interaction do not sufficiently describe real world negotiations, where we see both types of interaction intertwined all the time. In international negotiations, it has been shown that they are inseparable due to the social necessity (i.e. norm) of giving reasons for subjective claims (Holzinger 2001). It is therefore necessary to consider both modes in an empirical study on negotiation communication and to extend on their relationship.

Müller makes three main points regarding the role of argumentation in negotiations. First of all, strategic action is compatible with arguing. If rational utility maximisers perceive argumentation as an action with a positive expected utility value, they have no choice but to argue, i.e. they act rhetorically. In that case it is however questionable if they can reach understanding.

Second, if rational utility maximisers engage in argumentation without, at least partly, committing themselves to the better argument and thereby approach the assumptions of

---

22 The discussion is largely represented in the so called ZIB-Debate (Zeitschrift für Internationale Beziehungen, German Journal of International Relations) since 1994.

communicative action, their refusal to reciprocate will damage their reputation. Most negotiations are not single-round games and reputation or social capital is therefore of rational interest. As Müller continues (p. 409):

> "Our strategist must eventually be guided by the 'logic of communicative action' if he wants to achieve his strategic objective."

Third, there are procedural norms in effect during bargaining such as common rules of diplomacy, language or reciprocity (i.e. fairness is a basic concept in game theory). Negotiators can refer to these and further enter into a normative discourse in order to establish or question such norms – a strategy that is, while essentially driven by communicative action, a core component of the prescriptive negotiation literature, e.g. the Harvard Concept (Fisher et al. 2004).

Habermas has been criticised for normatively privileging communicative over strategic action through the strict distinction of a common lifeworld and the system world in his original work on communicative action from 1981. The archetypes of arguing and bargaining have blurred since the first development of the communicative action concept. As Müller (p. 415) states it:

> "He [Habermas] himself finds arguing - and people submitting to the better argument - in what he used to describe as the realm of the 'system' (Habermas 1996). The sharp demarcation line cutting through the social world is no longer there."

Risse makes a similar point (2000, p. 14). In summary, it can be concluded that negotiators regularly operate both with arguing logics and bargaining logics (Risse 2000, Müller 2004). A struggle for the better argument is ubiquitous in all kinds of negotiations (Sycara 1990, Müller 2007). Whether this combination is sequential or parallel and how far these logics of interaction are visible in an electronic negotiation setting remains to be investigated. An inclusion of both of these logics into an explorative study on business negotiator behaviour appears to be well justified.

2.4.2 An Integrated Perspective on Negotiation Support

Depending on the discipline authors are rooted in, their interpretation of what a negotiation is differs widely between the tight, technically grounded definition from artificial intelligence (a path in a joint decision space) and negotiations' significant role for society and norms (Strauss 1979).

The elegant definition in the negotiation agent section is implicitly assuming that a search space can be specified a priori and that there is a joint understanding of the concepts (ontology), which allows joint search activities within the search space. These premises are too narrow for the empirical purpose of this study, considering most business transactions today. The definition in the auction section is focussed on distributive 1:n or n:n negotiation problems and stresses the role of mechanisms for goods and services that can be reasonably described a priori. Not all negotiation problems fit into this schema, especially bilateral negotiations and renegotiations of existing contractual relationships.

On the other side, Raiffa's illustrative description of negotiation as an art and science is very open and leaves room for a number of different negotiation problems and protocols, but stresses the importance of the dynamic interaction process between agents. In contrast to a pure *joint decision* view of negotiations, the interaction process aspect of negotiations can be more easily documented, observed and reflected upon.

The definition of an electronic negotiation provided by Ströbel and Weinhardt (2003) is applicable to the three clusters of systems introduced and does not collide with the definitions of negotiation given for the three schools of negotiation support. This study will mainly concentrate on one special type electronic negotiations in the defined sense, namely the reverse auction paradigm. However, present auction systems partly incorporate NSS features. Electronic negotiation agents are not further investigated in the study, because it is meant to focus on complex, and less structured business negotiation problems, which are out of scope of current agent based systems. Here, technical communication problems regarding e.g. ontology handling must be addressed before impacts of the technology in other than highly structured and stable scenarios can be subject to empirical research.

Furthermore, the degree of automation can be considered as orthogonal to a number of other ENS design decisions (Ströbel, Weinhardt 2003), which will be addressed.

2.4.3 Existing ENS Research and Research Opportunities

Three types of ENSs, which exist as distinct schools of thought in the conceptual and empirical literature, have been introduced and three theoretical perspectives have been described. They form a matrix, which we can use to classify individual empirical studies on ENS application and give an overview of the state of the art in Table 4.

ENS type	Theoretical perspectives in empirical research on ENS		
	Decision and game theoretical perspective	Communication and media perspective	Social sciences perspective
Negotiation agent	Scarce	-	-
E-Auction	Common	Scarce	Less common
NSS	Common	Less common	Scarce

Table 4: Empirical research from different perspectives (excluding conceptual work).

The classification is fuzzy and not disjoint – especially newer studies employ elements from multiple perspectives simultaneously. An integrated view on the three modes of electronic support for negotiation tasks is lacking, although especially electronic auction and NSS technologies are integrating, the according research streams hardly are.

Empirical research on the application of negotiation agents is in its infancy across all perspectives, as practical application of the technology is as well. Empirical research on ENSs and E-Auctions including experimental approaches commonly employs either a decision / game theory perspective (such as for example Foroughi et al. 1995, Delaney et al. 1997, Kersten, Noronha 1997, Rangaswamy, Shell 1997, Goh et al. 2000, Filzmoser, Vetschera 2006), scarcely a communication centric perspective (Yuan et al. 1998, Köhne et al. 2005) or a social science perspective (Lim et al. 2002). If social / relational aspects are addressed, empirical studies often employ a cross-cultural perspective only (Kersten, Noronha 1997, Vetschera et al. 2003, Graf et al. 2006). The wider Information Systems and organisations perspective that enables an analysis of behaviour beyond simplistic, direct technological determinism is scarcely used, with few exceptions such as from DeSanctis & Poole (1994).

Nearly all of the empirical work regarding agents, auctions, and NSS is based on experimental data gathered in artificial negotiation situations. Studies based on field data are very scarce and limited to the auction type of support (such as Carter et al. 2004), because only auction systems have reached sufficient diffusion for field studies. They apply social science and decision theory perspectives. The communicative view is under-represented.

A second problem is related to this: The majority of electronic negotiation studies frame negotiations as the activity performed at the (virtual) table, possibly including preparatory activities. Two important aspects are thereby ruled out, namely the ex post evaluation of negotiation results after all obligations resulting from a negotiation have been carried out and the interactions between negotiators and their constituents (Turner 1992) including back-end negotiations. The situation is similar to the one criticised by Putnam regarding the framing of research on traditional face-to-face negotiations:

> "To understand the basis of interaction sequences at the table, researchers must extend their work beyond the bargaining dyad into the intergroup relations that constitute the negotiation event." (Putnam 1985, p. 236).

More than twenty years later, this critique still applies. Either aspect is highly relevant for the success of organisations and is quite probably subject to technology induced changes yet unknown. Turoff (Turoff 2006) provides a fresh view on this problem: He points out parallels between the environment in which decision and negotiation support systems are operated and the environment of emergency response Information Systems. For many companies, negotiations may actually be emergencies, i.e. situations of social interaction characterised by time-pressure, fragmented information and the demand for quick decisions, which may have potentially disastrous effects for the future of the companies. This analogy highlights the distance between the assumptions regularly made in empirical ENS research and the life-worlds of business negotiators.

2.5 Deduction of Research Questions

In summary, the limits of experimental research on ENS impacts have been approached and there is a lack of rich, qualitative knowledge of the socio-technical effects of all kinds of ENS in the field, which will therefore be mainly in focus of the research question to be derived.

Furthermore, present research does not fully recognise the emergent, communicative nature of electronic negotiations. Thus, the goals of the study, which guide the framing of the main research questions, are to ground the discussion on ENS impacts in the life-worlds of business negotiators, consequently to question strict automation as the main paradigm of E-Negotiation research and to extend the theory portfolio of E-Negotiation research with aspects of communication theory. Drawing on the lack of communicative knowledge on ENS use and its growing importance in business negotiations, the main research question of the study is best summarised as *"How does the utilisation of auction-type ENS in B2B exchanges impact organisational communication?"*

Because only auction-based ENSs have reached a sufficient diffusion for a field study, the empirical investigation will concentrate on this model. Findings that apply to ENS in general are pointed out explicitly. The view on ENS technology implied here is not that of a market mechanism (the traditional view considering decision theory driven research), but rather that of a special socio-technology,[23] which is subject to interpretative flexibility in and interacts with some organisational context. Inter-organisational effects are included in this question while the type of transactions is explicitly limited to trade and service related negotiations, the most common types of transaction. The cases of for example mergers and acquisitions, dispute resolution and collective labour agreements are hence not investigated further.

The question has an explorative, open character and can not yet be operationalised to propositions, but it can be detailed however. In line with the emergent process view of

---

23 Taking the language action perspective, it can be argued that the main impact of computer technology is to support communication and not computation in a strict sense.

communication media impacts (Markus 1999), intended and unintended effects can be distinguished and a number of constructs to investigate can be identified a priori.

In order to answer the main research question, the following sub-questions have to be addressed in line with it:

1. *What are the structural features inherent in the technologies applied, the organisational context and the task?*

2. *How are these features appropriated in social interaction?*

Investigating the first two questions is a prerequisite for investigating the following ones, because similar technologies may be understood and appropriated very differently by different actors. Building on knowledge how actors understand and use the technologies, their effects can be evaluated.

3. *What is the effect of the appropriated technology in terms of communicative quality?*

To some extent, these effects may be reflected and evaluated in practice. Compensation strategies may be developed, which would be of particular interest in order to understand different ways the technologies are used and the reasoning behind this use.

4. *How are these effects reflected in the organisational environment?*

Given such an understanding, we can better inform both the choice as well as the design of negotiation support technology.

These questions are exploratory, open and consider constructs difficult to observe in human interaction. This raises some philosophical questions, which are addressed in the following chapter.

3. Methodology

The literature review shows that, on the one hand, empirical work in electronic negoti-ation research is still scarce and often based on experimental data, disregarding the emer-gent organisational and communicational implications of the technology. On the other hand, more general theories hardly have explanatory power in their present form, because the specifics of electronic negotiations are yet disregarded in existing theory. The main goal of the study is, therefore, to research the (non-) utilisation of ENS in the field and initially generate a theory on its appropriation and effects without these deficiencies.

3.1 Epistemological Considerations

Every piece of scientific work is based on a philosophical position of the researcher regarding his/her understanding of reality and of how to answer research questions. Since there is no *escape* from such assumptions in the Social Sciences (Hammersley, 2002), they need to be considered and documented. As there are a number of positions and the choice of position is of major importance for the consistent conduct and especially for the evaluation of research, the underlying philosophical position of this study will be made explicit in the following paragraphs.

With regard to each basic *paradigm* or research tradition, three components must be described: On the ontological level, the researcher's view of the nature of the universe of discourse is defined. The epistemological level defines the individual researcher's place within it and the range of possible relationships between knowledge and the world (such as truth) and what we can actually know. Finally, on the method ontological level it needs to be operationalised how knowledge can and should be acquired (see e.g. Schülein, Reitze 2002, p. 26).

These philosophical questions have been subject of discussion since Aristotle. Important contributions have been made by Albert and Popper among others. These two described the limits of human knowledge seeking very clearly. Thereby they provided the building ground for the critical rationalism position, which stresses the preliminary nature of knowledge and proposes falsification as the scientific way of producing new knowledge. The mathematical, quantitative research tradition is rooted in this basic idea and has become the dominant modus operandi of modern science. Its major weakness lays in its reductionism – social science phenomena can not be covered in their full breadth and contextuality in the quantitative paradigm.

This leads to the development of qualitative approaches in Sociology and Social Psychology (such as Glaser, Strauss 1967), which extended research beyond behaviourism, i.e. the exclusive study of visible behaviour. Table 5 gives an overview of the quantitative and qualitative research paradigms (based on Krotz 2005).

Quantitative paradigm	Qualitative paradigm
Strictly sequential research process: Conceptualise and operationalise hypotheses, sample and collect data, check and analyse data, interpret results.	Iterative process based on minimal prior knowledge, sampling and analysis are repeatedly informing each other.
In order to make variables measurable they are precisely defined in order to avoid ambiguities, i.e. factor analysis drops items that appear not to be interpreted homogeneously, as they would invalidate inferences.	Assumes that not all relevant aspects of the world, such as sense and meaning, can be meaningfully reconstructed in mathematical terms. Inhomogeneous interpretations are taken up as opportunities for investigation.
Results are preliminary and open to further attempts of falsification using the same conditions.	Results are preliminary and open to scientific discourse.
Data analysis is an operation of data reduction that describes variables across cases.	Data analysis as an operation of data reduction that takes the context of cases into account, because sense making in the field is contextual.
Goal: verification of theory in the form of if-then or the-more type assertions.	Goal: discovery, understanding and verification of contextual (i.e. rich) theory.
Use of quantified data – i.e. surveys or frequencies in content analysis.	Use of qualitative data, i.e. observation scripts or quantitative data (this is not the usual case, but qualitative research is not necessarily limited to qualitative data).

Table 5: Overview of the quantitative and qualitative research paradigms (based on Krotz 2005).

It should be noted that despite the ongoing discussion between researchers of either paradigm, the two paradigms are not necessarily in competition. It is often useful to address a single research question using both paradigms. Results will certainly differ and may inform each other due to their complementary strengths and weaknesses, but the approaches are not comparable, because of their different goals. They rather are complimentary. In line with this integrative view, Iivari (1991) makes the point that epistemological monism can coexist with methodological pluralism. Yin and Fitzgerald & Howcroft (1994, 1998) also point out the context dependency of scientific methodology and the possibility of a methodological pluralism.

Other, more specific philosophical positions have evolved. The constructivist paradigm (Denzin, Lincoln 1994) can not be disregarded in an Information Systems study focusing on communication processes on the object level: *Reality* is not itself constructed, but multiple perceptions of reality (lifeworlds, in the words of Habermas) exist and must be dealt with, i.e. they must be shared (in fact negotiated) in order to reach understanding.

On the *ontological* level of this study, this means that only perceptions, and how individuals interpret these perceptions, can be subject to research. Constructivism assumes a Relativistic ontology (Denzin, Lincoln 1994, p.13). A Relativist ontology accepts that interpretations of reality are not more or less true in any formal sense, but simply more or less informed or sophisticated. Sharing test persons' perceptions of reality and finding differences among them is one of the main challenges for the present research.

Constructivism stresses that research is more a process of subjectively sculpturing knowledge than a process of discovery of something objective (Mir, Watson 2000). This basic Constructivist assumption is sometimes labelled as post-positivism and leads to the question of epistemology. Reality is not only a mental construction however. There may be an objective and true reality considering the effects ENS utilisation has on organisational processes, but it can not be fully described and understood due to its complexity and the variety of its subjective perceptions.

This holds for the actors in the domain and researchers as well. Regarding *epistemology*, the question of what can be known, it has to be considered that the strong Positivist axiom of mechanistic causality and replicative truth does not fit to social science research in general. Access to the world is difficult and limited. Understanding and technology appropriation in social interaction are inherently interpretative and thus call for interpretative, relativistic research that collects knowledge through a process of communication.

Research itself is then an interpretation as well - a relative construction of reality.[24] Table 6 places the paradigms mentioned in a comprehensive framework.

	Realism	Relativism
Ontological level	Positivism, Subtle Realism	Interpretivism
Epistemological level	Positivism	Interpretivism, Subtle Realism

Table 6: Zones of research paradigms (based on Mir, Watson 2000).

The author, following Huberman and Miles (2002, p. 2), takes the subtle realism position introduced by Hammersley (2002) for ethnographic research. As Hammersley argues, the only distinction between a (relative) researcher's perspective and any other relative perspective is that the researcher is obliged to make his or her perspective relevant and visible (cf. Charmaz, Mitchell 1996). This can be achieved only by embedding it into existing research and through the careful application of research methods, which will be addressed below in more detail. Another important strategy to gain knowledge from such a perspective is a focus on unintended, emergent issues that are potentially not admitted as being related by the community under study (Giddens 1984, p. 8).

If a theory can be created and generalised through interpretative means, it may lend itself to testing and should reach for 1) intersubjectivity and 2) applicability, two weaker forms of truth more suitable for social science research. To close the circle towards communication theory, Habermas' ideas can be applied here. His consensus theory of truth proposes that we should (and in fact have no choice but to) consider to be true, what those who act communicatively accept due to reasoning, argumentation and discourse – i.e. he evaluates knowledge based on the process of its creation.

This leads to the question of methodology for the researcher, which will be discussed in more detail below. On this level, it is clear that the methodology applied needs to be

---

24 Glaser (2002) might object here that a constructivist point of view must not be used to legitimate forcing researchers' ideas e.g. on interview partners, because there would be little to lose if all data was constructed anyway. This is a critique of relativistic constructivism on the ontological level in Grounded Theory studies, which is not assumed here. (Bryant 2003) reflects on the relationship of constructivism and Grounded Theory in more detail.

rooted in the discussion with electronic negotiation practitioners and established E-Negotiation theory. Further, there is a pragmatic notion of truth that can not be disregarded in management related research: The truth is what works. Beyond the claim of *Verstehen* in the sense of interpretative Sociology, this study is meant to provide useful contributions for industry decision makers. However, its usefulness as a decision guide can not be meaningfully evaluated within the study. Pragmatism and applicability are thus goals, but they are not used as an evaluation criterion. In one key aspect, Habermas' and Peirce's notion of truth overlap: As society advances, the truth of our thinking can only be preliminary and in need of revision – it is a matter of discussion.

Thereby, interpretative research does not necessarily conflict with the methodological ideas of Critical Rationalism. But interpretative empirical work is not certifiable in a strict sense. Hence, falsification (for example through experimentation) is not a workable *methodology* for most social science studies (Krotz 2005, Goulding 2002, p. 16). This study will, therefore, have a primarily interpretative and theory generating methodology. The need for an open, process-oriented method can also be directly derived from the symbolic-interactionistic base of the research question. The method to be applied is discussed in the following chapter in more detail.

If appropriate field data is available or the generated theory lends itself to further experimental investigation, falsification based methodology can later be applied to parts of the theory generated in the study.

3.2 Selection of a Methodological Framework: the Grounded Theory Method

First of all, the communicative analysis of electronic business negotiations is a novelty. Although a number of existing theories from different research areas can be argued to be of potential relevance, a strictly deductive approach is insufficient for the specific research questions, because no dedicated theory does yet exist. Further, communicative problems in business negotiations often become visible only after a contract has been signed and is being fulfilled, which is hardly possible in to achieve in quantitative experimental research.

On the other hand and with for example quasi-experimental approaches in mind, we need to consider that business negotiation processes are strongly intertwined with aspects of organisational structure, social structures, national and company culture and the idiosyncratic nature of the problem at hand, i.e. its context (Johns 2006).

This is most obvious considering the example of the often applied *my hands are tied*-strategies, in which negotiators directly use their relationship with their constituents in an organisation for strategic purposes. The way a negotiator is embedded in an organisation and interacts with it has however many more facets, which need to be considered regarding technology impacts. This aspect of negotiations is adequately illustrated by Hopmann, who reflects on his research on international negotiations and concludes as follows.

> *"Much of the real negotiation process takes place on the margins of formal negotiations and does not appear in the verbatim record. [...] After more than 30 years of visiting and observing negotiations, I have come to the conclusion that this is not an exception, but is in fact typical of most negotiations [...] Quantitative analyses of negotiations, therefore, have often been most fruitful when the negotiation process is highly transparent and mechanistic." (Hopmann, 2002)*

Therefore, and due to the reasons already mentioned, a study which targets complex negotiation problems has to allow for the analysis of context dependencies. A *qualitative and theory generating method* appears most suitable. There is a need for flexibility and openness, because it can not be anticipated where the investigation of the research question based on the structures and subjective views in the field will eventually lead.

Suchman (1987) stresses the value of such ethnomethodologies for understanding work environments and the application of technologies. The proponents of ethnomethodologies (see for example Cicourel 1973) criticise the idea of establishing social science theories without recognising the everyday life-understanding within the field of study, since this is a precondition for any meaningful interpretation of research observations. Consequently, methods of data collection and analysis need to be carefully chosen and possibly adapted, depending on the field of application.

There is a wide range of qualitative research methods with the above goal of sensitivity. While this variety is useful and allows research on a wide range of very different phenomena, the approaches, their fields of applicability and their justification are still not clearly structured (Krotz 2005, p. 57). Thus we need clear cut argumentations for the choice of qualitative research methods. A number of methods are potentially suitable for this type of research judging from their use and the discussion of qualitative methods in Information Systems research: mainly Grounded Theory, Ethnography, Phenomenology and Action Research.

In this case, Grounded Theory combined with ideas from Ethnography can be argued to be the preferred method of research as follows:

1. The Action Research school of methodologies in its different versions criticises research on the relationships between isolated sets of variables in Information Systems and organisational research and stresses the importance of an idiosyncratic, more holistic view. The basic idea is that researchers in organisations can only learn by iteratively introducing and observing change processes (such as in business processes or technology features), i.e. through their *actions*. Action Research is therefore most effective if immediate problem situations are given (e.g. for E-Negotiation service providers, cf. Turel, Yuan 2006) and a researcher is involved in a process of interactive problem solving while carefully informing theory (Baskerville 1999). This is also the fundamental problem in Action Research studies. Although generalisability is not intended in the meaning of the quantitative research view, Action Research results are intrinsically subjective and data collection covers mainly researcher-subject interactions instead of more unobtrusive observations.

   With the high frequency of renegotiations and our lack of understanding regarding this variable (Schoop et al. 2007a), an immediate problem situation is given in the field of reverse auction applications. Their use context parameters can, however, not be influenced or changed by the researcher – i.e. there is no option for action in the above sense. Accordingly, the Action Research approach is not suitable for this study.

2. In contrast to Phenomenology, the Grounded Theory approach and the Ethno-graphic approach (in the sense of Hammersley 2002) allow a wider spectrum of data to be analysed, including but not limited to interviews, direct observation, company reports, secondary data and even statistics (Glaser, Strauss 1967). As the access to empirical data can be expected to be difficult, this methodological flexibility is very valuable.

3. Further, the Grounded Theory method is an action oriented model and is thereby "broadly consistent with traditions within economics that have actions and pro-cesses as explananda [..]" (Finch 2002).

    It is further rooted in the Symbolic Interactionism position of Sociology. Grounded Theory, therefore, inherits what basically can be considered to be a communicative point of view and is hence appropriate for the study of interaction and communica-tion processes in electronically conducted business negotiations. Strauss himself analysed social relationships [25] in a number of face-to-face negotiation case studies (Strauss 1979).

4. Finally, unlike other interpretative approaches and despite ongoing arguments on that topic, the Grounded Theory method provides an established set of guidelines and procedures for data analysis, meant to add rigour and security into a dynamic-ally evolving exploratory study. It is more elaborated and thus more easily applic-able than those of Ethnography and Phenomenology. As Brynant (2002) puts it, to date the Grounded Theory method "has been widely misused; often as a catch-all that can be evoked as a justification for methodological inadequacies, [...] But this should not be allowed to detract from its strengths, and in particular its value for IS research."

Further, the Grounded Theory method has been successfully applied across a number of different research areas, including Management Science and Information Systems. Import-ant examples are the works of Orlikowski et al. (1993, Kellogg et al. 2006), or Allan

---

25 Giddens' conceptualisation of social relationships and organisations (Giddens 1984) is similar to that of Strauss: individual reflection and reproduction of meaning – through negotiations.

(2003) and Carter et al. (2004) from the research area of Information Systems.[26] Through these applications and reflections of them, Grounded Theory is provided with a solid epistemological ground (see Table 6, p. 60) suited for economic studies (Finch 2002) and Information Systems studies (see Bryant 2002).

Regarding the operational application of the method, Glaser and Strauss have developed different interpretations of *the* Grounded Theory methodology. Both of these versions are applied currently. While the basic properties of the approach, namely the constant comparison of data and derived concepts and categories, gradual abstraction, the use of memos and the need for saturation remain unchanged, Glaser stresses the interpretative, contextual and emergent way of theory development while Strauss emphasises highly complex and systematic coding techniques (Goulding 1999). There has been an extensive discussion between the authors (and others) regarding this point and both versions appear to have their justifications. At this point of the study, the Straussian approach to data analysis is felt to be too inflexible. It is preferable to let the data tell their own story.

3.3 An Introduction to the Grounded Theory Approach

The Grounded Theory approach is open to adaptation and subject to different interpretations and criticism, it is briefly reviewed here and critical aspects relevant for the study at hand are addressed. This chapter can serve as a first introduction to the methodology, but not as a complete account of its application, its strengths and weaknesses.

3.3.1 The Research Process

Data Collection

Theory generating research generates knowledge inductively. It corrects and improves, extends or details a pre-understanding of a new domain. Thus, the role of the researcher's pre-understanding needs to be explicated and reflected systematically in a first step (Krotz

---

26 Carter et al. investigate electronic reverse auctions. Orlikowski analyses IT enabled organisational change processes with a structuration perspective. Due to the methodological and conceptual parallels, their works will be revisited subsequently.

2005, p. 32, Hammersley 2002). This aspect is revisited later. It leads to the conception of research questions and to the selection of first cases for analysis. Grounded Theory studies then start with data collection very early.

The key characteristic of the Grounded Theory approach[27] is the constant comparison strategy whereby theory is derived inductively: Emergent theory (codes and constructs) and new data are compared iteratively. Thus, the process of data collection and analysis are intertwined. These iterations continue until theoretical saturation has been reached, i.e. until the point of diminishing returns from any new analysis (Gasson 2004, p. 80) is reached.

In further steps of analysis, the researcher aggregates and links the aspects found and gradually abstracts from the data. Thereby, all inferences made remain transparently *grounded* in the actual data. This is the second key characteristic: Theory is based on patterns found in the empirical data and not on inferences made from existing ideas.

Grounded Theory is a strictly inductive, reflexive process. All actions of the researcher regarding the subject of analysis are considered to be interactive and reciprocal, i.e. the researcher is in an investigative dialogue with the field data (Krotz 2005). While in positivistic research, the appearance of contradicting or unclear findings in data analysis is an indication of an erroneous research design, it offers valuable guidance for selective sampling during the iterative process of interpretative research. Questions raised can be addressed directly (Krotz 2005, p. 173).

Especially the first steps of data analysis have an exploratory character; they are approached very openly and initiate the process of purposeful sampling, minimizing or maximizing the differences among the cases in order to either further differentiate categories or in order to confirm findings from earlier iterations.

---

27 A full account of the method and its history can not be provided here. References to 'the' Grounded Theory approach refer to its present state of methodological development as described here, if not indicated otherwise.

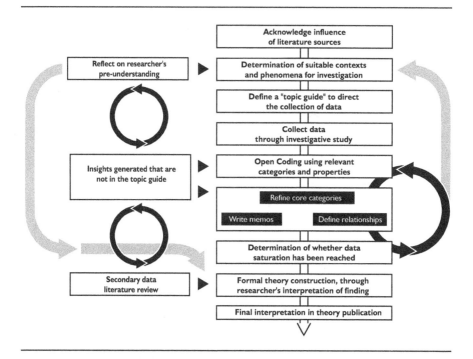

Figure 6: The Grounded Theory research process (based on Gasson 2004).

Once saturation is approaching, an in depth literature review is conducted in order to embed the Grounded Theory generated in the existing knowledge and to thereby make a theoretical contribution. This is the basic idea of iterative Grounded Theory analysis[28] as illustrated in Figure 6, which culminates in a final interpretation and aggregation of the findings in a research publication.

Data Analysis

Grounded Theory coding is a form of content analysis often performed on interview data. This process is not to be confused with quantitative coding methods, which require a stable and valid coding scheme deduced from existing theory. Glaser and Strauss (1967) insist that existent ideas should not be forced on the data. During analysis, the researcher

---

28 See also (Krotz 2005) for a detailed description of the process.

will become aware of reoccurring phrases or patterns of interest leading into the same direction, then group and compare them – i.e. a coding scheme or code dictionary is created during the coding process. Glaser (1992)[29] introduces a set of useful definitions regarding this process in order to make it more transparent:

> "**Coding** is the conceptualisation of data by the constant comparison of incident with incident, and incident with concept, in order to develop categories and their properties.
>
> A **Concept** is basically the underlying meaning, uniformity and/or/pattern within a set of descriptive incidents.
>
> A **Property** is a type of conceptual characteristic of a concept or a category.
>
> **Categories** are higher order concepts. They have much wider explanatory power, and pull together all the identified concepts into a theoretical framework."

More than one code may emerge from the same text and data will be regularly revisited after new data has been collected (Constant comparative method, Glaser and Strauss 1967). Over time, different versions of this analysis process have emerged.

Glaser proposes a so called open coding process and stresses its openness here (Glaser 1978). Further, he recommends abstracting from codes to categories into a consistent theoretical network right from the beginning. The mechanism for this abstraction is the constant comparison of interpretations and data material. The theoretical sampling must be executed with these comparisons in mind. Further, it needs to be flexible enough to be guided by emerging categories on the other hand (as summarised by Truschkat et al. 2005). Operationally, the coding starts with a line-by-line analysis. Key phrases are identified, which provide insights into the behaviour under investigation. These codes are then highlighted and gradually abstracted from (Goulding 2002, p. 76). It should be noted that the goal of coding is not the complete categorisation of the data material, but a selective analysis guided by the research questions (Krotz 2005, 182, 183).

Strauss and Corbin (1990) provide a three staged coding process that consists of open coding, axial coding and selective coding. The open phase is necessary to break up the data. Later phases are meant to inter-relate the codes and categories found. In contrast to

---

29 Taken from (Goulding 2002).

Glaser's approach, the later stages are far more deductive and reduce the likelihood of emergent findings (for example through the provision of predefined questions). Glaser criticised this as dropping the very purpose of the Grounded Theory method. Using axial coding, a researcher develops a category by specifying the conditions that gave rise to it, the context in which it is embedded and the (interactional) strategies by which it is handled (Goulding 2002, p. 78). More structure is imposed on the data than in open coding. Selective coding is then directed at the development of a core category, i.e. a backbone for theory. Strauss and Corbin here allow the application of selective sampling that is guided by theoretical preconceptions, which is again criticised by Glaser:

> "Strauss looks for his paradigm in the data, and data collection in his method is not guided by the emergent, but by testing his logically deduced hypotheses in service of his paradigm. This is just conventional verificational methodology [..]." (Glaser 1992, p. 103 – as cited by Truschkat et al. 2005)

While this critique is of a fundamental nature it may indeed be the case that the Strauss and Corbin approach may lead researchers to close their open, inductive coding phase too early, by reusing existing concepts. On the other hand, a more structured coding process is very valuable to inexperienced researchers.

At about the time Glaser's and Strauss' path diverged, a third approach of analysis – namely Dimensional Analysis[30] - was proposed by Schatzman (1991), a collaborator of the original authors. His main goal was to facilitate the articulation of the interpretative process in order to allow for more transparency in qualitative research. Therefore, he employs a process similar to axial coding and bases the analysis on conditions, processes, context and consequences, which can be shown to effect the outcome of the informant's story (Goulding 2002, p. 79, Kools et al. 1996). New data is collected and analysed until a critical mass of dimensions with explanatory power is identified and illustrative examples for the dimensions have been determined. For the process of theorising from this point on, Schatzman explicitly points out the necessity of an existing theoretical framework to help construct the story (Goulding 2002, 82).

---

30 The coding approach is also referred to as *Natural Analysis*.

	Open Coding	**Axial Coding**	**Dimensional Analysis**
Process	Single stage	Multi-Stage	Multi-Stage
Abstraction	Early abstraction	Abstract later	Abstract later
Primary Goal	Maximize emergence	Maximize ease of use	Maximize transparency
Theoretical sensitivity	Avoid contamination as far as possible	Question set, partly deductive	Question set, theoretical framework for writing down the story

Table 7: Overview of Grounded Theory analysis techniques.

Beyond these differences the coding methods are not necessarily in competition. All of them begin very openly, axial coding (as well as selective coding, which is therefore not part of the above comparison) operates on a set of codes and categories. It is therefore a candidate for the later phases of analysis. Grounded Theory practitioners point out that a guided coding process as provided by Strauss and Corbin or Schatzman is desirable, as long as the need for openness is respected. Mixtures of these techniques are commonly found (Truschkat et al. 2005, Krotz 2005, p. 185). The initial analysis strategy in this study will be open coding in order to benefit from its flexibility. It is guided but not limited by the concepts given in chapter two, in order to concentrate on the concepts that are important to practitioners.

The coding and grounding processes are extremely time consuming activities and hence benefit from computer support. The analysis in this thesis was conducted technically with the mark-up and commenting workflow tools in the Adobe® Acrobat® software package[31] on transcripts and notes of interviews, while indices of codes have been collected in a database.

A useful tool, which accompanies the coding process, is the writing of memos: the explication of inferences made on the material, a consideration of problems and contradictions as well as ideas for further sampling. They play an essential role in Grounded Theory research, because they document the iterative research process with all the decisions made.

---

31 Adobe and Acrobat are registered trademarks of Adobe Systems Incorporated.

Although interpretative methods are becoming more established in IS research since the 1980ss, a shared understanding of how such research should be assessed is not established, compared to the one reached in the positivistic, often quantitative, paradigm.

Two aspects of Grounded Theory are subject to systematic evaluation: process and result, while the quality of the latter naturally depends on the quality of the former. Further, Klein and Myers (1999) offer a set of general principles[32] for interpretative studies compatible with the Grounded Theory approach, which this study will be evaluated against during its conduction.

Glaser, who emphasises the emergent inductive nature of Grounded Theory generation, recommends constant comparison and self-reflection as a way of ensuring quality. Strauss, on the other hand, emphasises repeatable methods to data selection and analysis around formal (heuristic) coding schemes. They agree that emergence is central to the approach and the debate boils down to the underlying perspective, i.e. a Positivist or Interpretivist perspective (Gasson 2004). Positivist criteria can however not be meaningfully applied to qualitative studies, which leaves us with Glaser's criteria and the goal of maximal transparency (Schatzman 1991). A Grounded Theory can only be as good as its grounding.

Originally, three criteria were proposed to evaluate Grounded Theory results in a tradition of Pragmatism (Glaser, Strauss 1967): Fit, relevance and the ability to work, i.e. the concepts and categories should be grounded in the data and the theory derived should explain what was observed. Therefore, as far as possible, data, coding and interpretations are discussed with practitioners and other researchers (member and peer checking) in order to ensure the credibility of the interpretations made (Goulding 2002). Memos are a necessary part of this discussion as well as for the constant process of introspection and reflection that actually drives the Grounded Theory method – the ability of a theory to just work is insufficient; we must be able to understand the way of its construction and the theory must be systematic, extensive and precise in its terminology (Krotz 2005, p. 166).

---

32 In the philosophical distinction used by Klein and Myers, this study is an interpretative one. Thus their principles apply.

3.3.2 Critical Reflection of the Grounded Theory Method

Grounded Theory refers both to the approach (i.e. the set of approaches and assumptions) as well as to the results of the approach – this has lead to some confusion. One of the major criticisms of Grounded Theory approaches is that it rests on inductive reasoning and not on deductive reasoning. But as Gasson illustrates, it is by induction that we learn to avoid hot stoves (Gasson 2004, p. 85).

The most important practical shortcoming of the approach with "data needing to converge in a triangulation fashion" (Glaser, Strauss 1967, Yin 1994, p. 13) lies in the associated risks. The research process is characterised by high effort and a more or less vague criterion for the termination of the iterative comparison process. Convergence is not necessarily approached; studies are often found steering towards new aspects considered to be relevant or interesting in the field. While this flexibility is valuable and leads to a concentration on issues of practical relevance, it carries the risks of loosing focus. If convergence is approached as planned, Grounded Theory studies are still difficult to schedule a priori – the time of convergence can hardly be predicted.

On the other hand, pressing the data for closure and drawing conclusions to early leads to incomplete and sketchy theories.

Grounded theory is a method of theory generation, wherein theory evolves over the time of analysis and is a product of continuous interplay between analysis and data collection (Glaser, Strauss 1967). This has often been interpreted in the way that the researcher needs to enter the field with a completely blank canvas to start from (Goulding 2002, p. 42). Researchers, qualitative as well as quantitative, regularly work in their respective areas of expertise repeatedly – hence the expertise. However, researchers can hardly abandon prior substantive or methodological knowledge in the pursuit of understanding a complex social phenomenon (Goulding 2002 citing Kools et al. 1996).

Glaser (2002) and Eisenhardt (Eisenhardt 1989) propose that the a priori specification of constructs can help to shape the design of theory building research to sensitise the researcher to the significance of emerging concepts. Existing theory allows the researcher to measure constructs more accurately, given that they prove to be important in the study. No construct is however guaranteed to be part of the resulting theory and the focus of the study may shift in a data-driven way. Further, the hypothesis generation task is undertaken openly, attempting not to constrain the data collection or not to contaminate it by predefined perspectives and propositions, as far as possible:

> "These backgrounds of assumptions, experiences and knowledge can at best only imbue our open coding; they do not dictate it." (Glaser 1992, p. 50)

This is the viewpoint of Glaser – Strauss takes a more open position towards reading relevant literature a priori. He sees the method more as a combination of theory generation and verification. In summary, Glaser's and Strauss' positions on this topic mainly differ in their advice as to when theoretical sensitivity is needed in the Grounded Theory process and what kind of literature should be used: Glaser limits theoretical preparations to the use of abstract literature. Pragmatically, Goulding (2002) recommends treating the relevant literature as a non-dominant informant for the emerging interpretations.

Hammersley (2002) offers an epistemological argumentation that explains the role of existing knowledge in inductive research. He shows that for interpretative research the Realist position can not hold and that the Relativist position can not be either. Arguing that in social science research all perception of the world including qualitative research is idiosyncratically constructed, he raises the question what it is that makes the researchers' relative view so special that it is worth writing down. This argument is part of the base for the subtle realism position introduced. One of its main conclusions is that, while the circularity can not be resolved, one major difference between a researchers' point of view and any other point of view should be to make one's relative, constructed point of view carefully *explicit* and *relevant*.

After discussing the use of existing theory and the general compatibility of existing theory with the Grounded Theory method, as well as the impossibility of a clean canvas approach for a researcher who was already active in some field of research, the problem of contamination, as Glaser framed it, is still present. The most valid way to address this problem is to explicate the researcher's preconceptions and his/her lenses in order to make the argumentation transparent and relevant (Krotz 2005, p. 32). In this study, the literature review (see p. 12) and the argumentation for a communication perspective as well as the careful adherence to a research method precisely serve this purpose.[33]

3.4 The Interview as a Data Collection Method

Rubin and Rubin (1995) use the metaphor of a vacation plan to illustrate the process of qualitative interview design: One has an overall idea of what should be seen and takes maps and plans along, but it is unsure which of those will prove useful. There is sufficient flexibility to explore what appears along the way, as long as the final destination is kept in mind.

An interview blueprint is expected to evolve iteratively as necessary, as new opportunities for inquiry open up. The questions below are the first iteration in the sense of Rubin and Rubin's iterative process of qualitative interview design, during which the final design emerges:

> "At each stage of the interviewing, you gather information, analyse, winnow, and test; then, based on the analysis and testing, you refine or change your questions, and perhaps choose a different set of interviewees, and repeat the process. Each iteration focuses more on the core points the interviewees are trying to convey." (Rubin, Rubin 1995, p. 44)

Forschauer and Lueger (2003) propose a similar process. They stress that mainly through this process the emerging ideas are confronted with the logic of the field – which is the main point of interpretative research. This flexible, semi structured interview process, which is also immanent in the Grounded Theory method, allows questioning to be adjusted to individual interview partners according to their style of discussion and their expertise in specific areas (Rubin, Rubin 1995). It thereby provides richer and more vivid data than fixed interviews or questionnaire data would provide.

Regarding the practical issue of whether to tape research interviews or to take notes, there seems to be a consensus in the Information Systems research community[34] that first of all tape recordings do not substitute notes and second, they are very valuable, but

---

33 This argumentation goes hand in hand with a definition of *preliminary* truth based on credibility and plausibility (see Hammersley 2002, p. 73 or Habermas' definition) as sketched above.

34 See http://www.qual.auckland.ac.nz (last accessed 2007-07-29).

under certain circumstances only. That is, interview partners need to agree and to feel comfortable with tape recording. Krotz (2005) pragmatically adds that this problem is often overestimated, as well as the fear of missing certain details in written notes. A detailed analysis of how certain statements are made is only useful for special research questions, more often, as in this case, what was said is of importance. Further, important aspects can be expected to reoccur.

The sensitivity (and possibly confidentiality) of negotiation issues indicates that taping interviews might not be acceptable, or worse, that interview partners may agree, but limit or adjust their answers accordingly, yielding a biased view. For the same reason, individual interviews are preferred over group discussions.

3.5 Research Approach of the Present Study

After choosing and introducing a research method, a number of practical decisions need to be addressed and documented. This is the purpose of the following sections.

3.5.1 Time Frame of Analysis

A longitudinal data collection, as proposed by Bannister (2002), can only take one of two forms, due to organisational research constraints: snapshot-data of negotiation events collected at different times over approximately one year or historical data collected from documents and ex post interviews, i.e. participants' introspection of past events, especially after agreements have been implemented and misunderstandings have been identified and clarified.

Because negotiation skills often are a critical and strategic asset of companies, empirical research on primary negotiation data in the field is particularly difficult. Interview partners can be assumed to be more easily accessible for reflection. Hence, the reflecting interview approach is preferred.

Due to the nature of the methodology, a precise schedule for the study can not be given – the time needed to reach saturation of the data is unknown a priori. In this case, the data collection and analysis was conducted during a period of 16 months until July 2007.

The data collected during this time-frame does not suggest changes of perceptions to an extent that would invalidate the conclusions made. It is a period of rather rational post-hype technology use and most cases analysed fall into this category as well.

3.5.2 Selection of Data Sources

Richness and diversity of the data collected is an inherent feature of the methodology applied. Case studies, Grounded Theory studies in particular, rely on different sources of evidence.

Ethnography is the richest and deepest form of data collection available. It is however the one causing most effort as well. The basic idea is to spend large amounts of time in the field of interest, generating first hand observations, abstracting from those and iteratively refining the knowledge collected by resolving from breakdowns, i.e. observations that contradict the ethnographers' preliminary theories, which can occur naturally or can be facilitated on purpose. First hand observations in the area of electronic negotiations are especially scarce, because it is difficult for scholars to gain access to the sensitive area of inter-organisational decision making. Whenever available, ethnographic observations should therefore be used. Especially in the early stages of the research, first hand observations are useful in order to become familiar with the context and e.g. specific terminology before interviews are conducted.

As personal experiences and reflections are valuable data sources regarding the communicative impacts of ENS, the study will primarily rely on semi-structured interviews using open questions (see Allan 2003) discussed with decision makers and negotiators such as members of marketing and procurement departments and additionally utilise primary observation, ethnographic data and text analysis wherever possible, but does not depend on a specific source. These groups are chosen as they are most likely to provide insights into the research area and guidance regarding further data sources. Rubin and Rubin provide the following three main requirements for the selection of qualitative interview partners:

"They should be knowledgeable about the cultural arena or the situation or the experience being studied; they should be willing to talk; and when people in the arena have different perspectives, the interviewees should represent the range of points of view." (Rubin, Rubin 1995, p. 66)

Due to the third requirement, it is advisable to gather data from buyers as well as from sellers – the two major perspectives involved in a negotiation setting. It is desirable to gather data from technology or marketplace providers as well, in order to increase variety and capture a third point of view. Intermediaries play an important role in the eProcurement market, but will probably be less knowledgeable regarding the technologies' effects than those players with first hand experiences. Due to the difficulties of primary data elicitation, the use of secondary data will be necessary at least in parts of the argumentation.

Following the advice of Rubin and Rubin, a fourth group of persons whose personal reflections on business negotiations would be of interest. It is the group of those procurement or sales representatives who carry out negotiations exclusively via *traditional* media such as face-to-face, via phone or fax or via electronic mail. Especially in the early phases, it may be useful to study their behaviour in order to capture a further point of view and to allow contrasting their views with those involved in electronic negotiations.

3.5.3 Subject and Level of Analysis

As Yin (1994, p. 20) puts it, case studies are a particularly useful method of inquiry when the phenomena of interest – in this instance technology use patterns and communicative impacts of technology – cannot be clearly separated from the social, technological, and organisational context in which they occur. In the research of inter-organisational systems these contexts are further blurred (Reimers 2002), which additionally calls for a careful and rich approach to data collection.

To allow for a seamless cross-case comparison of data, the main level of analysis will be that of single sourcing, especially negotiation processes, which can be easily discussed with people who have been involved in it. This level is also analysed by Carter et al. (2004, 2007). A wider level, such as the overall introduction process of an electronic negotiation system, is not appropriate, because it requires a much greater level of abstraction from the people interviewed and implies that they accompanied during the whole process. This would make it more difficult to find adequate interview partners. A finer level of analysis such as single document exchanges or speech acts can only be used when negotiation transcripts can be accessed or created from observation by the researcher, which turned out to be unrealistic.

3.5.4 Initial Interview Blueprint

The basic structure of all interviews conducted is that of a narrative interview (Schütze 1976). By explicitly asking interview partners for a narration, they generally tend to use an appropriate narrative structure, i.e. they introduce all players and the context of the narration, then report events and experiences chronologically and come to a conclusion finally.

This kind of structure is easy to follow for the interviewer. It contains all elements relevant to this research project. Further, interview partners naturally structure their narration to cover those details that are important to them (i.e. the core concepts), which are highly valuable for this study and further sampling steps. The narrative nature of the interviews is expected to decrease over time, after core concepts are identified.

In all cases the following aspects of the context need to be clarified:

- What was transacted?
- Was it a routine transaction or a special transaction carried out only once or seldom?

Once a basic understanding of the setting is provided, interview partners are asked to describe the negotiation process in its context. Special attention is drawn to:

- What kind of technology was employed to support the negotiation and why?
- What are the structural properties of this technology?
  (preferably off-site using documentation material)
- What was the role of the technology used?
- What makes this case a (non-) successful one for you?
- Was the mode of communication appropriate? What kind of problems occurred?

- How were those problems dealt with? Which strategies were employed to compensate the problems?

The final point is probably the most interesting and open one, as it accounts for the reflectivity of ENS users during transactions and the interpretative flexibility of the technologies. This path is extended in a final set of questions that takes changes in the context of transactions into account, such as:

- Do you think the technology was used in the way it was meant to?
- Is there anything you would do differently if a similar transaction was to be carried out again?
- What are the general 'lessons learned' regarding the use of such technologies in negotiations?

This blueprint is however not suitable for interviews with technology providers or people who do not use supporting technologies in their negotiations.

With the above interview blueprint, all components required for the actual conduct of the Grounded Theory study are introduced. We will continue with the presentation of its results.

4. Results - A Grounded Theory Field Study of E-Auction Appropriation and Communicative Impact

In this chapter the result of the analysis of the field study, i.e. the Grounded Theory developed, will be presented. This theory will be linked with existing knowledge. Writing Grounded Theory results is an ambiguous process regarding writing style. Charmaz and Mitchell (1996) point out that in a presentation of such results the author's several selves need to be visible - reflecting, witnessing, wondering, accepting - all at once. Furthermore, this reflection needs to embed the findings in existing theory in order to make clear what kind of contribution is made. At the same time the writings need to be evocative of the experiences and views of the interview partners, in order to actually provide a grounding in the sense of Glaser and Strauss.

The structure used to present the results is thus primarily arranged around the core concepts identified. At that level, pointers into the data as well as into existing theory and to other core concepts are integrated, in order to provide a more dense and understandable text than a sequential, i.e. chronological or case-based, presentation of these topics would allow. The observations made are backed up and linked by citations from interviews[35] and references to the other data collected in an anonymised form for reasons of confidentiality.

However, this style of writing puts the iterative process of data collection, coding and sampling into the background. For this reason, it will be sketched in a first step. The data collected and the conclusions drawn are presented as follows. First, the business context of electronic negotiation processes is sketched to provide a framework for the core results. As ENS technologies have been found to yield impacts in different roles, these roles are henceforth used as a top level structure for the presentation of the grounded theory. On a more detailed level, contingencies and consequences of the technology in its

---

35 Note that a dedicated index offers lists all interview excerpts included and all references made to them throughout the thesis (see p. 234).

respective role will be analysed – a number of concepts used resembles the coding families that Glaser and Strauss described drawing on their experience with the newly introduced Grounded Theory method such as the *Six Cs*.[36]

Throughout the presentation of the results, references to relevant theory are made in order to *embed* the conclusions drawn from the data collected theoretically. Interview data is also included in the text, to ground each particular point made.

4.1 Steps of Inference and Inquiry

Initially, the research process began with informal discussions with practitioners on fairs, in order to become familiar with the field of research in an ethnographic way, while observations of actual electronic negotiations were not possible.

The initial interview sampling draws on the contacts made in a 2005 survey study at Hohenheim University (Schoop et al. 2006b, Schoop et al. 2007a). While the survey did not provide rich data suitable for qualitative analysis, it initiated first contacts with potential interview partners and allowed for selective sampling. At that time, a small number of participants, addressed as N_1 to N_4 subsequently, agreed to participate in an open interview regarding their (electronic) negotiation habits and experiences. Since this initial sample includes both seller and buyer perspectives, as well as the perspective of an electronic negotiation intermediary and one company that does not use E-Negotiation technologies in the strict sense, it provides variety. Thus, it is a very useful starting point for the analysis. It yielded a considerably broad set of concepts of potential explanatory value.

Table 8 gives an overview of the key differences among the four initial datasets, which were selected to cover the main roles involved.

---

36 Namely Causes, Contexts, Contingencies, Consequences, Covariances and Conditions (Glaser 1978).

	N_1 (Buyer, non-electronic)	N_2 (Seller)	N_3 (Seller)	N_4 (Intermediary)
N_1	/	• Indirect goods – strategically relevant in N_1. • While N_1 was highly confident regarding structured exchanges N_2 saw this as a major problem, i.e. understood technology as a barrier he struggled with and as a relationship threat.	• Both large deals - about equal strategic relevance. • A different communicative setting: 1:1 and about equal power distribution and existing business relationship. • Technology as a productivity tool in the background.	• Technology both as an enabler and a barrier • Trade with large quantities of different goods of low complexity, while N_1 was about a single highly complex service.
N_2		/	• Selling through argumentation and joint work • Partly electronically, approach worked in N_3, while N_2 complained that an opportunity for discussion was lacking.	• Similar situation descriptions • Different strategies: Adapting the ENS iteratively (N_4) versus circumventing the ENS (N2).
N_3			/	• N_4 also described a setting, in which electronic media play the same role as in N_3 – without its project character. • High frequency low value transactions in N_4 versus low frequency high value N_3.

Table 8 : Selected differences found in the initial set of four samples.

Interestingly, there were little differences between the perspectives regarding some aspects. For example, all interviewees had communication structures that were far more complex than the traditional two-step model of two negotiators with one constituent on either side. They shared a number of goals, such as reaching a joint understanding and grounding the deal onto a solid legal foundation. N_1 and N_3 employed dedicated specialists to reach this goal during the respective negotiation events. Other goals were unevenly distributed. There is a complex set of goals and heuristics which (e-) negotiators are operating with. Considering this variety, the communicative and motivational setting of e-negotiators needs more exploration before a useful theory can be derived. This issue was addressed in further rounds of data collection.

Further observations resulted from these first interviews. It was already argued that before consequences of negotiation technology appropriation can be identified, it needs to be clarified what these technologies mean to their users and how they frame it (Orlikowski, Gash 1994), i.e. what the role of the technology is. Drawing on the first interviews, it is already evident that negotiation technology carries multiple divergent meanings. For different negotiating parties, a technology may either present itself as useful tool or as a threat for successful communication and relationship management, as already indicated in the example of HypoVereinsbank provided in Chapter 1. These aspects provide the starting point for the main part of data collection.

Regarding the technologies employed, the initial sample does not contain data on dedicated bilateral negotiation support systems in the strict sense, although N_3 heavily (and for some time exclusively) relied on computer mediated communication. Further, the settings are archetypes of the negotiation models presented, i.e. either 1:n or 1:1 settings, with auction or bargaining processes respectively. The following data collection was thus also guided by the search for NSS applications in the strict sense and multilateral bargaining cases – a hybrid setting that can be useful as a reference for further comparisons. The search for NSS application cases was not fruitful; hence electronic reverse auctions are the main focus of the study. Table 9 provides an overview of the data sources used in the study and serves as a reference. All data sources are listed chronologically, i.e. in the order of data elicitation and consequently in order of data analysis.

Three interviews were conducted in a more confirmatory manner towards the end of data collection: one with a buyer, one with a seller and one with an intermediary respectively. Triggered by a narration of negotiation events, the researcher presented and discussed selected conclusions made, in order to verify both relevance and plausibility of the Grounded Theory. These partly narrative, partly confirmatory interviews are marked explicitly. Finally, several discussions within the scientific community, for example at research conferences and other occasions, served to verify and clarify the conclusions drawn.

Identifier	Short description of the data set
P_1	This is a set of short, open interviews each of about 10 minutes conducted with a number of technology providers at the eProcure 2005 convention. Options for follow up interviews were opened.
P_2	Two interviews of about 90 minutes each regarding negotiation practices and options for technology based support (no dedicated technology was applied so far) were conducted with a professional juridical negotiation consultant from the ICT industry.
N_1	The head of procurement department of a large company in the financial sector (85 min, personal with field notes, covering IT-streamlined transaction processes and a successful, complex RfQ carried out via CD-ROM exchange).
N_2	The head of marketing in a large manufacturing company that mainly delivers to the construction sector (60 minutes presentation + 30 minutes telephone interview covering procurement platforms).
N_3	A project manager (key account, sales) in a large IT service company with a web focus (30 minutes telephone interview, covering email and Shared-Desktop interaction as well as face-to-face and telephone calls).
N_4	Marketplace / auction technology provider, CEO (20 minutes telephone interview).
N_5	The head of procurement (IT) in a large company in the financial sector with experiences in E-Auctions as well as electronic mail based RfQs (35 minutes telephone interview).
N_6	This interview was conducted in an SME level IT firm specialising on public administration projects, which are regularly awarded electronically (120 minutes face-to-face interview, 3 interviewers). A follow-up narrative interview that includes an analysis of project documentation is planned.
S_1	Secondary Data. The interview of a consultant with the CPO of a reverse E-Auction early adopter from the US-American electronics industry: Scientific-Atlanta, conducted in 2006 and published online: http://web.archive.org/web/20060430000115/http://purchasingautomation.com/articles/articles163.shtml last accessed (2007-08-07).
C_1	Series of discussions with the section manager of an eProcurement and Supplier Relationship Management software provider of about 5.5 hours (face-to-face) in total.
S_2	Secondary Data collected from the web regarding a specific reverse E-Auction case of a complex service bundle: HypoVereinsbank auctioned the handling of their customer magazine Wealth Management in September 2006. through the I-Faber platform.
S_3	Analysis of an online forum discussion with an intermediary and technology provider.
N_7	Open discussion with narrative interview elements as well as some following confirmatory elements (2x30 minutes, face-to-face and telephone respectively) with two procurement managers in the electrical industry.
C_2	Online forum discussion on reverse auctions with a procurement manager from the automotive industry.
N_8	Open discussion with narrative interview elements with two entrepreneurs of a negotiation support technology provider start-up (120 minutes, face-to-face interview).
N_9	Web cast presentation session including discussion (70 minutes) of a procurement case study presented through a senior sourcing manager and a representative from Emptoris Inc. They applied a combine E-Auction-negotiation model in a US-wide sourcing project for temporary labour.
S_4	Analysis of an interview published by Forbes.com (Feb. 2007) with the leader of e-sourcing at Heinz.
S_5	Position paper by Adrian Griffith, Director of Vendigital, Swindon, UK in the Journal of Supply Chain Management (Griffith 2003).
N_{10}	Face-to-face interview (50 minutes) with a sourcing manager for indirect material in large manufacturing company.
C_3	Face-to-face interview (120 minutes) on eRfQs and reverse E-Auctions with the Head of Key Account Management and E-Commerce in a medium sized trading company, which mainly delivers indirect goods to a broad set of industry sectors.

Table 9 : Chronological list of preparatory open interviews (Pn), narrative interviews (Nn) and confirmatory discussions (Cn) as well as secondary data used (Sn).

With most interview partners, non-disclosure agreements were made. The descriptions of these companies are therefore on an abstract level, which does not allow to deduce the identity of the respective market players. For the sake of clarity, the identifiers from the above table are used as references to the interviews subsequently, whether there is a non-disclosure agreement or not.

Perspective	Buyer	Supplier	Intermediary
	9	5	5
Data source	Primary data	Secondary data	
	78.95%	21.05%	
Data collection	Face to face	Phone / Audio	Textual
	8	6	5

Table 10: Aggregated overview on perspectives and data sources.

Table 10 provides an aggregate overview on the data sources used. Most interviews are on the sourcing side and conducted face-to-face, supplier and intermediary perspective are represented equally. Secondary data plays a complementary role only.

4.2 Business Context Factors and the Roles of Negotiation Technology

The following pages serve two purposes in the line of argumentation. First, a description of the setting in which business-to-business electronic negotiation actually takes place provides relevant context. Second, as an orientation in the broad dataset e-negotiator's goals are analysed, in order to shed light particularly on those aspects of ENS use and effects that are relevant and of interest to practitioners in the proceedings of the study. Further, this step is necessary to be able to see the findings from their point of view.

4.2.1 Communicative Setting of Electronic Business-to-Business Negotiations

The question of how to define the relevant context of negotiation technology for analysis is difficult, as any particular border among (sub-) organisations can be argued to be arbitrary (see Reimers 2002). Similar claims can be made for other dimensions.

Following the exploratory line of research, along with some obvious context parameters, only key aspects of negotiation context will be investigated, i.e. those aspects that carry explanatory value for the practitioners who mentioned them in their explanations of individual negotiation cases, precisely because of their explanatory value (see Table 11). Note that the values provided are the results of the coding procedure – information on specific context parameters could not be identified in all cases. Some interview partners refer to more than one case or did not argue narratively, i.e. on a case-by-case basis, at all.

Power distribution	Buyer	Buyer / Supplier	Supplier
	16	6	-
Existing relationship	Yes	No	
	15	2	
Strategic relevance	High	Medium	Low
	5	4	11

Table 11: Business contexts of the cases analysed.

Although the products and services negotiated in the cases mentioned range from potatoes, mechanical and electronics components to temporary labour contracts, facility security services and construction contracts, some common patterns of ENS application can be identified.

First, buyer-markets prevail. In most cases, the buying organisation holds the market power and brings this power to the (virtual) negotiation table – usually in the form of an auction model.

Second, the argumentation of technology providers regarding the ease of finding new suppliers is misleading since transacting with new businesses partners is an exceptional case. In nearly all cases observed negotiators had some form of business relationships already. Previous studies paint a similar picture. It is for example proposed that (even during the hype time) half of all companies participating in online auctions in the aerospace market have not won new customers (Emiliani, Stec 2004).

Third, while the majority of electronic negotiation cases are about indirect goods procurement, this mode of interaction is not limited to this category. Strategically relevant complex goods and services are also transacted this way – sometimes successfully, sometimes not.

Another aspect in which the average business negotiation setting investigated consistently and strongly deviates from the common practice in electronic negotiation experiments is the communication network. The common chain model including two negotiators which represent one constituent each is too simple to describe actual business settings (Turner 1992, Webster, Wind 1972).

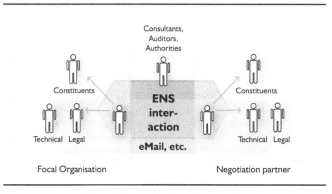

Figure 7: Communication setting overview.

As summarised in Figure 7, further stakeholders such as legal departments, specialist departments, external legal or technical consultants and auditors may come into play, regularly through electronic mail or telephone, as well as the authorities, consultants or negotiation technology providers. It is also not uncommon to find multiple constituents for a single negotiator, most often business-to-business negotiators operate as buyers or sellers and thereby in the role of internal service providers for different departments, besides having a formal constituent such as their respective head of department. All of these parties potentially interact with each other (through traditional media or directly), with the ENS or through the ENS.

A typical example for inter-organisational interaction which involves other players than the negotiators and their respective constituents is the direct interaction between legal experts in two companies through electronic mail using attached contract versions. This was observed in the datasets P_2, P_3, N_1, N_3 and is a common occurrence in business practice.

Nevertheless, usually key negotiators can be identified, who mainly take the boundary-spanning role. The interaction between negotiators and constituents in which preferences are communicated, new information and views are formed and exchanged is referred to as intra-organisational bargaining in the theory.

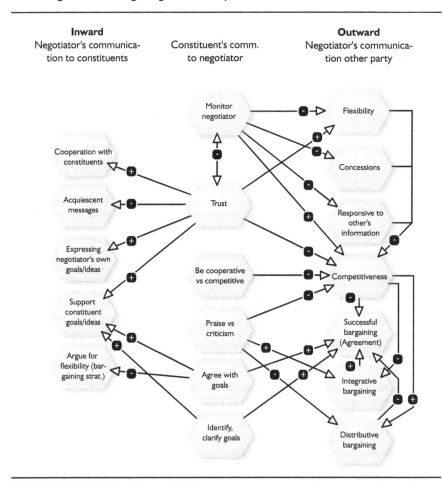

Figure 8: Inward and outward directed communication in business negotiations (based on Turner 1992, p. 245).

Turner (1992) gives a comprehensive overview of the inner workings of intra-organisational bargaining and negotiation related communication respectively (see Figure 8). The role of a boundary spanning negotiator, e.g. a sourcing manager, is largely characterised by conflicts. While constituents' expectations and those of negotiation partners are often oppositional, the boundary spanner needs to maintain a productive working relationship with each of them. Business negotiator roles involve three inherently communicative functions: representative, information processing, and agent of influence (Turner 1992, p. 235).[37] All of these functions are bidirectional. That is, the sourcing manager interacts with constituents and business partners iteratively, as an intermediary.

4.2.2 Operational Goals and Heuristics in E-Negotiation Behaviour

The traditional economic view of negotiation analysis abstracts from the multifaceted structure of goals that negotiators are operating with. By application of utility functions, which negotiators are assumed to optimise with different degrees of rationally, it reduces strategies to uni-dimensional concession patterns. Only recently authors such as Curhan and colleagues (2006) stressed the predictive worth of subjective value, a multifaceted construct in itself, in an empirical study that also started with a phase of qualitative coding. The business-to-business context analysed here will probably inherit such complexities from their claims made for negotiation situations in general, but is likely to include further goals specific to inter-organisational E-Negotiation settings.

A number of concepts emerged from the open coding analysis of the interview transcripts, further iterative analysis and coding clarified that many interview partners were giving reasons for their behaviour, while weaving the narrative structure of the interview. While initially these were coded as important statements individually, it soon became clear that many of these statements were examples of goals or heuristics the interview partners operated with. The coding process, therefore, iterated in order to provide a more com-

---

37 Webster and Wind (1972) distinguish similar functions, which persons involved in a buying centre may have inter- and intra-organisationally.

plete view of these concepts in the different business negotiation settings. Table 12 gives an overview of the frequency with which the goals were mentioned.

Goals, i.e. what people actually try to do, are obvious candidate aspects of business settings which may carry explanatory power for technology use and effects.[38] Goals are an important aspect of the negotiation context. The multi-faceted character of operational goals is clearly evident from the data collected. These goals operate on different levels. For example, achieving good prices can be seen as a subgoal of an overall utility maximisation goal. In this dataset, this is not mentioned explicitly as an operational goal and is thus not useful for explaining technology use behaviour.

---

38 See (Zumpe, van der Heijden 2006) for a similar argumentation.

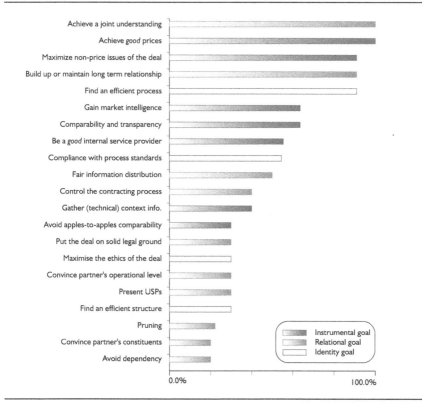

Table 12: Prevalence of negotiator goals and heuristics in (e-) negotiation cases.

A dedicated study on negotiator goals (Wilson, Putnam 1990) identifies three primary high-level goals: instrumental goals of resource distribution, relational goals and identity goals such as face saving. While resource distribution goals (such as to achieve good prices or to collect information, marked in green) and relational goals (building up a long term relationship or pruning on the other hand, grey) are often present in the dataset, identity goals (such as to maximize the ethics of a deal or to find an efficient structure for the procurement department, white) are less frequent.

However, it should be pointed out that it might be less acceptable for interview partners to discuss motives other than rational, economic self-interest (Curhan et al. 2006, p. 495). It is also plausible that interview partners explicate official goals or socially desirable goals rather than their own, which is why the completeness of the given list can not be argued for.

Naturally, some of the goals are interdependent if not mutually exclusive. As Griffith (2003) points out, the goals of the main stakeholders of sourcing managers in the industry, finance and manufacturing, may have directly opposing goals (that is price versus quality and continuity of supply), which forces sourcing managers into a process of juggling their interests.

Established negotiation and auction theory is mainly concerned with resource distribution goals and a considerable breadth of model driven and empirical research, leaving the other two sets and their interaction open as opportunities for exploratory research. Consequently, because relational goals are dominating identity goals in business negotiators' mindsets, they are mainly in the focus of the following analysis.

As Blumer (1969, p. 69) puts it, a tree is not the same to a lumberman, a botanist, or a poet. Concepts are socially defined with respect to what people do with them, i.e. what their goals are. This is especially true for innovative technologies. Consequently three conceptions of ENS technologies in use can be identified.

4.3 Auction-based ENS as Process Tools

Beyond potential savings in indirect material costs, which were the main driver of the first wave of reverse auction applications in B2B electronic commerce, such systems are meant to increase process efficiency. After introducing the process tool role of auction-based ENSs, we will investigate antecedents and likely consequences of systems, which are applied as such.

4.3.1 The Process Tool Role and its Prevalence

De Moor and Aakhus (2006) point out that communication technologies are not necessarily tools. Only those devices and technologies that contribute to the purposes of their users, i.e. if they help to reach their users' goals, can be considered to be tools.

As will be shown, these goals are usually process related and we consequently speak of a process tool. This point of view is naturally the view of those who consider their respective application of ENS to be *successful*. The rhetoric of application providers is quite similar, but not grounded in scientific analysis and must be further assumed to be biased towards an organisational imperative, i.e. towards the assumption that Information Systems are conceived to fulfil an organisation's information processing needs – a position of considerable optimism regarding the control of human influence over the capabilities of (inter-organisational) Information Systems and their introduction processes, including organisational changes (Markus, Robey 1988).

The analysis of negotiator goals shows that the (operative) conception of efficient negotiation processes is of importance indeed. Consequently, the (more strategic) efficiency of negotiating (sub-) organisations is as well. Judging from the data collected, ENS may indeed serve these purposes in certain contexts, as will be shown below.

4.3.2 Antecedents of the Process Tool Role

Descriptiveness

All electronic auction models share the assumption that the good or service under consideration can be described in sufficient detail a priori. The same is true for most NSS approaches such as Inspire or SmartSettle.

Findings

Interview partners (in consensus) stress that the key to success in electronic auctions lies in the preparation phase, in the creation of an *apples-to-apples* decision scenario, or in other words in the adequate descriptions and specifications. E-Auctions require detailed, precise and stable specifications of goods and services and may require extensive supplier selection and bid evaluation processes that generate high volumes of data, either quantitative or qualitative.

☐ *(S₁ line 105) Your requirements must be clearly documented. [..] you'll need drawings that contain dimensions and plating specifications, so your suppliers understand what they are going to bid on.*

☐ *(N₈ line 26) If it is good to specify, then I'm running an auction.*

☐ *(N₉ line 20) [For successful online auctions] You need to make sure that you know your requirements. [..] Such a high volume of data. [.. we used a] distributed analysis team to evaluate supplier coverage as well – we require presence.*

☐ *(N₁₀ line 49) [..] and you can quantify that. We try to create a real comparability [of offers].*

☐ *(C₂ line 31) I made the experience that E-Auctions and E-RfQs can yield completely different results. Relevant factors are the product category, the structure of the market and the quality of the specification.*

The HypoVereinsbank case illustrates the effects of lacking descriptiveness in an electronic auction case: Flexible, creative services can not be meaningfully specified on the same level of detail as physical goods, such as office supplies. For highly standardised goods, on the other hand, auction technologies can provide efficiencies and transparency improvements. Take for example the diffusion of electronic stock exchanges such as the German XETRA, which have largely replaced traditional trade procedures. It is an electronic, open-cry double auction of homogeneous and easily describable goods and can hence create efficiencies from IT use. To sum up, these findings can be generalised to form the following hypothesis:

(Hypothesis 1): Electronic auction success, reliability of auction results and procurement process efficiencies are positively related to the descriptiveness of the goods and services to be transacted.

This factor seems to be more important in online, open-cry auctions than in sealed-bid auctions, i.e. eRfQs. In fact, sourcing managers use the hypothesis as a heuristic evaluation of their reverse auction projects. They discover incomplete or misleading auction specifications through the careful observation of variance in bids. Thus, this hypothesis is inherent in the theory-in-use of electronic business negotiators, but it is subject to pragmatic experimentation.

Related Work

The traditional economic literature abstracts from the descriptiveness factor. We find it in similar form in the New Institutional Economics. Williamson (2000) concludes that, due to bounded rationality and scarce resources in the process of producing contracts, negotiated business contracts are necessarily incomplete in that they do not cover all possible contingencies regarding future events. Because the auction protocol requires that this not the case and that all relevant aspects of the transaction can be specified a priori, the above hypothesis appears plausible and reasonable.[39]

Similar hypotheses have been derived in the empirical literature on electronic auctions. The CAPS research group (Beall et al. 2003) identifies specifiability (based on item specificity and different aspects of complexity) as a strong predictor of electronic auction success in their discussion of E-Auctions in strategic sourcing. It is pointed out that complexity stems not only from products, but may include e.g. special logistic requirements, which make a transaction difficult to describe and plan. Similar findings are presented by Kaufmann and Carter (2003) as well as Smeltzer and Carr (2003) and Gattiker et al. (2007) for the auction case.

It is unclear under which circumstances and how far NSSs could successfully be used in situations of uncertainty and tacitness regarding the issues to coordinate, as no field data is available yet.

Supplier Training

Findings

Another requirement for ENS to work as a process tool emerged from data analysis: supplier training. Consider the following interview excerpts:

---

39 Below, it will be shown that often transaction partners have no incentives to cooperate in creating such a specification which further supports the hypothesis. For extreme cases of non-descriptiveness the expertise of the transaction partner may be required however. This usually either leads to a more cooperative model of coordination or a dysfunctional form of electronic auction, where influence on the specifications and information advantages are used strategically.

☐ (S_1 *line 92*) *I also recommend using a very consistent sourcing process for your suppliers'*
sake. It's stressful enough to put them through a reverse auction: you don't want the process to
be different for them every time.

☐ (N_9 *line 23*) *[..] Training of suppliers was very important.*

☐ (N_{10} *line 128*)
Q: You mentioned that suppliers have learned a lot. What does that mean for supplier training
regarding procurement platforms? Is that still a critical success factor?
A: Absolutely. Mastering the platform is strictly necessary.

Despite the prevalence of electronic trade, the transaction platforms and protocols appear either not to be similar enough or to be widespread enough for suppliers to let a general media competency replace platform specific training at the time of writing. Consequently, supplier training is a critical success factor for ENS projects. Both in experiments by the Negoisst team and by the Inspire team the experiences made by the support teams while conducting the experiments can be seen as confirmation of this finding for the NSS case. Therefore, we derive the following hypothesis:

(Hypothesis 2): Supplier training is positively related to the process efficiency of ENS transactions.

Although the data mainly points towards supplier training, E-Negotiation skill seems to be a specific skill both on the supplier side and on the sourcing side. System training plays an important role in establishing it, but is not identical with it. The ability to compensate for weaknesses of such systems is relevant as well. The section on overconfidence contains examples of such specific issues and the consequences of a lacking understanding of the platform (see p. 115).

Related Work

The empirical literature on electronic auction use supports this finding. Training, in this case on the supplier side as well as on the buyer side, is proposed as an effective means of overcoming electronic auction implementation barriers (Carter et al. 2004). This is a prerequisite for extracting rents from process efficiencies or increasing competition. Dedicated service companies have been founded to satisfy the need for supplier training regarding E-Auctions (such as www.e-three.com). Further evidence exists for the effectiveness of training in general, equivocal decision making tasks performed through computer mediated communication (CMC) channels (Cornelius, Boos 2003). Experiences from experiments both by the Negoisst-team and the Inspire-group confirm this finding for the NSS case.

It should be further pointed out that platform specifics turn supplier training into a relationship specific investment for them.

Trust and Transparency

Findings

Due to the high level of specialisation and interdependency of industrialised business operations, maintaining a trusted relationship is of primary concern in general. Auction-based models regularly give rise to suspicions of unethical behaviour such as e.g. phantom bidding. In other words, the auctioneer may secretly be acting as a bidder, in order to induce competition artificially. Hence, trust is of special concern in electronic auction settings.

Because negotiation platforms are often controlled by buyers or buyer consortia, suppliers have little means of controlling such behaviour and that means, they need to rely on trust. Further, since participation and competition are core success factors in all auction-based negotiation models, buyers regularly have a strong incentive to facilitate trust building and to build up auction-related credibility. The following excerpts show such considerations.

☐ *(S_1 line 16) We were concerned, but we also believed we could mitigate the risks by making our sourcing policies fair. For example, we made it clear that [C_1] would never award business on price alone.[line 101:] We didn't want to damage our reputation.*

☐ *(N_5 line 35) [..] All in all it's very transparent; we do this rigorously and the suppliers all know: it will be two rounds – they really acknowledge it.*

☐ *(N_9 line 405) [..] has found that auctions also provide transparency to suppliers—they know without a doubt where they stood against the competition and can walk away knowing they were given a fair shot at the business (we have had supplier feedback to support this).*

☐ *(N_{10} line 90) Bonus and malus systems often appear very subjective [..]. We develop a decision matrix with the respective department involved [..] and in summary the process is transparent and credible.*

Transparency of procurement processes is the main contributor (and requirement) for trust building in this sense, which in turn is a key success factor in electronic auctions and ENS use in general. Building on the goals of negotiators, which have been analysed above (see p. 89), the operational success in this context is twofold. It has a direct savings component and a more indirect component of process efficiencies and frictionlessness. While the benchmarks for the components may vary from case to case, the following hypothesis appears to hold generally.

(Hypothesis 3): Process transparency and supplier trust are positively related to process efficiency of ENS transactions.

The actual software implementation and its trust related features, such as encryption and digital signatures, play a small and complementary role in trust-building only. Trust in ENS contexts is more a conclusion of experiences made over time during particular episodes of interaction, both within software systems and within other channels of interaction.

Related Work

Transparency and the ability to control are important concepts in the New Institutional Economics (Williamson 2000). In a business sourcing context, buyers' choice to use open, rank order or sealed bid auctions for example may arouse suppliers' suspicion that the buyer is using the auction opportunistically against the supplier (Jap 2003). This may motivate her to apply additional safeguards and hence increase transaction costs – the same argumentation holds vice versa.

A recent empirical study which uses a structural equation modelling approach shows the role that trust plays for supplier non-price performance in electronic auction settings

(Carter, Kaufmann 2007). It thus confirms the above hypothesis, since process efficiencies and transparency are important aspects of such a general performance measure. Jap (2003) adds that suppliers may benefit from trust and implicit understanding of a buyer's needs and constraints, in order to make auction events successful. Specific concepts such as transaction costs or process costs need to be explored further, in order to clarify what success means in this context empirically.

The fact that dedicated trust-building technological solutions have not been mentioned at all fits into the schema of the general, much discussed theory of a commoditisation of business IT infrastructure (Carr 2003). The basic idea is that, given the ubiquity of IT, it ceases to offer strategic opportunities for business, i.e. it is a commodity - with some similarities with electricity. Companies strongly depend on IT, which therefore carries risks that need careful evaluation and management.[40] Therefore, as the technology itself is basically perceived as trustworthy, further technological improvements will hardly change the situation.

4.3.3 Consequences for Negotiation Processes

Re-Design in Adjacent Processes

Findings

Interview partners comment on the effects of an ENS introduction remarkably often in a context of broader organisational change. The following interview excerpts exemplify this.

☐ *(N, line 37)*

> A: There are also problems with the back end-integration to [..] the logistics partner; to keep them up to date regarding different negotiated contracts, to make sure everything actually arrives where it is supposed to. [..] In the course of eProcurement we also plan to provide efficient means for controlling and spend management. We are planning a new project now [..].

---

40 Two such risks, the communication barrier and the relationship threat, are introduced below in Chapter 4.

> Q: What is your primary goal – how would you know whether the new solution was a good one?
> A: Processes that are as frictionless as possible. [..] For a service company such as we are procurement is not as important as for other industries. 'How many employees do I need to maintain the supply' – that is the core question.
>
> □ *(S₄ line 30)* The savings benefits are confidential but substantial, but the real impact is in process improvements and reliability. I like to think of it as value engineering

Consequently, it appears that reverse auction systems, or more precisely the process of their introduction, trigger or enable process redesign in adjacent intra-organisational processes, such as controlling, logistics or contracting. Moreover, the frictionless conduct of such processes is an important criterion of ENS success.

This kind of spill-over effect has not been mentioned in interviews with suppliers. It seems to be limited to the buy-side. On the supplier side, however, the introduction of reverse auctions into a business relationship is taken up as a driver for cost-cutting and efficiency improvements (e.g. in C_3). Thus, we present the following hypothesis.

(Hypothesis 4): ENS introduction offers an occasion for intra-organisational re-design in adjacent processes.

Following this aspect into the adjacent organisational units in order to evaluate whether such changes generate transaction cost efficiencies in the long run, would be interesting, but requires a conduct of further interviews with persons that do not have a boundary-spanning negotiator role. We will not continue this chain of argumentation and rather concentrate on the consequences for those directly involved in inter-organisational negotiation processes.

Related Work

The idea of technology as an occasion for organisational change (Barley 1986) is a key conclusion of the structuration perspective and the Information Systems perspective in general (see Markus, Robey 1988, Orlikowski 1992). Barley (1986) shows in a longitudinal study how technology triggers organisational change.

Note that the changes induced in this study are not deterministic, but divergent in the two organisations involved, depending on how the particular technology is framed (Orlikowski, Gash 1994). Because the technologies analysed by Barley (computer tomography scanners) are not inter-organisational technologies, and thereby have a more arte-factual, tangible character than ENS, a broader range of framing and effects can be expected here. One pattern of organisational change has been observed repeatedly however.

Centralisation of Competencies in the Negotiating Organisations

How is the mentioned occasion for redesign employed in practice? Information Systems have long been predicted to yield a centralisation of competencies, to deprive middle management of flexibility and to strengthen the role of top management (Leavitt, Whisler 1958). This idea has undergone extensive debate and especially internet-age Information Systems have been shown to actually yield the opposite effect, i.e. to decentralise decision making and to flatten hierarchies (see also Barley 1986). How do ENSs play into this (ongoing) discussion?

Findings

In N_9 highly complex service contracts for temporary labour were sourced nationwide in a single event by a centralised sourcing project team that collected and compiled job descriptions as well as information from the potential suppliers and awarded business to a subset of these using electronic negotiation support technologies. It was pointed out that this form of negotiation was clearly enabled by the technology:

> ☐ (N_9 line 15) We could not have done such a (auction and negotiation) process a few years ago – the tool was very helpful.

It needs to be pointed out that the auction tool in this case was not applied under strict auction rules, but to select a subset of bidders for further negotiation. Nevertheless, it increased the cognitive and communicative capabilities of the sourcing team enough to run the negotiation project centrally.

Another aspect of centralisation is that specialised competencies of procurement and sourcing departments and other departments can be accessed more easily in an electronic, asynchronous negotiation setting than in a face-to-face negotiation setting. This argument is driving centralisation of sourcing processes in general and can also be applied to the supplier side: Technical, economical or legal expertise can be accessed intra-organisationally in a more efficient way in a centralised environment with ENSs deployed. We find this on the supplier side as well.

> ☐ (N_6 line 64) Our customers are mainly from the public sector [online RfQ is common]. First we broadly specify what the customer wants; which components and partly for what price. Functional details are not specified at that time. Up to now really everything is in one hand. Usually we offer to create a contract [..] and before any contract goes out to a customer he [the sales representative] will send it to me to check it for any problems.

Drawing on these findings it is concluded that negotiation support technologies with their codified procedures and asynchronous communication facilities contribute to centralisation of decision making within organisations that make use of the technology.

(Hypothesis 5): ENSs enable centralisation both in sourcing and supplying organisations. While desktop purchasing, i.e. eProcurement on an operative level, effectively is a form of de-centralisation, the electronic support of negotiations yields the opposite effect.

Related Work

The aforementioned study by BME and Siemens (2006) claims a large potential of savings that could be accomplished through a complete centralisation of sourcing activities, because non-traditional categories such as patents, financial or consulting services, marketing, research and development etc. do not yet benefit from professional sourcing expertise (Wannenwetsch 2006, p. 2). Weigand et al. find centralisation as the key reorganisation issue in strategic sourcing (Weigand et al. 2004).

It can be assumed, that this is a consideration that drove HypoVereinsbank (S_2) to reverse-auction their marketing project. As illustrated in this example, centralisation is not valuable in itself as long as it does not yield efficient processes. Furthermore, centralising additional procurement volume requires additional domain specific expertise (or ready access to it) in the respective procurement departments or associated centres of competence respectively (such as in N_{10}). In these non-traditional fields of procurement other factors such as flexibility need to be investigated and evaluated against potential efficiency gains from centralisation.

Long-term Process Efficiencies

The procurement function is currently shifting into the focus of strategic management (hence "sourcing"). Multiple interview partners report of reorganisation projects with this background. Therefore, process evaluation in the sense of spend management and transaction cost analysis is of concern and we will concentrate on these non-price issues.

Findings

Interestingly, practitioners do not see ENS, E-Auctions in this case, as a tool for process cost reductions per se. On the contrary, running an E-Auction is regularly considered to be an additional effort in a procurement process, for a number of reasons: Although E-Auctions are technically an exchange of messages (specifications and bids) through a restrictive, asynchronous medium, they are enacted as synchronous interaction events. Appointments are made and members of the procurement staff make sure to attend and observe the auction process, in order to make sure everything runs as planned.

Furthermore, the auction setting critically depends on high-quality specifications. Creating these is causing additional process costs compared to interactive face-to-face or telephone-based bargaining or RfQ processes. The following excerpts exemplify, that sourcing managers take this effort into account when choosing negotiation models.

☐ (N_7 line 44) Those savings in X percent generated through E-Auctions [which you find in the press] - they are realistic from time to time. [..] But you always need to take your time and ask: is it really worth the effort?

☐ (*N₉ line 378*) *Whether using a reverse auction or simply an electronic RFP, the tool has forced us to be more organised and precise with our information. When suppliers have better informa-tion, they are able to "sharpen their pencils."*

☐ (*N₉ line 383*) *All sourcing information around a project is captured and maintained in the tool. When we are ready to source the project again in a few years, we will be able to find all of the info quickly and used relevant templates.*

☐ (*C₂ line 34*) *E-Auctions are an excellent tool to create some dynamic in a negotiation, to speed it up and make it reproducible such as for annual purchasing processes.*

From an intra-organisational process point of view, transparency and improved process documentation are *bought* with this additional effort as well as future benefits, which can be realised by reusing or analysing the datasets gained.

(Hypothesis 6): ENS support in negotiated business sourcing events increases the internal, ex-post transparency of the process.

While that effect is positive and intentional, the short term evaluation of ENS use is neither. As the investments and operational costs in technology infrastructure and training have not been explicated as considerable or decision relevant, they are considered as marginal. Because most ENSs are available in the form of services over the internet, this is plausible, which leads to the following hypotheses regarding short term cost effectiveness on the buyer side of a transaction.

(Hypothesis 7): Regarding a single negotiated business sourcing event, auction-based nego-tiation support yields no decrease in buy-side negotiator workload compared to an unsup-ported process, which relies on electronic mail and/or traditional means of negotiation.

While ex-post transparency is an important goal in itself regarding negotiator goals men-tioned, long term transaction cost effects of increased process transparency are subject to numerous contingencies, such as transaction frequency or the negotiation support model in use.

Regarding the transaction cost effects described so far we have mainly taken a sourcing point of view. Consequently, an evaluation of sell-side effects follows. Consider the following interview excerpts.

☐ (*N₂ line 9*) *We receive many requests to integrate us into some [buy-side] procurement platforms. First of all, it needs to be clarified whether we are talking about a catalogue and ordering platform or whether it is only "you are allowed to bid", which we try to avoid. [..] Often the costs for the integration are prohibitive, considering the integration and especially the maintenance of say 6.000 articles. We can't do that if there is not enough transaction volume to be expected.*

☐ (*N₆ line 156*) *eRfQs are associated with process costs that may well exceed the amount of revenues. We, along with a consulting partner, have spent around 400.000 € in process costs to prepare our participation in such an event – to no success.*

As auctions live trough competition, based on the number of bidders, it is straightforward to find suppliers to be invited more frequently through the advent of online reverse auctions ceteris paribus, which also translates into an increasing workload for the respective negotiators. Further costs may be induced by communication problems typical in reverse auction settings (see p. 108) and the technical integration into buy-side catalogues. Beyond the workload on the supplier side, regularly an integration fee applies. Therefore, the following hypothesis appears reasonable.

(Hypothesis 8): Regarding a single negotiated business sourcing event, auction-based ENS support yields an increase in supplier-side negotiator workload compared to an unsupported process, which relies on electronic mail and/or traditional means of negotiation.

In summary, the *red tape* involved with reverse auction models increases transaction costs on the supplier side of a transaction. It appears that, surprisingly, suppliers are paying for the increasing transparency on the sourcing side in the electronic B2B markets, which exemplifies the current distribution of market power.

Related Work

All of the above statements surprisingly indicate an increase in process costs as a consequence to the introduction of auction-based ENSs compared to established processes. This is consistent with other findings (Emiliani, Stec 2004, Emiliani, Stec 2005), which show an increasing overhead burden through the application of electronic auctions on the supplier side and on the buyer side, e.g. associated with the people required to work on the bidding process. Especially open-bid auctions increase the supplier's bargaining costs (Jap 2003). Regarding transaction costs auction models, in the strict sense of competitive bidding, seem to be at a disadvantage compared to less automatic bargaining procedures, which is surprising.

An earlier study that compares these modes of transaction found choosing a contractor using negotiations (in the sense of bargaining) to involve less *red tape* than competitive bidding protocols (Bajari et al. 2002), such as online reverse auctions. The explanation underneath lies in the nature of business relationships – while the negotiation case assumes that there is an incumbent supplier or a new one is selected based on reputation or similar mechanisms, the competitive bidding case assumes that at a transaction with a new transaction partner is considered. This implies search costs such as for advertising a contract and the cost for creating and understanding some kind of specification. While traditional economics, due to a full information assumption, would consider the result to be the only efficiently allocated solution, what we see here is an argumentation with transaction costs and a return on social capital (see p. 153), which is perceived to compensate for possible inefficiencies such as price premiums.

Repeated E-Negotiation events may reduce negotiation process cycle time. These effects regarding negotiator productivity replicate earlier findings (Carter et al. 2004, p. 239). However, a core problem of transaction costs economics, which Williamson addressed but could not solve, is still the lack of operationalisation regarding the transaction cost and efficiency terms. This severely limits the use of transaction cost argumentations for predictive purposes, while many phenomena can be explained ex post (Schreyögg 2003, p. 74). The transaction cost approach has been heavily criticised for its basic assumptions. A central point of critique is the extremely narrow perspective. Basic economic aspects such as relevant costs and especially all kinds of benefits (esp. aspects like collective dynamics and innovation, cf. Goshal, Moran 1996) are disregarded.[41] There is no room to argue in term of competitive advantages and strategic resources. Traditional transaction cost theory abstracts from power relationships, goal setting processes and the internal organizational behaviour. The internal organisation is seen as mechanistic and "a priori", i.e. it is basically irrelevant when transaction costs come into play (along the lines of Schreyögg 2003, p. 74).

Because the above findings are rooted in the observation of reverse auction settings, it is difficult to make predictions for electronic negotiation support in the sense of bargaining (such as SmartSettle or Negoisst). As the hypotheses derive from specific properties of auction models, it can plausibly be assumed that they do not hold for the bargaining case – a symmetrical decrease in transaction costs could be expected instead, drawing on experiences with video conferencing described in N_3 and N_6.

4.3.4 Contingency Model of the Process Tool Role

The contingencies and consequences of the process tool role of electronic auction tools are summarised below (see Figure 9). The effects apply to buyers and sellers alike, while the negotiator workload effect is different for the two roles. Due to the appropriation of auction events as synchronous and the increasing workload for specifications, process efficiencies are of an indirect, long-term kind. They mainly arise after repeated interaction or from secondary use of the obtained data. Further, an externalisation of process fragments and the associated costs from buyers to sellers currently seems to take place.

---

41 We will investigate both below.

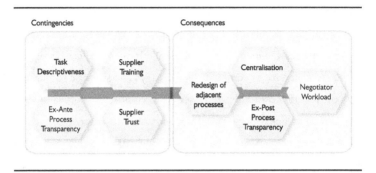

Figure 9: Contingency model of the process tool role.

Process transparency is an importance goal in itself as it provides the ground for controlling, spend management, market transparency as well for process standard compliance. The process tool role appears to gain importance, which confirms the transaction cost driven model of auction application by Pinker (2003, see Figure 3, p. 33). Online auctions clearly enable an extension of the portfolio of dynamically priced goods.

However, the comparison of electronic auctions with traditional auctions is misleading. It appears to be more difficult to obtain process efficiencies from the introduction of electronic auctions than generally assumed, if compared to (electronic) RfQs or an e-mail driven process, which more closely represents the decision situation procurement managers face. As already stated, the single transaction falls short as a level of analysis regarding these effects. Overall, these findings largely match the early evidence from other qualitative studies, where the following aspect is hitherto disregarded.

4.4 Auction Platforms as Communication Barriers

The relevance of communicative quality in electronic negotiations, a term which has only been vaguely defined so far (Schoop et al. 2006b), has been motivated and sketched from a theoretical point of view already. Drawing on the data collected, we find that business (e-) negotiators actually have communicative goals in mind when they interact with each other and that they experience negotiation support technology to get in the way of reaching them.

Excerpts of interviews demonstrate that such goals are relevant (4.4). Further, our finding will first be embedded into and contrasted with existing theory. The ideal communicative setting is revisited as a point of reference in greater detail (4.4), before it is evaluated how far the communicative goals in E-Negotiation interaction are reached and what pathologies ENS technologies potentially yield (4.4). With that in mind, the identification of antecedents (4.4) and especially the socio-technological contingencies (4.4) follow. Understanding both is necessary to speak of a theory of use and appropriation.

4.4.1 Communicative Goals in Electronic Business Negotiations

The following excerpts illustrate the relevance of reaching a joint understanding of the goods or services to transact, as well as the application scenarios in the decision makers' mind-sets, because they all appeared during the presentation of usual business procedures or special events and not on request by the interviewer.

☐ *(S₁ line 93) At [S₁], we try to make things as open, honest and communicative as we can.*

☐ *(N₃ line 79) [..] in order to make sure that both parties are really talking about the same thing, you know? Otherwise you quickly get some kind of Chinese whisper phenomenon.*

☐ *(N₅ line 47) Those are companies we are working with on a regular basis. Misunderstandings occur quite often – we then need to make sure not to exclude someone from the process, because of a knock out criterion which was not correctly interpreted, or because we interpreted something wrong. There is a very intensive communication taking place.*

☐ *(N₆ line 149) When the quality check of the contract reveals something strange, clarifying why is the next step. [..] We prepare all documents and keep them at hand, so you can see who is referencing what.*

As we can see from these statements (which are collected and compared with other goals in Table 12, p. 91), communicative goals are quite common in negotiator's mindsets and they thus can be assumed to shape negotiation processes.

This supports the line of argumentation presented regarding the inseparability of the communicative and the strategic modes of interactions, which seems to translate into electronic business negotiations. If we analyse these statements in relation to existing theory, it appears that (e-) negotiators are actively operating in a communicative action modus, while working on an inherently strategic process – this was proposed for international negotiations (Risse 2000, Müller 2004), but has not been investigated in business-to-business interaction. These excerpts are selected to illustrate that the distinction is not clear cut. The two modes appear intertwined in practice.

4.4.2 Theoretical References on Ideal Communication

The ideal speech situation, which is based on the abstract reference point from Jürgen Habermas' communication theory, will be used as an illustration of the communication pathologies identified. Grice (1975) offers a comparable instrument,[42] but in this case Habermas' theory is preferable due to his focus on the action component of speech, as the root of negotiation is the coordination of actions. Habermas argues that in an ideal, dialectic speech situation communicative action takes place: a process of communication wherein all participants submit to the better argument. In interaction, they collectively assume an objective world to refer to, as well as a social and a subjective world. These systems (or spheres) are interrelated, yet distinct. The individual's lifeworld is made up of his or her contacts with everyone and everything else. It thus intersects all three spheres. With this system of reference, the communicators delineate what communication is possible at all (Habermas 1981, p. 126). They make the four well known validity claims for each of their utterances either explicitly or implicitly, which is the second formal pragmatic requirement for communicative action. In consequence, it means that communicators make utterances in full awareness that the validity of their claims may be questioned by other parties.

---

42 According to Grice (Grice 1975, as summarised by Holtgraves 2002, p. 170) all conversations are guided by the cooperative principle and corresponding maxims of quality (be truthful), quantity (be appropriately informative), relation (be relevant), and manner (be clear).

Habermas continues to sketch the ideal speech situation in more detail by introducing a reflective element as follows:

> "[..] in discourses the participants of an argumentation need to make the (often untrue) presupposition that the conditions of the ideal speech situation are actually in effect. I will speak of discourses only, [..] if participants are urged towards assuming that fundamentally a rationally motivated agreement could be found, whereas 'fundamentally' expresses the idealised retention: if the argumentation could be carried out openly and as long as necessary." (Habermas 1981, p. 71)

This reciprocal assumption of rationality is the third requirement and completes the idealisation of rationality and accountability. He further points out the role that this assumption has for argumentation by stressing that without a communication situation of such rationality that enables the better argument to count, no argument whatsoever can count (Habermas, 2005, p. 31).

Communicators are supposed to be reflective, i.e. they are in principle able to identify incorrect, manipulative or insincere messages and emancipate themselves from those. This means, there is an option to evaluate validity claims in a discourse if necessary (see Figure 1, p. 26 for an overview).

Similar reference points are used in the marketing literature. Bruhn (2004, p. 705), for example in his discussion of communication strategies in industrial markets, speaks of the necessity of an active and credible communication as well as a competent and trustworthy self-presentation of the company, which basically describes Habermas' validity claims of truth and truthfulness for communicative action.

Such ideal situations, which are constituting properties for the public sphere in the sense of participatory democracy in its original conceptualisation, are mainly characterised by the following properties or norms (Habermas 2005, p. 89):

- *Inclusiveness*: Every subject with the competence to speak and act discursively is allowed to take part in a discourse

- *Equal distribution of communicative freedom*: Everyone is allowed to question any assertion. Everyone is allowed to introduce any assertion. Everyone is allowed to express his/her attitudes, desires and needs. No speaker may be prevented, by internal or external coercion, from exercising his/her rights as laid down above.

- *Sincerity*: Participants of the discourse mean what they say.

- *Absence of compulsion*: The yes/no statements regarding all kinds of validity claims may be motivated only through the argumentative power of reasons.

In combination, the constituting properties yield a fully symmetric relationship among the communication partners (Habermas 1981, p. 70). Habermas acknowledges the counterfactual nature of these assumptions, but insists on their factual, operative role for the structuring of communication processes (Habermas 2005, p. 30). As McCarthy continues:

> "Cooperative interaction is seen to be structured around ideas of reason [..]. As idealizing suppositions we cannot avoid making while engaged in processes of mutual understanding, they are actually effective in organizing communication and at the same time counterfactual in ways that go beyond the limits of actual situations. As a result, social-practical ideas of reason are both immanent and transcendent to practices [..]."
>
> (McCarthy, 1994, p. 38)

Note that these assumptions are commonly considered to be far more realistic in the Internet than in traditional social interaction. Habermas considers communicative action to be greatly facilitated by modern communication media (Habermas 1981, vol. 2, p. 274).[43] In a business negotiation context this has not yet been investigated in detail.

4.4.3 Identification of Communication Process Pathologies

After sketching an ideal setting and demonstrating that it is at least partly congruent with the goals of the decision makers involved, we conduct a diagnosis and analyse how far the

---

43 Recently, Habermas critically pointed out that on the other hand the intellectuals seem to be suffocating from the broadening of the media sphere, as if they were overdosing. The blessing seems to have become a curse. He sees the reasons for that in the de-formalisation of the public sphere, and in the de-differentiation of the respective roles (see http://www.signandsight.com/intodaysfeuilletons/649.html, last accessed 2006-09-18).

abstract ideals are realistic and what role negotiation technology plays for communication in business negotiations.

Reciprocal Assumption of Rationality – A Common Understanding

Collectively assuming a single objective reality to refer to as well as the other's ability to understand is a precondition for successful communication in general. Such reciprocal assumption of rationality is not made unconditionally. It is subject to reflection and can be revised if communicators experience opaque or paradox behaviour of a communication partner and draw their conclusions accordingly (Habermas 2005, p. 44). Regarding electronic business negotiation, it was a surprising observation that one of the most fundamental assumptions of Habermas' communicative action proved to be wrong on a regular basis.

According to Grice's (1975) theory of conversational implicature, people generally communicate with the expectation that others' contributions will be in line with the basic maxims of relevance and manner, i.e. clarity. This is not the case in (electronic) business negotiations. In fact, practitioners quite distinctively differentiate between two different, distinct worlds – e.g. a pragmatic one, where business is actually conducted, and a legal one. While both are essential for the negotiation process, they are assumed to be independent and thereby irrelevant for each other respectively. More such worlds exist, e.g. in different departments. The following excerpts illustrate the observation:

> ☐ *(N₂ line 58)*
>
> A: *[..] We reduced that to six candidates [..] and scheduled a bidder meeting [face-to-face]. And in that meeting, we do not speak about the contents of the contract.*
>
> Q: *I don't quite understand that. What do you talk about then?*
>
> A: *At that point we only speak of conditions such as schedules, prices etc. The contract is prepared before among the legal specialists.*
>
> Q: *Ah – I see.*
>
> A: *Otherwise you wouldn't know what kind of things you would trigger or what you might commit to [laughs].*

☐ (*N₃ line 53)*

> Q: And that interaction was also frictionless and without any misunderstandings?
>
> A: [Pause] Yes. Basically yes. But let's say: As soon as the legal people come into play... a machinery is set into motion on both sides. It should be clear that you will never need those paragraphs, as long as you understand each other. In this case it was like some wanted to stress their subjective perception [pause] but anyway. But it was always constructive anyway.

☐ *(C₃ line 46)* Especially the larger companies increasingly employ strategists, strategic sourcing specialists. They know their processes and analyses – but they are far away from the product [..]. It's all about prices then, sure. In the long run, it may be at the cost of quality.

Of course the consultation of contract specialists with dedicated skills may be useful without fully integrating them into the process, or in other words without bringing them to the (virtual) table. But a sequential process, like the one sketched above, introduces an artificial barrier between two supposedly separate topics, which likely leads to suboptimal results. Potential improvements might have been reached by logrolling qualitative contract details against each other.

The ideal condition of shared lifeworlds is thus not given. That appears to be an aspect which is not introduced, but only reinforced through negotiation support technology with its respective workflows. It was also found in traditional negotiation settings, but the codification of roles that may or may not change contract clauses and the use of contract templates in present ENS tools is actively maintaining this communicative disconnection.

(Hypothesis 9): ENS systems reinforce an artificial separation of professional lifeworlds.
While price-issues and non-price issues can be discussed simultaneously in the traditional negotiation settings or NSS driven settings, they are typically dealt with separately in the electronic auction model (Kaufmann, Carter 2003).

The following interview excerpt shows an example of a dedicated ENS impact regarding non-shared meanings and divergent mental models.

☐ (**N₇ line 67)** We set up an an online auction once at nine o'clock – European Time [on an international procurement platform]. Consequently, invitations where sent out via email for a time X am, which the suppliers naturally interpreted in terms of local time. At nine, there was only one bidder and submitted a bid. Yes. A second one then later called me and complained that he could not login for the auction and so on. Well, I also communicated that personally, but you can't do anything more. Who is reading that closely? It is always the same time zone, but [..] even for me this is error-prone.

In this case, the ENS governs the schedule of interaction in a counter-intuitive way – it lacks the ability of a human to anticipate and prevent such misunderstandings. The system carries a spirit of overconfidence in its users that may be perceived as ignorance of their needs, i.e. the mental models of the process that system operator and supplier have, clearly differ.

This pattern, as illustrated using an obvious example, reoccurs in similar form regularly: E-negotiators fail to establish a joint understanding and at least one them is aware of that fact – the assumption of communicative rationality is dropped. In contrast to traditional communication settings, the means to recover from such a communicative breakdown are limited, if present at all. This leads to the following hypothesis:

(Hypothesis 10): Current ENS systems do not offer sufficient means for recovery from communicative breakdowns.

The mode of interaction seems not to be discursive – it is partly assumed that what is auctioned is indeed clearly specified and that the usual business practices do apply as a heuristic.

The idea that a discussion is potentially open and may take as long as necessary in order to reach a rational agreement in the sense of commitment to the better argument is reverted as well, since right after initiating an E-Auction or eRfQ-process the schedule for final decision making is fixed.

Making and Questioning Validity Claims

Are participants of electronic negotiations enabled to carry out an interactive model of communication, where all kinds of validity claims made in speech acts can be freely introduced and questioned? This turned out to be the most important communication pathology identified.

In the case of negotiations about services or complex goods, the communication between buyer and seller is a vital part of the value creation process. Suppliers may take the role of a sparring-partner that questions decisions and assumptions in a *constructive discourse* (Strauß 2006). The business partners need to enter a *communicative action* mode of interaction before a detailed specification of the goods or services to transact can be provided. Unidirectional communication processes such as in electronic auctions can not provide this and are thus perceived as communication barriers in this complex and strategic case (Strauß 2006). Bajari et al. (2001, 2002) point out that auctions stifle communication of relevant knowledge compared to bargaining, because they reduce the incentive to do so. But in general suppliers have a strong incentive to differentiate and thus to communicate their selling propositions.

A barrier perception is given in this situation and it is not limited to strategic goods. Already in case N_2, an important communication pathology in both an auction-based and an RfQ-based ENS was witnessed. The interview partner explicated the role negotiation technology plays for him in the case of a buy-side electronic marketplace including electronic auction facilities as follows:

☐ (*N_2 line 20*) *That platform is just another intermediary that is constraining me.*

This clearly contradicts the Habermasian ideas of inclusiveness and equality. It should be pointed out that direct interaction with customers is part of the primary strategy employed in this case – the company is actively investing in research and development and thus depends on explaining innovations and their benefits. Its products are commonly indirect goods that draw little attention and are hard to differentiate for non-experts using other attributes than price. The interview partner continues:

☐ *(N₂ line 24) There are projects – such complexity can not be represented on the platform.*

This complexity of goods and situations is perceived to be not recognised on the buyer side in this case, i.e. there are information asymmetries typical for principal-agent relationships. The system strictly limits the interaction to a predefined set of speech acts.

In N₄ a similar case was described from a marketplace provider, which makes the statement particularly interesting and reliable, because he has no incentive to present the situation like that, on the contrary.

☐ *(N₄ line 98) There are platforms using the E-DIN standard. [..] things that are ultimately comparable. Take for example a switch. What are the innovative parts of a switch? [..] There are some soft criteria, such as the power-on time or the durability of a compensator. But this is simply not offered as a decision criterion on the platform, because: It is not part of the standard. A standard is always the lowest common denominator.*

The discourse ideas that assertions of any kind may be both introduced and questioned through all communicators are reverted – the communication process is unilaterally controlled and interaction is highly constrained. Suppliers are unable to freely introduce product quality specific assertions or question aspects of the specification. As already described, negotiation support systems are not exclusive communication channels, but they may play a critical role as such if negotiation processes are designed accordingly. By formally defining and organisationally enforcing (electronic) sourcing processes (see p. 101), negotiation systems are shifted into the centre of interaction and their role as a communication channel is strengthened. Thus, besides the presence and use of complementary communication channels, this leads to the following hypothesis of a communication barrier.

(Hypothesis 11): The use of electronic auction systems impedes the discursive making and questioning of validity claims in the negotiation process.

This finding is consistent with the impression made by Carter and Kaufmann (2007), though their argumentation is more relationally framed and not based on a theory of communication. In their survey study, they find a significant relationship between supplier opportunism as a consequence of auction use and dysfunctional conflict, i.e. a conflict that is not resolved or a situation, in which one channel member perceives another channel member to be engaged in behaviour that is preventing or impeding him from achieving his goals (Stern, El-Ansary 1977, p. 283).

The dataset contains examples of reflective compensation approaches. For example N_6 provides a series of high quality workshops in areas related to, but not identical with their product portfolio, in order to establish a discursive interaction despite the fact that their public institution customers can not freely choose their modus of negotiation and the respective technologies.

Pragmatics in Negotiation Support Settings

The basic credo of the language action perspective, which is that people use language to *do* things, to achieve actions through communicating, is particularly visible in business negotiations. The mechanism of exchanging and interpreting illocutionary acts is of vital importance, consequences of a misinterpretation can be fatal for a company. Can illocutionary forces such as commitments, promises etc. be adequately communicated and understood in ENS enabled settings?

There is one communicative act whose illocutionary force is regularly called into question: the invitation to a bidding event or auction on an electronic platform. Does this include a credible commitment to send out a purchasing order to the best bidder determined in the event? Because the effort for analysing specifications and preparing offers and strategies may be considerable for smaller enterprises, this question converts into an investment decision.

Drawing on the present dataset, the answer is *no* on a regular basis. Either the buyers' ability to draw back is an inherent feature of the auction model applied or there is no commitment to the model at hand. The understanding (and expectation) of such actions depends on culture (see p. 159). Misunderstandings of the pragmatic component of bidding invitations easily become emotionally charged and may damage the reputation of the buyer.

> ☐ *(C₃ line 9) At first it was not bidding, but pricing a product portfolio on their platform and an RFI regarding delivery etc. We had a good feeling: "It just fits, I think we get the deal." Then suddenly, they said: "let's make it an auction" – on the European level. [..] Of course suppliers get mad about this. That was a really large cake to share. I really thought it would be going right to the limit [..]. We made our calculations – personally, I was quite concerned. [..] Finally, we did not even approach the initial offer, since there were only two bidders competing for all tenders [..] and made the deal based on the initial offer.*

The application of the (reverse) auction term is questionable, if we do not speak of a resource allocation mechanisms in the strict sense. Practitioners use the phrase in case of a protocol for offer exchange with competing bids with mechanistic decision making.

Data source C_2 and the following bad publicity point out the relevance of a shared understanding of the illocutionary aspects of auction models. Reputation and trust building (see also p. 140) are the mechanisms that compensate in credibility, what present negotiation support technology can not provide (Carter et al. 2004, p. 244). Regarding the overall set of negotiation technologies in use today, we come to the following hypothesis.

(Hypothesis 12): Present ENS technology in use does not provide sufficient actability to make credible commitments on allocation rules; credibility in this sense is instead largely a function of reputation.

Actability is a concept, which incorporates the idea that software systems should enable their users to carry out (communicative) actions. From this LAP based position further requirements can be derived, e.g. the principle of elementariness of actions or the principle of action potentiality. (Ågerfalk 2003, 2004). Present reverse auction systems seem to violate both: nor do they clearly separate the proposition of a specification, the directive of participation and the commitment to award business nor do they provide means to resolve such uncertainties. Credibility largely needs to replace both.

Griffith (2003) explains the consequences of a culture of non-committing auctions as follows. It is difficult for sales managers to distinguish non-committing bidding events and committing events. Buyers regularly conduct *auction* events in order to gain insights into present market prices for a renegotiation with an incumbent supplier. Suppliers need to identify events that represent real opportunities regarding the buyer's willingness to switch suppliers. Hence, they may engage in a process of token bidding. They participate, but do not compete in order to minimise their share of transaction costs, while not rejecting the potential customer's request for a quote. Given the large number of contracts that actually are awarded to incumbent suppliers, this behaviour is understandable.

4.4.4 Antecedents of the Communication Barrier Role

The last chapter showed that there is considerable variance in discursiveness, the conceptual distance to ideal communication in electronic negotiation settings. It still needs to be investigated under what circumstances these pathologies arise, what the contingencies are and what economic effects may be explained by this variance.

Technology Properties and Spirit – A Process View

Findings

In the course of the interview process, the technical subject of analysis was narrowed down since most technologies in use are actually quite similar from a communication media point of view. In the case of traditional face-to-face negotiations, the definition of the mode of interaction is regularly an interactive process, wherein the rules of interaction are jointly defined or redefined. This is different in the electronic negotiation case. Here the protocol is unilaterally chosen (regularly by the buying side) and enforced through the ENS.

Given this decision, the negotiation environment yields a certain level of restrictiveness, which may or may not fit the task at hand for a given negotiator. Regarding the problem of time zones illustrated above (see p. 115), this was clearly not the case. A deep mismatch of task and technology fit was also perceived by the marketing agencies and the procurement department in the example case (see p. 8). In N_2 a general lack of admittance for the need of discussion and the complexities of the seemingly homogeneous goods under discussion is claimed, i.e. supplier and buyer have different mental models of the subject under negotiation. Understanding does not occur; the level of coordination accomplished is suboptimal.

In this sense, the technical properties of ENS are of great concern for the communication process. However, the spirit of restrictiveness regarding the overall interaction process that is associated with a certain technology appears to be far more important than individual features. With repeated use of negotiation support systems, the negotiators' perceptions are undergoing a development in the sense of structuration, which is a perceived construct. This may mean that low discursiveness e.g. in simple auction systems is either actively compensated or reinforced if bidders get used to this form of interaction. A norm of non-discursiveness emerges or is being reinforced as a structure.

During the analysis of the auction and electronic request for quotation (eRfQ) based procurement platform used in N_7, a non-standard component was found. Bidders are enabled to accompany monetary bids with small texts in order to e.g. explain their bids or argue on product quality in a field labelled *comment*. From a theoretical point of view, this constitutes a new negotiation protocol, which deviates from common auction properties – if comments are considered to be relevant (and they obviously are, given the prominent position of the field), the allocation mechanism is questioned.

☐ *(N_7 line 105)*

> Q: I have a question regarding the comment field in the auction form next to the field for the bid. Do suppliers use this field? And if yes – what do they use it for?
> A: That is easily answered – that field has never been used, it lies idle completely.

In practice, this is not the case – the bidders' expectations or the rule of non-discursiveness in auction settings leaves no room for this. Economically speaking, they do not hope to realise additional benefit through commenting and thus avoid the additional effort. Such mechanisms of re-structuration make it difficult to conceive negotiation support settings that are highly discursive and include auction-like technologies, since this would be inconsistent with existing structures.

Therefore, we find a synchronous process of perception, mental modelling and complexity evaluation that aggregates to an evaluation of fit between the two (task-technology fit). However, only one party decides on the mode of negotiations. Thus, we propose the following hypothesis.

(Hypothesis 13): The communication barrier perception is an emergent structure iteratively shaped by the communicative richness of technology, task-technology fit and negotiators' expectations.

All of these cases show the relevance of adequate information richness and flexibility for negotiation support systems, which is not an objective property of the technology, but a socially constructed property. The perception (or construction) of a communicative barrier may be the result of this evaluation as well as the restructuring of the socio-technological system in the long run, for example towards combination models.

Related Work

Different communication media allow different kinds of interaction (Daft, Lengel 1986). For example regarding feedback immediacy, the number of social cues, language variety and personalisation – in this view, electronic auction systems are rather restrictive, lean media (Gattiker et al. 2007).

The socio-technical system ENS, at least in the sense of auction-based technologies, seems to have an inherent property, or spirit in the adaptive structuration theory wording (Giddens 1984, DeSanctis, Poole 1994), of (non-) discursiveness shaped by user expectations. Unlike the idea of media richness (Daft, Lengel 1986), this property is not inherent in the media technologies, but is largely constituted by both social rules and norms as well as technically enforced rules of interaction (e.g. on how binding commitments are made). Hence, it transcends the borders of the ENS application software and carries over into the above text-field the interaction via telephone or electronic mail.

The following table directly compares different understandings of communicative richness. Negotiators evaluate the discursiveness of the ENS technology and the discursive load (i.e. the need for discussion, based on object complexity or equivocality) – these are both individual evaluations, not rational ones like in media richness theory. This means that both the system discursiveness and the object complexities are socially constructed.

	Social cues...		An increase of social cues...		Research focus on...			
	... are necessary to maximise communication richness.	... can contribute to but are not necessary to maximize communication richness. It can readily occur in the total absence of social cues	... increases communicative richness correspondingly.	... not necessarily leads to a corresponding change in communicative richness	... features of the process of communication (cues, capacity)	... whether or not mutual understanding occurs.	... whether or not the listener or reader critiques the validity claims of what is communicated to her and emancipates herself from distortions if needed.	... social construction of communication technologies.
The Positivist conduit perspective of media richness	●		●		●			
The interpretive perspective		●		●		●		
Ngwenyama and Lee's CST, Actability theory		●		●		●	●	

Table 13: Comparison of definitions of communicative richness (based on Ngwenyama, Lee 1997).

Knowledge on communication media effects in negotiations has been collected since the emergence of negotiation support (see Putnam, Roloff 1992 for an overview). So far, research has failed to provide consistent practical implications due to heterogeneous and contradicting findings (Swaab et al. 2006). One explanation for this, which the present study is supporting, is that it is insufficient to analyse technologies alone – their context of application shapes their use and thereby shapes the effects of their utilisation.

A meta-analysis of experimental media impact research in negotiations suggests that synchronicity facilitates information exchange especially when multiple issues need to be negotiated (Swaab et al. 2006, p. 22). Asynchronous communication, as experienced in document centric E-Auction / RfQ processes and message based ENSs, can, therefore, be expected to discourage information sharing with increasing complexity. This is reasonable considering the additional effort of e.g. text-based interaction, which usually goes hand in hand with asynchronicity.

On the other hand, asynchronicity enables negotiating parties to carefully prepare and process argumentations to an extent that would not be possible in synchronous exchanges do to limited cognitive resources, which leads to the paradox of richness (Robert, Dennis 2005) and disconfirms a simple, monotonic relationship between ENS success variables and media richness in the original sense. For communicative richness in the above sense, such a relationship holds for measures of effectiveness. However, efficiency is taken into account and hence negotiators apply a kind of task-technology-fit reasoning (Goodhue 1995, Dennis et al. 2001) based on their own expectations.

Such a model of media choice can also be applied for the dominance of electronic mail interaction in business negotiations (Schoop et al. 2006b). Given appropriate tasks and adjacent expectations and use patterns of negotiators, electronic mail can be (but is not necessarily) amazingly rich, which explains earlier findings on media richness in business negotiations (Schoop et al. 2007a) and leads to a different aspect of E-Negotiation communication processes to be addressed separately: communicative overconfidence.

Institutionalisation of Norms

Findings

Rules are a constituting property for electronic negotiations. They are meant to clarify and facilitate the interactions necessary to achieve a coordination and a synchronisation throughout bargaining phases. This would in principle translate into a high communication quality during a rule guided negotiation process. However, electronic business negotiation settings form a genre of organisational communication (Yates, Orlikowski 1992), which is in fact regularly characterised by rules and norms that directly oppose the principles of discourse and contribute to the overall restrictiveness of the interaction process (Schoop et al. 2007a), beyond the properties of the negotiation support technology in use.

This is obvious in the case of S_2 (HypoVereinsbank) and its rules regarding communication media (see p. 8) or auction deadlines, which may cut off the (possibly not concluded) discussion of contract details.

While the example case on HypoVereinsbank and their customer magazine shows a lack of interactivity, in the case of N_5, a highly discursive negotiation process is established although both apply a process of competitive bidding. The main differences between the two settings are summarised below in Table 14. The comparison of these cases is of particular interest, because both stem from broadly similar organisations (that is from the financial services market) and describe a similar procurement task.

Case: HypoVereinsbank	Case: N$_5$
Complex service-product bundle, strategically relevant	Complex service-product bundle, strategically relevant
Partly existing relationships, the bidder selection process was intransparent for the bidders.	Existing relationships only (small market), decision-makers stress fairness and try not to exclude bidders if they can meaningfully contribute to the process – bidders realise that.
Reverse E-Auction, no direct interaction – switch to bargaining in a second phase that was not announced initially.	RfQ with elements of electronic communication as well as a joint meeting with all bidders and domain experts.
Insufficient amount of information provided	Information distribution policy, process ownership is shared between domain experts and the purchasing department
Questions are explicitly discouraged through the mechanism and the rules of conduct	Questions are encouraged in an open forum meeting, all questions and answers are distributed to all parties
Prices[44] are the only content of messages provided by bidders	Bidders provide quotes in two versions that suggest solutions with and without prices, intra-organisational discussion is then carried out while prices are kept confidential

Table 14: Analysis of discursiveness in two similar E-Negotiation cases using an E-Auction and a hybrid RfQ respectively.

While the conceptual and technical difference between the two technologies[45] is only marginal, the way the technology is applied and embedded in the business procedures is quite distinct. The difference lies in the compensatory actions in N$_5$ that accompany the auction process. Similar compensatory actions can be found on the supplier side with different means. If potential deals are attractive, the sales force in N$_2$ tries to circumvent the auction system in creative ways in order to initiate an open, argumentative dialogue with the potential buyer, to facilitate the creation of long term, exclusive contracts and partnerships.

Another important aspect of regulation naturally lies in the respective incentive structures. Procurement management is often paid by or receives bonus payment based on savings. Therefore, they have no incentive to engage in inter-organisational discourse in order to settle efficient deals in the broad sense; time is better spent on further cost

44 HypoVereinsbank refused to provide additional data on the case. Price bargaining between industry and marketing agencies regarding customer magazines is regularly carried out on prices per page designed, in case of long term business relationships.

45 A reverse e-auction is iterative while an e-RfQ is essentially a single-round, sealed bid auction. From a communication process point of view, the according processes of publishing specifications and receiving bids is largely identical.

reduction efforts. The conscious application of negotiation support software to create a communication barrier is perfectly rational for an individual decision maker with such incentives. From the organisational point of view, the return on communication in procurement is possibly positive, depending on the issues at hand.

Consequently, organisational rules and norms can be hypothesised to contribute to the communication barrier role of ENS as follows.

(Hypothesis 14): Strict deadlines, over-formalisation and intra-organisational incentive structures contribute to the establishment of ENSs as communication barriers.

With this in mind, the careful management of both the incentive structures for business negotiators (both traditional and electronic) and the other organisational rules and norms that constitute the communication setting of a business negotiation appears to be required in a way that is not yet common business practice. It can however be found in selected best-practice cases.

Related Work

Collaboration is much easier if parties have a set procedure (agenda) that coordinates the moves (Poole et al. 1992). Walther and Bunz (2005) suggest that the mere following of any rules and norms whatsoever may reduce uncertainty and enhances trust in communication of distributed work teams and thus should enable productive interaction. In the case of electronic business negotiations, this hypothesis can not be supported in its breadth, in that particular rules show dedicated negative effects resulting in a communication barrier perception of the overall system. Procedures designed to avoid conflict or to better organise the interaction process of multi-party negotiation also reduce the opportunities for negotiators to learn about each other's interests and to thereby find integrative gains (Bazerman et al. 1988), they prevent flexibility and dynamic processes of creative improvisation (see Valley et al. 2002).

Acknowledged and institutionalised norms on the other hand, such as in Table 14, contribute to discursiveness in the sense that any party can refer to them – the interaction is less power-driven and approaches communicative rationality. The situation is similar to that of international negotiations, where (beyond diplomatic protocol) communication is only weakly institutionalised, because acknowledged norms are emerging only slowly (Habermas, 2007). The application of ENSs in general is weakly institutionalised as well and thus exacerbates the questioning of validity claims. If such ideas hold for the business context, the institutionalisation of norms regarding a (limited) discursive mode of interaction would be beneficial, due to the fact that it yields a higher degree of rationality in these processes.

An exploratory survey study conducted in 2005 took up the ideas of rules in business negotiation processes and their communicative impact and provided similar results for a broader sample, which support the above findings (Schoop et al. 2007a).

In short, the more closely the negotiation settings applied resemble an auction setting, for example if awarding is guaranteed and the awarding decision is made at a fixed deadline, the more likely is the occurrence of renegotiations. Note that the impact of the fixed time schedule (deadline) rule matches the results in Social Psychology research on communicative overconfidence under time pressure (Horton, Keysar 1996).

Communicative Overconfidence in Electronic Negotiations

Findings

One code that appeared very early in the process of data analysis, and regularly reappeared later, is the great confidence that some negotiators express regarding the ease and effortlessness of electronic negotiation communication. Both N_1 and S_2 showed great confidence in asynchronous, textual exchanges in a unidirectional communication of specifications for strategically relevant services in E-Auction and eRfQ settings. It is unclear whether the confidence was justified in N_1, but at least in S_2 this confidence was clearly not justified.

Other interview partners explicate their own or their partner's confidence in electronic communication means directly:

☐ (**N₆ line 73)** *If there are irregularities, it's obvious. [..] I don't see a problem of coordination there: It's the age of electronic mail and we have a central file storage here on our server.*

☐ *(N₇ line 81) And he just said: "Maybe next time". He had no idea what it was all about. The auction was about some security services – he might have made a really good deal with follow-up transactions and all. He really missed that point.*

Certainly negotiation support technologies have the potential to communicate documents during a negotiation with unprecedented ease, but the processes of technology use needs to be critically evaluated: In some cases communicative overconfidence seems to be present while in others it is not. How can that be interpreted with reference to established theory? First, interpreting the above statements, it could be argued along the lines of Social Psychology that communicative overconfidence is a property or an attitude of individual persons (Holtgraves 2002, p. 133).

Another idea is voiced in the first narrative interview.

☐ *(N₁ page 4) [..] It is all the small things that cause most of the trouble.*

This is an indication of such a communicative overconfidence attitude in relation to transaction volume or strategic importance, with a pointer to difficulties of intra-organisational communication where overconfidence also seems to play a role. Considering the fact that electronic auctions are regularly applied to commodity goods, communicative overconfidence can be argued to be of relevance with considerable frequency.

The attitudinal interpretation as sketched so far does not cover the emergent, interpersonal nature the construct may show in interaction with negotiation technology. Consider the following excerpt.

☐ *(N₇ line 57) [..] That platform is completely in English – that is taken for granted. But we are talking about MRO [Maintenance, Repair and Operations] and local suppliers here, which partly do not have personal e-mail addresses. Those are the info@something addresses, which are checked only from time to time. [..] The system sends notifications and invitations for newly created auctions in English automatically. [..] They [the system developers] did not show any sensitivity to these issues.*

In this case (N$_7$), the overconfidence is induced through a negotiation system, while the procurement manager who uses it is fully aware of the problem and actively tries to compensate it. But understanding communicative overconfidence as a property of a certain negotiation support technology would be overly simplistic as well.

The notion of a certain spirit which a system brings into the respective processes, describes the data collected more adequately. Overconfidence is then an emergent structure in the sense of adaptive structuration theory. Given this definition, the following is hypothesised.

(Hypothesis 15): Communicative overconfidence in narrow, electronic channels facilitates the role of ENSs as communication barriers.

It is non-admittedly inherent both in individual's presuppositions and actions as well as in larger structures, such as a particular process or technology, while the two levels recursively shape each other.

Related Work

While the phenomenon of overconfidence in negotiation situations has been studied extensively (e.g. Neale, Bazerman 1985), the data collected in this study points towards a different form of overconfidence: communicative overconfidence in E-Negotiations.

This finding is of major importance in negotiation processes. The Harvard Concept (Fisher et al. 2004) extensively describes the importance of perspective taking[46] in negotiations. Further, laboratory experiments show that message senders in description tasks are more overconfident under time pressure. They tend to fail to use common ground and use privileged information in descriptions instead (Horton, Keysar 1996). This is a

---

46 In spite of the fact that perspective taking in negotiations is generally considered to be a reasonable advice, a recent study (Epley et al. 2006) indicates that it may actually increase the risk of impasse, when we expect other's to behave selfishly and then reciprocate (see also Thompson, Nadler 2002 on the *sinister attribution bias*). Therefore, perspective taking should be carried out with great care. In this chapter, it is discussed in its fundamental, unquestioned role for communication.

common context parameter in procurement departments. Further, according to Mead the ability to take another persons' perspective is a requirement for the development of a self and intersubjective dialogue (Hesse 2001, p. 81) - in any case the mechanism of reciprocal perspective taking is fundamental for language use (Mead 1934). For example, seeing the world from another person's point of view lies at the core of speech act recognition. Without perspective taking, threats might not be distinguishable from assertions. Further, more basic communicative tasks, such as identifying which part of the world an illocutor is referring to, ultimately depend on the successful perspective taking of the hearer. It is, therefore, a precondition for any kind of coordination or joint action (Mead 1934, Clark 1996, p. 92). But although it is an omnipresent process, it may well be difficult for a speaker in a business context to take the perspective and knowledge of the hearer adequately into account, e.g. during the conceptualization of an offer or a request with numerous technical details and different levels of confidentiality etc.

Generally, people tend to overestimate the extent to which others are similar to them and have similar knowledge (Holtgraves 2002, p. 131) and adapt the amount of information provided in communication accordingly (Fussel, Krauss 1992). Recent neuroscience studies have indicated that the same regions of the human brain are active, when reasoning about the self and the other respectively (David et al. 2006), which adds a neurological explanation for the surprising difficulty of keeping aspects of these separate.

A systematic overestimation of communicative success in narrow communication channels has been shown in Social Psychology research (Newton 1990) and translates to informal interaction through electronic mail (Kruger, Epley 2005). Here message senders systematically overestimate the proportion of sarcastic statements that receivers correctly identify in their messages. In both cases, it is argued that senders *hear their song* while communicating it – that they are egocentric, i.e. can not see the lack of cues in a self-composed message, because they do not really experience it. In consequence, we often can not communicate a message through narrow channels as well as we think.

Drawing on the data collected in this study, a similar condition seems to exist in electronic negotiation settings. It yields highly restrictive communication processes – the need for interaction and clarification, possibly improvisation, is not seen as the creators of documents and messages overestimate their understandability for other persons or organisations. The effects of this bias are probably increased by a *temporal synchrony bias* (Thompson, Nadler 2002) on the level of multiple message exchanges: Negotiators have a tendency to behave as if they were in a synchronous communication setting, when in fact, they are not.

4.4.5 Consequences of the Communication Barrier Role

At this point it can be concluded, that ENSs as a socio-technical system regularly do appear in a communication barrier role with considerable impacts, such as buyers missing an opportunity for innovation or other kinds of economically inefficient deals. These consequences will be investigated in greater detail below.

Inefficient Deals

Findings

Drawing on the judgements of the interview partners, the efficiency of procurement departments is largely evaluated on per product savings and transaction costs compared across years. These savings determine the procurement managers' bonus at the end of the year, thus they play an important role in operative decision making. Strategically, this criterion is obviously insufficient if used in isolation.

> ☐ (*N$_s$ line 8)* We are not doing many auctions any more. [..] I remember one about two years ago. [..] Basically everything went well. There were two auctions – PCs and printers. The suppliers really drove down the prices but had some difficulties to implement that. You could see that they must have bid below the threshold of pain. Quality and delivery schedules where [..] not quite what we have been used to. [..] Right now we are conducting a lot of negotiations via e-mail.

Consequently, total cost of ownership calculations are taken into account, which transforms the auction setting with clear cut rules into a more ambiguous process. A communication driven inefficiency in the sense of unrealised unilateral revenue was coded for an E-Auction case as follows:

☐ (N_7 **line 11**) *[After an E-Auction initiated by upper management] we talked to the winning supplier and cut another 5 percent [laughs] - that was basically the point where it was finally decided to no longer use reverse auctions.*

Further investigation shows that unclear specifications and the lack of a pre-auction inter-active argumentation urged suppliers to make their cost calculation very cautiously, based on worst case assumptions. In an open ex post discussion, or renegotiation, this became clear quickly. In a sense, this (potential) inefficiency was induced by the use of the negotiation technology.

If the parties involved do not develop a joint understanding or a shared mental model, inefficient deals are the consequence. It should be pointed out that situations like this may contain hidden integrative potential not realised – a symmetrical inefficiency in the above sense. The following excerpt describes such as case. The supplier quoted below was asked to participate in a reverse auction for an MRO (Maintenance, Repair and Operations) good specified in detail with high quality standards for a construction project. Supplier's experts claim that the quality requirements are probably overly high for this project and that the high quality products offered by the suppliers have additional quality features unsuitable for this case – in consequence they can not bid competitively.

☐ (N_2 **line 28**) *We are looking for direct contact to our customers and therefore avoid intermediaries [..] We try to clarify that directly. In this case the context of application needed to be clarified. Maybe they don't even need the high quality they specified – there are a lot of things we could offer.*

In summary, we arrive at the following hypothesis.

(Hypothesis 16): ENSs that are in a communication barrier role induce economic inefficiencies both in the societal and in the unilateral sense of unrealised gains.

Such inefficiencies are probably consequences both of the technical barrier, which such systems pose, and of a fixed-pie bias inherent in reverse auction technologies, as far as they do not consider multiple attributes simultaneously. The procuring party assumes the existence of a *pie* of costs and supplier margins of fixed size, which is being divided. Through the auction process and the communication barrier role of the auction system, this perception is fixated, potential trade-offs for mutual gain (such as the use of adequate quality goods for even lower prices in this case) can either not be found or worse, they can not be communicated, which is a frustrating experience for the supplier.

Related Work

Before a supposed impact on negotiation outcome efficiency can be evaluated that term needs to be clarified. What does efficiency mean in detail? Two points of view need to be taken into account to answer this question:

1) the symmetrical, societal view of efficiency,
2) and the asymmetrical view of the individual negotiator or his organisation respectively.

The traditional economic theory 1) proposes Pareto efficiency as the primary measure of efficiency. This is a symmetric property of a resource allocation. The application of the measure is dependent on the existence and explication of utility functions of all parties involved. Leaving problems of preference elicitation and computation aside, this means a disclosure of all private information by all parties to the evaluating party, which renders the measure useless for practical application in most business cases. The more general idea of societal efficiency as the absence of unrealised gains from trade (Krishna 2002, p. 5) may be useful to investigate however.

Further 2) in unilateral economic analysis the direct revenue (i.e. savings) of a transaction is used to evaluate it. Here it is further assumed that decision makers decide rationally, solely based on revenue expectations. Hence, the first of the above excerpts clearly matches what is described as the *winner's curse* in the literature (see e.g. Milgrom 1989). It is assumed that a good, or a contract in this case, has a common unknown value for all bidders. If all bidders have similar information, it is likely, that the winning bidder overestimated that value.[47] Hence, the result is not efficient for that particular bidder.

Similar findings as sketched above regarding communication have been made in more recent experimental studies on bargaining and double auction games. In contrast to predictions of normative theory, they show significant efficiency effects of pre-phase communication, i.e. coordination, which is reduced in case of written communication (Valley et al. 2002). A positive association between the congruence of negotiators' mental models of the situation and the likelihood of reaching optimal settlements has been found in another experimental study (Van Boven, Thompson 2003).

If negotiators fail to share the spirit of the deal, that is the implicit expectations of all parties (Fortgang et al. 2003, Perrone et al. 2003), in a productive form of conflict, further inefficiencies may occur in fulfilment and after-sales. In that case, supplier performance is found to be limited (Carter, Kaufmann 2007) and renegotiation occurs frequently.

Renegotiations

Findings

Renegotiation issues, a term which will be defined shortly, appeared repeatedly in the interviews conducted for the present study. In contrast to experimental settings, the success of a negotiation is evident only after the respective fulfilment and after sales phases of the respective business transaction, and not after reaching some (initial) agreement. The key excerpts of the relevant statements are listed below.

> ☐ (*S₂ cp-wissen.de*) *Also auction guidelines were provided – all in all about 30 pages. Letters are accepted exclusively via confirmed mail. On the other hand i-Faber has the right to use all communication channels [..]. Fairness looks different. [..] Meanwhile [in a follow-up newsletter] a number of suppliers have been invited for further negotiations.*

---

47 The Vickrey auction (Vickrey, 1961) addresses this inefficiency. It requires, that the winning bidder pays / charges the price of the second best bidder (Second Price Sealed Bid Auction). However, suppliers appear to have improved their bidding strategies for first-price (English) auctions in the recent years (also see excerpt on p. 168).

☐ (*N₇ line 92*) I also care for things like cleaning staff and call centre services – there it (E-Auctions) is a commonality. They know it, they know the process. But I always try to do a review conversation with the supplier afterwards. There is for instance a price that was offered – I take the time to write a spec usually and that contains payment terms for example. Often questions arise like "Why discount? We have never been told about that." and I can just refer them to the specs.

☐ (*C₁ line 136*)

   Q: What are the evaluation criteria for electronic procurement processes?

   A: [..] Savings – this is where the bonus comes from [..]

   Q: What about renegotiations? Quite often they seem to indicate misunderstandings or problems.

   A: Yes. But that can also have strategic reasons.

☐ (*N₅ line 98*) You have detailed service directories there – VOB [48] – and everything is in there. Basically you can insert prices into it, alternative solutions from time to time. You can also load them into a specific software and edit them. Often such directories are incomplete. If you then cooperate with a company with the experience of [experienced company]; they will see at once what is missing and prepare the first change order right with the first offer.

☐ (*C₃ line 28*) [..] after three bids, he withdrew. Afterwards, the three best bidders were invited for further negotiations. Getting there, and then somehow 'bending' it to be profitable – I know that many run such strategies. But it is not fitting for us.

All of the statements refer to E-Auction-based negotiation scenarios. Two patterns, i.e. codes, have emerged and both appear to be consequences of the communication barrier role of certain ENS features.

First of all, the lack of discursiveness and interactivity inherent in most auction and RfQ systems yields misunderstandings and unclarity, things remain unclear until the negotiating

---

48 'Vergabe und Vertragsordnung für Bauleistungen' (VOB). A set of rules that governs the awarding of construction projects through the public administration in Germany as well as the structure of the contracts involved. The latter part is regularly used in private procurement as well.

parties (or a subset) get into discussion after an auction event. This problem is not limited to complex cases as we learn from N_7, although it may be more frequent there. The second code relevant in this regard is strategic renegotiation. Leveraging information asymmetries might be an important aspect for implementing such strategies. This strategy seems to be common.

In open bargaining cases, these two flaws disappear if cost based contracts are designed; however, contractors need to be selected by reputation in that case. In summary, we arrive at the following hypothesis.

(Hypothesis 17): ENSs that are in a communication barrier role induce an increased likelihood of renegotiations – both unplanned and for opportunistic purposes.

Related Work

The analysis of renegotiations is not a new idea as such. The concept appears regularly in economic analysis of principal agent contracting models. Here renegotiations are regularly assumed to be of homogeneously strategic nature.

Salacuse (2001) clarifies the term by distinguishing three distinct forms of renegotiations, namely post-deal renegotiations, intra-deal renegotiations and extra-deal renegotiations. All three forms have in common that they describe a subsequent negotiation which is related to a prior negotiation between the very same parties. The type of relation to this prior negotiation is what distinguishes the three forms. While in post-deal renegotiations the second negotiation is conducted after the expiration of a negotiated contract in order to possibly renew the business relationship between the parties, intra-deal and extra-deal renegotiations are conducted during the fulfilment of a business contract. Intra-deal renegotiations are the anticipated form of handling contractual changes such as in change order procedures, which are regularly described for example in engineering contracts. Renegotiations that are not anticipated in an active contract are thus considered to be extra-deal renegotiations.

In contrast to initial negotiations or post-deal negotiations, where all negotiation partners decide to enter into exchanges, intra-deal and extra-deal renegotiations often involve at least one party that is reluctant to negotiate. As Salacuse (2001) points out, these types of negotiations often aim at allocating losses based on 'shattered expectations' or all kinds of problems. For these forms of unwanted renegotiations two main reasons are proposed by Salacuse: (1) incomplete or unclear contracts (Hart, Moore 1988) and (2) changes in the environment that were not anticipated in the contract. A third reason lies in (3) power relationships between the negotiating parties. A powerful party might successfully demand renegotiations for strategic reasons only. This goes back to the new institutional economics that introduced the idea of incomplete contracts and opportunism (Williamson 1975). This contract theoretic perspective is regularly used to analyse renegotiations conceptually (e.g. Hart, Moore 1988, Fundenberg, Tirole 1990), while other perspectives are largely disregarded in the literature. Here, usually incentive schemes and contract properties such as the degree of flexibility in a contract are analysed in order to prevent strategic renegotiations of agents with varying degrees of rationality assumed. The idea of renegotiation-proof contracts derived from that point of view (used e.g. in Zhao 2006) may be misleading however, because it does not allow predictions regarding type (1) and type (2) renegotiation likelihood.

Empirical analysis of renegotiations and their antecedents in work practice as a qualitative component of negotiation results is very scarce. Scholars have shown the role of renegotiations in the development of a business relationship with a case-study approach (Ariño, la Torre 1998). Hanna et al. (2002) analyse antecedents of change orders, a kind of intra-deal renegotiation, in construction projects. It is, however, unclear how to generalise these findings to B2B negotiations in general, as they are specific for project organisation: percentage change, manpower estimations etc. Tadelis and Bajari (Bajari et al. 2001, Bajari et al. 2002, Bajari, Ye 2003) point out that auction structures stifle communication between buyers and sellers, preventing the buyer from utilizing the supplier's expertise when designing the project. In the case of RFQs and E-Auctions the communication is usually unidirectional: The buyer creates and sends a specification while suppliers submit bids or send more complex formalised offers (also see page 32).

If suppliers have relevant additional information, such as errors found in the specifications, they (1) are not expected to share the knowledge, because there is often no dedicated communication channel for this case (such as in S_2) and (2) they will be more likely to use this information in order to win the auction and capitalise on expected changes in a renegotiation. This is precisely what happened in the case quoted above. Emiliani and Stec (2004), in their study of electronic auction impacts on the US aerospace market, find over 70 percent of the suppliers responding to actively seek opportunities to charge their customers higher prices ex post as a direct result of participation in online reverse auctions, e.g. by invoicing complimentary services that were including in a fixed price a priori (Carter et al. 2004). In summary, different streams of literature offer explanations and support for the idea of ENS induced renegotiations.

Missed Opportunities for Innovation and Collaboration

Findings

Regarding negotiation support technology, a problem arose in the discussion with practitioners: It seems to be the case that restrictive ENSs introduce an innovation barrier. The interview partner in N_4 came to a conclusion similar to the one reached in N_2 (see also p. 117) and added that a technology, which facilitates decision making on prices exclusively, possibly by using standards and norms et cetera, thereby constrains communication and is ultimately also a barrier to innovation.

☐ (N_4 line 105) *Any standard is reduced to a least common denominator. You impede innovation that way - I have no idea how to solve that.*

In that case, innovation in different aspects of product or service quality is not recognised and consequently not adopted as long as it can not deliver price advantages. Opportunities are lost (Emptoris Inc. 2005). This is a consequence of the communication barrier effect. In that case, the negotiation technology actively reinforces the standard. While this allows efficient comparisons in terms of transaction costs and is an important factor for the work of engineers, it constitutes a barrier to open communication and supplier driven innovations.

(Hypothesis 18): ENSs that are in a communication barrier role or integrate with product and service description standards decrease a sourcing organisations' capabilities for future innovations.

Can an electronic platform offer the room for sufficient heterodoxy and flexibility to allow for innovation? Without heterodoxy, i.e. any opinions or doctrines at variance with an official or orthodox position,[49] there can be no innovation (Nooteboom 1992).

In N_9 this was judged as not feasible. Procurement was particularly interested in innovative add-on services regarding a large scale procurement project. In consequence procurement management tried to compensate this effect actively as follows:

> ☐ *(N_9 line 44) We sent a letter from the CEO's desk to all our suppliers and made three points: First, a commitment to internal communication [of values and offers], second the rule that the CEO must sign all large orders. So "make your value known!" At first, they didn't believe they would benefit from doing so – until the letter from the CEO with his signature and the CPOs signature on it.*

Note that this largely established a hybrid model between bargaining and auctions. This reflective strategy of avoiding ENS communication impacts worked sufficiently in N_9.

Related Work

Traditional economic models assume that each actor involved in economic exchanges has a stable set of preferences. They further regularly apply the ceteris-paribus assumption in order to abstract from factors such as technological evolutions or other more disruptive changes in an economy. Innovation is however an economic factor of increasing importance and frequency currently, i.e. dynamics drive markets. This therefore needs to be taken into account in inter-organisational interaction research. Communication is the key to innovations and *pie-expansions* (Jap 1996) of all kinds, as innovations are evaluated and possibly adopted throughout communities. In the manufacturing industry innovation is regularly a collaborative effort – the age of innovations by isolated individuals appears to

---

49 Definition from Wordnet.

be over (Westlund 2006, p. 89). Further, many innovations are carried up value chains and the relative importance of innovation sources outside a focal company compared to its research and development department is expected to increase further (IBM 2006). Effective collaboration across the value chain is therefore of great concern and recognised as a problem (Accenture 2006).[50] Competitive auctions and the perception of opportunism can negatively affect this aspect of supplier performance (Carter, Kaufmann 2007).

A survey study on research and development cooperations in Germany (Haribi 1998) has shown that the most common form of vertical integration regarding innovation processes is the informal exchange of technical knowledge. This stresses the importance of open, discursive exchange networks between buyers and suppliers.

This collaboration can be seen as a process of argumentation or learning, which is not necessarily explicit. It can be argued that this is a driver for companies to network, i.e. to cooperate with either similar or complementary organisations (Nooteboom 1992) - organisational learning then may happen on the fly, as a part of day to day interaction. Regarding this kind of organisational communication, Nooteboom pointed out the following aspect:

> "Note that the effect of cross-firm learning requires difference of perception and interpretation, but also a certain commonality of concepts, practices and procedures and perhaps organizational structure, sufficient to establish and maintain an effective linkage: a common [relationship specific] language has to be developed." (Nooteboom 1992).

This is essentially a symbolic interaction process par excellence – meanings of terms follow as well as precede communicative interaction (Blumer 1969).

A second aspect regarding lost opportunities is better represented in economic theory, namely in the new institutional economics: the lack of relationship specific investments. While in principle substantial rents can be obtained from relationship specific investments, both physical (e.g. in the case of adjacent plants) and immaterial (e.g. effort on learning about the partners capabilities and business processes), this is more difficult in practice. In

---

50 This aspect development is recognised and partly explained by social capital theory, to be addressed below. Social capital is known to be a key facilitator of innovation (see e.g. Westlund 2006, Chapter 7 and p. 56), hence the idea of *clusters* or *networks* for innovation.

this context, the opportunity to extract such rents from a business transaction is possibly lost if a transaction partner perceives the mode of negotiation as a business relationship threat. If this is the perception of a supplier, it is a disincentive for relationship specific investments.

Model Combinations

Business negotiators actively reflect on the communication barrier role of ENSs and consequently apply compensation strategies such as model combinations.

Findings

One result of the present study is the proliferation of negotiation model combinations in practice. Their application has fundamental impacts on negotiation strategy as the following excerpt corroborates.

> ☐ (N_9 line 23) As you can see [on a plot] there was some downward movement, but the compression of bids was more important. We can then focus on capabilities. Now interview the finalists and bring them in, have a final discussion. They just know that we're not gonna talk about mark-ups any more – that was really successful.

Thus not only media are applied in a mixed form, but there are combined processes models applied. Similar cases have been found e.g. in N_{10} and C_3.

As the procurement project team in the above case realised that an apples-to-apples comparability was unrealistic in this particular case, two negotiations were conducted sequentially – one on price mark-ups and one on service quality. Here the auction event served to compress the bids in order to reach a reasonable price level. Note that the competitive bidding was conducted on suppliers' margins in percent, which implies a cost-plus contract setting in the sense of Bajari and Tadelis (2001) and the buyer's ability to monitor suppliers cost. In this case of temporary labour frame contracts it translates into contracts with individuals which are comparatively easy to monitor, because of the large proportion of variable costs.

As already said, other aspects are decision relevant, ranging from a consideration of the geographical dispersion of supplier offices to innovative process integration features. Such aspects were negotiated in a second step of individual, iterative face-to-face negotiations with a set of suppliers, allowing them to present value propositions. The broad qualitative dataset obtained this way was handled using expert teams and multi-attribute decision support tools in the background – the project goal was to source based on best value and not on cost alone. Finally, multiple contracts were signed in different regions.

Similar negotiation support models have been found, although this case is the most complex and most illustrative one. Reverse auctions on Chemunity for example always end with the *choice* of a supplier, e.g. to allow a consideration of non-price issues (see also Wannenwetsch 2006, p. 52). For example, at www.sorcity.com, only sellers who can satisfy all terms and conditions can bid on a contract. The buyer will discuss details with the three lowest bidders at the end of an auction and choose from these (Pinker et al. 2003). Such processes have one commonality in that they are installed in order to compensate for communicative pathologies by combining features of different negotiation rule-sets. Thus, we speak of combination models. A business negotiation follows a *combination model* if its negotiation process is separated into at least two identifiable phases with distinct rules and norms that can be applied as stand-alone procedures in order to reach an agreement.

If a particular auction model is combined with a less structured bargaining phase like in the case presented above, the auction loses its function as a resource allocation mechanism – its process determinism – and the discursiveness of the overall process is increased purposefully. Thus we formulate the following hypothesis.

(*Hypothesis 19*): *The prevalence of combination models in the industry is a consequence of the communication barrier role of ENSs.*

Negotiators combine electronic models and traditional models of negotiation in order to compensate for the respective weaknesses of the models. In this case, it is the communicative barrier role of auction technologies that drives decision makers to include bargaining steps in the transaction protocol. The models applied in combination serve different purposes as summarised in Table 15, which associates the phases of combination models with operative negotiator goals as introduced above. Since a credible commitment is not the only goal, combining bargaining and auction steps is actually rational behaviour.

Function / Goal	Bargaining model (pre)	Auction model (potentially multi-round)	Bargaining model (post)
Instrumental	Supplier selection (quality) Market intelligence (innovation) Prepare apples-to-apples comparability	Price determination Price compression Minimal transaction costs	Identify potential of joint gains and trade-offs[51] Incorporation relationship specific issues into decision making Find ways to keep in budget after target prices have been missed
Relational	Create joint understanding Establish or maintain a working relationship and trust	Identify divergent interpretations (outlying bidders)	Communicate the spirit of the deal Achieve a trustworthy commitment
Identity	Sharpen requirements specification	Maintain reputation Find efficient processes	Maintain reputation
Relevant technology features	Supplier evaluation, CRM Rich, tractable communication Document management Decision Support	Bid analysis (bonus malus, charts) Back-End Integration Reliable and trustworthy platform	Rich communication Document management Decision Support

Table 15: Combination models: phases, their respective features and purposes.

The table further points out features of negotiation support technology of particular importance in the respective phases.

Related Work

While combination models are common practice, this is not adequately reflected in negotiation research. Moreover, game theory analysis predicts that, e.g. in a bargaining round prior to an auction, no credible commitments can be made and that thereby it must be considered to be *cheap talk*. Most research on electronic negotiation support applies archetypes of negotiation models in order to clearly depict characteristics thereof. In

---

51 A sealed-bid or rank-visible auction is said to be advantageous, when the buyer intends to conduct further, traditional face-to-face negotiations. Here the buyer identifies the best e.g. three suppliers based on bid price. There is no need to allow the low bidder to know, how much lower his bid is as compared to the second lowest bidder (Carter et al. 2004, p. 246).

practice this does not adequately reflect today's purchasing reality, where phone calls and face-to-face meetings do play an essential role in integration with electronic bidding events (Kaufmann, Carter 2004).

In the language of structuration theory, combination models are *emergent structures*. The causality at work is particularly visible in the HypoVereinsbank case (S_2), where the need for more discursive interaction arose during an auction process and the model then shifted into a combination model. The e-Sourcing strategy proposed by the CAPS Research group (Beall et al. 2003) implicitly relies on a combination model, as it advises sourcing managers to consider non-price variables in a separate process step after conducting a reverse auction. Of course, these changes of the basic (reverse) auction institution require a substantial element of managerial judgement and open possibilities for influence, favouritism and bribes (Milgrom, 1989), as well as in the case of multilateral bargaining. It appears, that the distinction between these two is not as clear cut in practice as the research on auction and negotiation archetypes implies.

Further scholars (Daly, Nath 2005, Shakun 2005) propose similar combination protocols, while Subramanian and Zeckhauser (2005) describe a kind of hybrid mode with different degrees of regulation and transparency in their negotiauction approach, which resembles some of the cases studied in this research. They further point out the importance of transparently communicated rules and the possibility that negotiators may strategically use the murkiness of negotiation processes to their advantage.

Hybrids are not considered as combination models, since they do not contain distinct phases. Other examples for comparable hybrid models are multi-attribute auctions and bonus-malus auctions, which may in turn be part of combination models.

Shift of Negotiator Roles

Because roles are major constraints and guides for all organisational behaviour, it is plausible to assume that the introduction of behaviour guiding technology will change the roles in their social context. How far is the role of the e-negotiator different from that of a traditional negotiator? Beyond requirements of media competence and an explicit negotiation model choice, the relative importance of their boundary spanning functions are changing as described below.

Findings

First, note that any organisational role is a structure in Giddens' sense, therefore organisational decisions and formal documents describe it only insufficiently – it is enacted by individuals and thereby possibly changed. Thus, the understanding of individuals' perceptions of their respective roles is vital in order to understand role changes.

Turner (1992) lists three functions of boundary spanning negotiators: namely an information processing function, a representation function and an agent of influence function. The latter may require a certain level of subtlety and informality that is unavailable within most ENSs. Further, there is a formalisation of subtle interactions through the very use of negotiation specific tools, because they explicitly frame the interaction as goal-directed, formal business tasks. In their own words, many business negotiators do not actually *negotiate*, but have strategic meetings with, call or e-mail suppliers to see what they can do on certain problems etc. - they avoid the negotiation term for its formality and negative connotations.

The pervasiveness of electronic mail based negotiations has been demonstrated already (Schoop et al. 2007a) and is confirmed here. While boundary spanners may efficiently achieve inter-organisational coordination through such practices that clearly are negotiations if a scientific definition is applied, they avoid the negotiation term which is associated with a fixed-pie bias and consequently winners and losers.

This formalisation effect (which is present regardless of whether an ENS is applied in a pool of other communication media or not) is not clearly visible in the interview transcripts. It emerged over multiple interviews: While in the first interview (N_1) the discussion was opened with the request for anecdotes on *negotiations*, the term did not appear again in the subsequent discussion of organisational context and cases. Later interviews have increasingly targeted *sourcing processes with flexible prices or specifications and inter-organisational coordination*. These terms cause a lot less confusion and uneasiness, while addressing the same entities and processes.

Another aspect of changing negotiator roles was best brought to the point in an earlier study citing a buyer comparing the electronic auction process with traditional face-to-face bargaining as follows (Kaufmann, Carter 2004):

☐ *This is as passive as watching fish in an aquarium, only with more excitement.*

An introduction of information technology into negotiation tasks, as far as it substitutes face-to-face interaction, clearly strengthens the information processing function. Further, the opportunities to represent are drastically reduced if not removed at all, like in the case of Chemunity where market players may act anonymously. In summary the following is hypothesised:

(Hypothesis 20): The communication barrier role of ENSs decreases the role autonomy of business negotiators.

Given this effect, it can be plausibly argued for a recursive effect: The decrease in role autonomy is not only an effect of the communication barrier role, but also contributes to it through negotiators' reflection. Functions performed by boundary spanning e-negotiators require a different set of skills than traditional negotiation expertise – this can be derived from the prevalence of consulting services or in-house specialists, e.g. for electronic auctions. The nature of these skills is not fully understood yet and may be required for example for the adequate preparation of electronic auction events, re-negotiations or combination models.

Related Work

Qualitative research in the construction industry (Schoop 2002), which resulted in the implementation of the Negoisst system, clearly supports the idea of a need for informal exchange in electronically mediated interactions (i.e. a green area, Schoop et al. 2003) and points out that there is no clear cut between informal and formal negotiations.

The concept of role autonomy is multi-faceted and describes the discretion and freedom boundary spanners have in interpreting and enacting their respective roles (Perrone et al. 2003). Generally, a role is not fully characterised by the set of rules, a person adheres to in enacting the role. In the case of ENS this is the case for at least one rule, which is enforced by the system (Ströbel, Weinhardt 2003) - Information Systems may play a vital role regarding role autonomy. The organisational definition of role autonomy for purchasing managers provided by Perrone et al. thus needs to be extended by a technology component.

In the literature, it is claimed that auction approaches automate the dirty parts of inter-organisational coordination and thereby take tedious and emotionally stressful bargaining processes from human hands. This view could not be replicated in the present study.

4.4.6 A Contingency Model of Communicative Impacts

The following contingency model summarises the communication related impacts identified so far. Factors such as individual strategies or the general and/or individual tendency for communicative overconfidence play into this process and influence the discursive load a negotiator experiences. Information asymmetries may exist; lifeworlds may be shared only partly. This explains, why negotiators perception of discursive load (i.e. the need to talk) may widely differ.

The same is true for the perception of the negotiation technology at hand and the rules and norms in the background. Negotiators bring these factors, along with their respective strategy, to the virtual negotiation table as sketched in Figure 10.

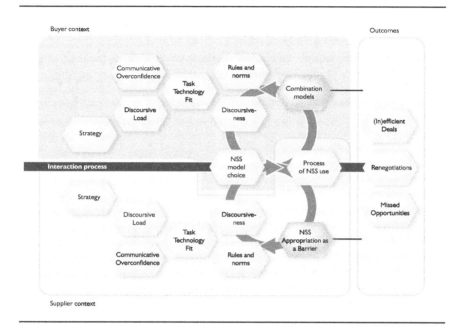

Figure 10: Contingency model of communicative impacts.

During and after the actual event we then find a synchronous process of perception, mental modelling and complexity evaluation. However, only one party decides on the mode of negotiations. In the case of traditional face-to-face negotiations, this is regularly more of an interactive process, wherein the rules of interaction are defined, but not in the electronic negotiation case. Here the protocol is unilaterally controlled and enforced through the ENS, which one party chooses according to strategic considerations and task technology fit considerations. The choice is actively reflected and may also emerge from a history of model choices.

Other parties may come to different conclusions regarding the discursiveness of the overall system and its fit with the respective task at hand, i.e. to carry out a strategy and reach a joint understanding. In case of incongruence, this may lead to the perception of the information system as communication barrier. It should be pointed out that this perception is not directed towards media or communication technology alone. In line with the understanding of Information Systems as a research discipline, the system includes the social components of the interaction process such as the partners perception of a low discursive load and consequently his unwillingness to communicate, or the positive perception of communication facilitating actions respectively. Therefore, poor communication media do not necessarily have negative effects in electronic negotiations if applied with care, which may explain the irrelevance of some puzzling findings with a negotiation media scope (Schoop et al. 2007a).

This leads to the second group of emergent issues. In N_9 and N_7 a combination of face-to-face bargaining and electronic auction processes was used. Such model combinations are the result of reflecting on ENS discursiveness and the rules and norms in effect – procurement managers are fully aware of the need for a joint understanding (see also Table 12, p. 91).

4.5 ENS as a Business Relationship Threat: Not Technology Alone

Whereas the importance of personal relationships and business relationships for successful negotiations in general has been recognised (McGinn 2004, Gelfand et al. 2006), there is uncertainty among buyers and suppliers about the effects that technologies, such as electronic procurement auctions, may have on the relationship between these parties, especially in the case of long-term strategic buyer-supplier relationships (Kaufmann, Carter 2003).

4.5.1 The Relationship Threat Role of ENSs and its Prevalence

One negotiation context parameter that is easily recognised is that, in contrast to most experimental studies on ENSs, most negotiations are conducted between parties that have an existing business relationship already. Dealing with new business partners is exceptional in the dataset, i.e. in only one case a new business relationship was initiated through electronic negotiation means. The existing, personal relationships are valued by the negotiators that were interviewed. They regularly stress the importance of these relationships explicitly, which can be seen as a kind of social capital thinking (Adler, Kwon 2002) as well as a relational self-construal: They acknowledge that negotiation is an inherently relational process for themselves (Gelfand et al. 2006).

Managers prefer direct face-to-face interaction to all forms of mediated interaction when sensitive or complex decisions need to be made (Mintzberg 1973). In an interactive negotiation situation between organisations, similar findings are documented in the literature. Experimental results indicate for example that media richness in a particular negotiation positively affects the desire for future negotiation interactions in the respective dyads (e.g. Purdy et al. 2000). Actually it is one of the basic propositions of media richness theory (Daft, Lengel 1986) that managers take effects like this into account and choose communication media accordingly in a rational manner. Naturally media preferences and positive effects thereof need to be evaluated against process costs and the needs that arise from a particular situation.

Beyond these well established preferences, interview N_2 indicated a relationship threatening aspect of ENS technology application in two cases that can not be explained with media effects alone – one in which the ENS technology had been deployed on behalf of the focal company to streamline the costly sales channel for small customers and the opposite setting of a buyer-side marketplace using E-Auctions. In the first case, the customers complained, because they feared that their established relationships to sales representatives – and thereby their individually negotiated discounts and services – were in danger, if not completely removed on purpose. This could be resolved only very slowly using a carefully designed loyalty scheme along with communication efforts. In the second case we can not speak of a resolution. Keeping up relationships despite the application of ENS technologies on the buyer side seems to be an ongoing process and a very pressing issue in this case, which calls for further analysis of the concept.

It has been argued that individuals, in contrast to economic theory, have negative perceptions regarding negotiation in general, i.e. that people regularly do not see an opportunity for one-dimensional utility gain, but a strain for an existing, multidimensional relationship (Greenhalgh, Chapman 1995, p. 181), because any negotiation is ultimately grounded in a (potential) conflict of interest. There seems to be an analogy on the inter-organisational level of interaction, which is driven by technology or its introduction.

(Hypothesis 21): ENS technology is perceived as a threat to established business relation-ships.

Similar findings have been made in earlier studies on E-Auction impacts (Carter et al. 2004). The threat perception seemed to have gained importance over time since Carter et al. found it among suppliers mainly. Based on these findings, it needs to be investigated if antecedents of this perception can be identified and what consequences it yields.

4.5.2 Antecedents of the Business Relationship Threat Perception of ENS Technologies

Why are ENS technologies understood as a threat to existing business relationships by some negotiation professionals? Beyond the obvious idea of increasing competition for and very purpose of reducing dependencies from personal relationships and skills through the use of electronic reverse auctions, the following antecedents can be identified.

Media Structuration

Findings

Increasing competition and transparency can not fully explain the threat interpretation for existing business relationships, as it was voiced in the interview. A recent meta-analysis suggests that synchronous communication facilities or the presence of visual cues (such as gestures) in negotiation processes do not necessarily result in better relationships (Swaab et al. 2006 p. 25), the perception of business negotiators regarding ENS and relationships is different however. Many negotiators interviewed in the present study implicitly reflect that negotiation technology, or more precisely the utilisation of said technology, might be some kind of threat for these relationships, and that direct interaction through rich chan-nels is both valuable and absolutely necessary. These aspects can be seen in the following excerpts.

☐ *(P₁ line 1)* *If we did everything through auctions – where would that lead us?*

☐ *(N₂ line 23)* *The platform is a tool, but you have to maintain a personal relationship as well.*

☐ *(N₄ line 52)* *Business relationships are not maintained through technology alone.*

☐ *(N₆ line 91)* *[Project manager]: For smaller projects nobody goes there [..] I know each of them [purchasing managers] personally. [CEO]: It's always like that; it needs to be.*

Therefore, it can be argued that business negotiators understand and appropriate ENSs as a potential threat to their valuable business relationships, especially in the case of reverse auctions.

(Hypothesis 22): Exclusive use of poor communication media in ENS scenarios induces a relationship threat perception.

Buyers and suppliers share this perception.

Related Work

Media choice and media effects theory make two references to social relationship developments. It is argued that on the one hand mediated or poor interaction media hinder the development of social relationships, most notably trust or social capital in a wider sense (Granovetter 1973, Purdy et al. 2000, Swaab et al. 2006, Gattiker et al. 2007).

On the other hand, social capital and trust are considered to be facilitators of effective and efficient use of such media (Purdy et al. 2000). The negotiators' awareness regarding the role of business relationships seems justified from a media theoretical perspective, especially if new relationships are to be established.

Experimental research clearly indicates that computer mediated negotiations develop less rapport, attentiveness and exchange information less readily than face-to-face negotiations (see for example Thompson, Nadler 2002, Gattiker et al. 2007).

Empirical field studies on the other hand indicate that media richness in business negotiations has no direct effects regarding misunderstandings or relationship quality (Schoop et al. 2007a, Leuthesser, Kohli 1995), the cautiousness and reluctance of business negotiators may be the *explanation* for these findings – they reflect and perceive the technology as a threat and act accordingly.

On the other hand, it needs to be pointed out that in the case of electronically supported business negotiations the technologies used not only have the role of communication media, but interact with their environment more directly and more invasive than mere communication technologies would, while other means of communication are in use simultaneously in order to compensate for media weaknesses.

Congruence of Relational Goals and Expectations

Findings

First of all, the relationship threat interpretation depends on the relationship goals of the focal company. Electronic auctions and eRfQs are regularly applied for supplier selection, that is to reduce the number of business relationships of a buying organisation (such as in N_5).

Beyond this obvious case, the perception is independent of the role of the focal organisation. Sellers as well as buyers and intermediaries potentially share this thought and in N_2 we have seen an organisation acting as a seller, both in the role of the threat perceiver as well as in role of the threat origin (more precisely the role that controls the technology, which is perceived as a threat). The auction paradigm inherently carries the spirit of *flexibility* – further, decisions are made mechanistically, soft factors are explicitly not taken into account.[52] While this setting is the norm in liquid commodity markets, many companies in B2B markets have developed a strategy of customer binding or networking in reaction to continued pressure for differentiation and price reductions. This includes dedicated relationship specific investments such as the synchronization of processes (SCM), the exchange of knowledge and possibly joint projects such as in research and development or in marketing. In the case of corporate publishing, such as in the case of HypoVereinsbank presented initially, practitioners argue for an open, trusted and interactive relationship, which resembles one with a *sparring-partner* (Strauß 2006).

---

52 There are auction models that discount bids based on soft factors through bonus-malus systems (e.g. on the click-2-procure platform, see Müller-Lankenau, Klein 2003, Griffith 2003).

Market players with such strategies, like in N_2 or S_2, are likely to perceive the technology as a business relationship threat. A side aspect of this is that the participation in electronic negotiation exchanges may be a relation specific investment in itself, despite ongoing standardisation efforts and technological improvements (see excerpts on p. 105).

The following excerpts shed light on the role of expectations and relationship goals regarding the perception of reverse auction application.

☐ (*Michael Höflich, Corporate Publishing Forum (CEO), Press Release, Munich - 14 Sept. 2006)* The HypoVereinsbank obviously does not value their customers and their customer service any more then ball pens and paper clips.

☐ (*N_7 line 1)* There was this just-in-time project – our service partner jumped in and helped to plan urgent changes, when it was clear that it can be done and the spec was written, the head of procurement insisted on running an E-Auction for the project [unexpected; goal-incongruence, not successful in the end].

☐ (*N_7 line 92)*
  Q: What about the relationship to the suppliers – is there anything that changes, when auctions are used?
  A: Yes and no. I'm also sourcing things like cleaning or call-centre services, and it's a common practice there. They know the game, know the processes and participate in auctions almost every day.

In summary, expectations of the negotiators obviously offer an explanation for a considerable share of variance in the relationship threat perception.

  (Hypothesis 23): Incongruence of expectations of the parties involved in ENS interaction determine, if ENS technology is perceived as a relationship threat.

More specifically, it is the lack of congruence of relationship goals and expectations that drives the relationship threat perception of ENSs. Drawing on the second excerpt, it should be noted that multiple parties within a single organisation may have different relationship goals, which adds further complexity to the problem.

Related Work

As far as suppliers define themselves as established business partners of a buying organisation or producing high quality goods and services (such as in the case of marketing agencies), which needs to be acknowledged, the introduction of auction technologies has a personal component. It carries the risk of loosing face, or in other words, of a clash between the suppliers' self-understanding (one's situated identity, Holtgraves 2002 p. 38) and the image communicated to him or her. This effect is hence closely related to the discussion on face-saving in negotiations, which is an important factor in negotiator cognition and behaviour (Wilson 1992). To fail to have one's identity ratified by others means loosing face. Hence, active maintenance mechanisms and social rules exist that regulate social encounters with respect to face-work (Holtgraves 2002 p. 39). In a way, these institutionalise the expectations mentioned, and cooperative face-work is generally assumed.

An incongruence between expectations has a facilitating effect on the threat perception for the dissatisfied party and their respective tactics. Similar models that use congruency as an explanatory variable can be found in the negotiation literature already (e.g. Gelfand et al. 2006). Also in reverse auction cases it appears that supplier's level of cooperation (a relationship specific investment) is contingent, at least in part, upon the expectation of continued interaction with the buying firm (Pearcy et al. 2007). However, since it is the lack of congruency that yields negative effects, the importance of clearly and transparently communicating expectations and rules can be concluded.

Rules of Conduct

Findings

As already indicated the threat perception does not apply for all kinds of negotiation support technology in the same way, and it depends on the way the technology is applied.

Human interaction is inherently symbolic. Our acts in relation to others are symbolic – we intend to communicate. Thus we may (mis-) interpret the acts of others as intending to communicate (Charon 1979, p. 130). For suppliers, the use of a semi-automatic decision, therefore, carries the message that they personally (as well as on an organisational level), do not deliver strategic value for the buying organisation and further that their goods and services are replaceable as well as the (possibly existing) business relationship as a whole. Again, analogous claims have been made on the level of individuals in negotiation situations. That is, a future relationship depends more on the process, on how the individual was treated than on the utility gain, as economic theory would predict (Greenhalgh, Chapman 1995, Thompson, Nadler 2002): on the rules of conduct.

Depending on the products and services under consideration this may be more or less relevant. In the HypoVereinsbank case (S_2) it was the main cause for the irritated and negative reaction in the media agency sector – similar reactions have been seen before.

□ (*Peter Haller, Henning von Vieregge (GVA, Gesamtverband der Kommunikationsagenturen), Frankfurter Allgemeine Zeitung, 14 Nov. 2005)* *Then a number of agencies were informed that they were allowed to participate in an auction, a bidding competition on the web with defined rules. The resulting list ideally matched the purchasing department's desires: the cheapest and most willing ones of the country. Whether this procedure helped the marketing department in their search for first-class communication professionals remains in comfortable half darkness [..]*

The main technology property that seems to yield the threat interpretation is mechanistic decision making – the determinism of the interaction process and the rules in effect. This is an inherent property of electronic auction (and agent) models, which are traditionally applied for indirect goods.

Another important aspect of procurement auctions, which has been pointed out as a success factor already, is that of transparency (see excerpts on p. 97). A lack of transparent rules of conduct that actually are effective, as seen in the HypoVereinsbank case, creates a climate of uncertainty and non-commitment. It is part of a relationship threat perception, which is, in a sense, the flip side of Hypothesis 3 (on trust and transparency). It is a key challenge for the auction initiator to create and communicate process transparency in this sense (see also the excerpt on p. 119).

☐ (**N₁₀ line 77)** In 95 percent of the cases we are sourcing according the result of the bidding
event. Otherwise [if target prices are not reached] we start negotiations. These follow-up negotiations – they are a real problem, I think.

Therefore, we pose the following hypothesis, which addresses both the technological and
organisational components of the problem.

(Hypothesis 24): Determinism of allocation mechanisms and intransparency in ENS
enabled processes facilitate the relationship threat perception.

Related Work

While rules are a form of social capital in the sense that they are institutions, which
increase the predictability of social interaction (Ostrom, Ahn 2003), this particular, formally institutionalised rule-set is ineffective, in that it leads to the perception of opportunistic behaviour of the buyer side. Its introduction is a violation of de-facto rules-in-use such
as a submission to the better argument (Habermas 1981), reciprocation or other established business practices.

Earlier survey research indicated that the auction process may explain an increase in
opportunism suspicion (Jap 2003). Bidding procedures are reflected by suppliers as a
means for opportunistic exploitation and not offering fair opportunities. Their ability to
create a level playing field is questioned (Emiliani, Stec 2004).

In auction procedures the negotiation is rather impersonal and strictly fact-based, leaving
nearly no room for personal interventions during the event (Kaufmann, Carter 2003). This
is an aspect of the buyers' individual role autonomy (Perrone et al. 2003), which has been
pointed out already. The reduced role autonomy, i.e. the determinism in auction settings
deprives buyers of opportunities to build and maintain trusted business relationships and
social capital.[53] This seems to be reflected by the decision makers, who consequently perceive the technology as a relationship threat.

---

53 The role of trust as a success factor in electronic reverse auctions and according references to the relevant literature have been pointed out already (see 4.3, p. 97).

Culture

The relationship threat interpretation seems to be culturally embedded. While on the one hand it is well known the Asian negotiators have a relation centric style of negotiating with a win-win framing of negotiations (Salacuse 1998), Americans for example have a more competition driven style of negotiating. This aspect has been raised in two separate interviews both quoted below. Two interview partners from a multi-national corporation bring it to the point through the following statement.

☐ *(N_7 line 15)*

> A: The Americans just love it [reverse E-Auctions].

☐ *(N_{10} line 119)*

> Q: Do you think that the role of negotiation support approaches is culturally dependent? That for example Americans approach them differently than Europeans?
> A: Oh yes – certainly. We have made some experiences there. Americans have bidding events in order to have an outcome afterwards. What happens with that outcome afterwards is a separate question and they may be happy with just knowing it. We usually try not to do that.

Thus the following is concluded.

> *(Hypothesis 25): The relationship threat perception of ENSs is moderated by the cultural background of the focal negotiators.*

Since the present study is based on a national sample, this factor can not be further explored here. It is an interesting point for future research.

4.5.3 Consequences of the Business Relationship Threat Role of ENS Technologies

The following chapters will evaluate consequences of the prevalent relationship threat perception of ENS technologies, both on an inter-organisational level and on an intra-organisational level.

Social Capital Impacts

Findings

Reducing the dependency on social capital seems to be a rewarding strategy from an organisational level of analysis, especially in indirect goods procurement. However, the effect of electronic negotiation support technology on social capital is not that clearly cut, but twofold.

First, most of the interview excerpts that stress the vital importance of personal interaction and business relationships (see excerpts on p. 153) were voiced as a reaction to discussing E-Auction aspects or E-Auction projects. It seems that both purchasing managers as well as product-, project- and sales managers see their social capital *discounted* through the use of auction protocols; supplier relationships are taken out of their hands as the following excerpts illustrate.

> ☐ (N_9 **line 272**) *Most of us work with internal project managers who 'own' the supplier relationship. While we can suggest ways to save money, new ways to do things, the biggest challenge is in changing out an entrenched supplier when the project manager is a fan.*

> ☐ (N_{10} **line 74**) *In my view the personal relationships stand not as much in the foreground as they used to, which is why we choose these instruments.*

This finding is hardly surprising and in line with the desired effects of the respective decision makers. For example in public procurement the irrelevance of social capital (in the sense of collusion) for purchasing decisions is a key benefit of electronic auction models.

Second, social capital (in the sense of networks and trust) is a highly important asset in the day to day interaction of businesses, which depend on cooperation and goodwill (Riemer 2004), visible e.g. as reliable and timely communication behaviour. Along with the unwanted dependency, these aspects seem to be affected by electronic auction models as well as the industry experts point out.

☐ (N_{10} *line 76)*

Q: What do you think does E-Auctioning mean to the personal relationship with a supplier?
A: It stifles communication – at least a bit – it is important to keep the awarding procedure
transparent.

☐ (S_4 *line 32)* You can drive savings in a damaging or a beneficial way. Squeezing margins is usually damaging and risky in the long haul.

Therefore, we arrive at the following hypothesis, which extends on the social capital
metaphor introduced earlier.

(Hypothesis 26): The application of auction-based ENSs discounts the social capital of the
negotiators involved.

Related Work

The economic role of social capital is well documented to be a facilitator of economic performance, investment and innovation on a national level (Knack, Keefer 1997, Beuqelsdijk
et al. 2004), which makes perfect sense, because these are long-term activities which
require economic agents to rely on the future actions of other agents. This situation incurs
control costs or costs through other activities required to avoid unilateral opportunistic
action such as carefully designed contracts – in addition to these propositions of the New
Institutional Economics, social capital and trust determine considerable shares of these
costs. Trust is a predictor for openness in intra-organisational communication and relationship investment (Smith, Barclay 1997), both of an increasing importance in the networked
knowledge economy.

Repetitive interaction among business partners, i.e. a robust network structure, provides
incentives to prove trustworthy and build up a reputation (Ostrom, Ahn 2003). A buyer
who strengthens his bargaining position by shopping with numerous alternative suppliers
may ironically undercut the incentives of any one of them to make non-contractible
investments and it may thus be optimal for a firm to employ fewer suppliers than the
number dictated from the trade-off between coordination costs and fit (Bakos, Brynjolfsson 1993).

Most suppliers in the well known studies by Emiliani and Stec (Emiliani, Stec 2004, Giampietro, Emiliani 2007) reported less cooperative relationships with their suppliers as a result of online auctions. In consequence, it was claimed that online reverse auctions have the capability to deconcentrate whole industry clusters (Emiliani 2004). A recent study provides further evidence (Carter, Kaufmann 2007). The authors speak of relationships as underlying, intangible resources at the inter-organisational level and point out that these can be eroded as a result of an auction driven perception of increasing opportunism. It is further anticipated that online reverse auctions decrease the supplier's willingness to make idiosyncratic investments (Jap 2003).

One operational definition of Social Capital is that of structural holes and bridges in a network structure of peers (Granovetter 1973, Burt 1992) as depicted in Figure 11.

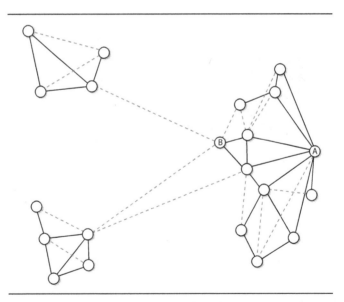

Figure 11: Business network including structural holes (based on Burt 1992).

Consider the strong and weak relationships of actors A and B respectively. Holes in such a structure create a competitive advantage for the boundary spanning individuals. They control information diffusion. Information on disruptive events such as innovation etc. reach these people faster than people that are involved in tight, closed networks exclusively, because these can be assumed to have similar, redundant information. The boundary spanning role of actor B opens opportunities for brokering if social ties of sufficient strength exist, which cross the holes to the left. In the terms of social capital theory, it appears that it is precisely such relationships that are weakened and hindered in their functionality as information conduits through the ENS threat perception.

In summary, the literature broadly supports the above hypothesis. Further, social capital in business relationships is a self-enforcing concept. Just like in the case of monetary capital, the presence of social capital yields new and more social capital (Riemer 2004). This is achieved for example by generating weak ties through co-presence (Granovetter 1973, Thompson, Nadler 2002) – a mechanism less available in electronically mediated interaction. Hence, the discount of social capital additionally deprives a party of this opportunity.

Intra-organisational Monitoring

Brokering information across boundaries is basically an intra-organisational function and at an individual's discretion – the intra-organisational aspect of ENS impacts and the resistance to ENS introduction often observed therefore deserves attention.

Findings

Reconsider Figure 8 and the relationship of constituent and negotiator in the light of electronic auctions. Trust plays a key role in the intra-organisational communication processes and influences all sorts of process and relationship variables. If a constituent decides to introduce E-Auction technology into a procurement department, this carries a message of distrust for procurement managers. It can be understood as an act of monitoring in a process hitherto controlled by personal interaction.

One purchasing manager, when asked for the performance indicators of purchasing processes brought this to the point by answering: "Savings! Savings! Savings!" This situation explains the reluctance many purchasing managers show regarding negotiation technology: They find themselves in competition with it.

☐ **(N₈ line 7)** *The idea that procurement managers are afraid of discovering savings sounds quite familiar.*

☐ **(C₁ line 157)** *There is definitely a problem of acceptance, because the established procurement managers find themselves in competition with the auction system.*

This perception has been found repeatedly in auction or SRM projects lead by interview partners N_8 and C_1. The idea of a competition with the system is only one aspect of the increasing ex-post transparency, which most types of ENS bring with them – they enable a more efficient controlling of negotiators' work, both in and in competition with the respective systems. Hence, we pose the following hypothesis.

(Hypothesis 27): Intra-organisationally, ENSs are perceived as devices for monitoring the performance of individual negotiators.

While given the often large scale and importance of negotiated agreements, the idea of a systematic control of negotiator efficiency is appealing, it needs to be carefully evaluated. Suppose a newly introduced auction process yields considerable savings. Even if these savings are generated at the cost of quality, the respective procurement manager is likely to loose face regarding the competition at first. Beyond the quality-effects in the sense of total costs, a decrease in intra-organisational trust is then likely to damage the working relationship of negotiator and constituent as well. Systematic controlling approaches therefore need to reflect the multifaceted nature of the *quality* of negotiated agreements, which is clearly a challenge. While ENS as data repositories can efficiently deliver information relevant for controlling (in the sense of spend management), appropriate means of evaluation and appropriate incentive structures for negotiator positions yet need to be conceived.

Related Work

The social capital theory, i.e. the theory of structural holes, argues that entities skilled in bridging structural holes in social networks have a competitive advantage over others – it is argued that business opportunities often arise around such structural holes and that consequently networked entities are likely able to benefit from participating in or mediating hole-spanning initiatives. If ENS discount social capital and work as threats to business relationships, they indirectly lead to business opportunities being lost – an effect caused through their communication barrier role directly (see e.g. Burt 1992).

Perrone et al. (2003) suggest a relationship that crosses the communication and relationship effects found in the present study: Role autonomy is positively associated with inter-organisational trust and hence social capital, which largely is an informal entity (Li 2007). Consequently, the decrease in role autonomy yielded through E-Auction introduction directly threatens business relationships and partly deprives purchasing and sales managers of opportunities to build up trusted relationships by making use of their discretion in a trust-worthy manner. Hence this problem escalates into the inter-organisational relationship as well.

Previous studies indicated strong resistance to the implementation of E-Auction technologies (Carter et al. 2004), and this resistance is likely to carry over to other negotiation support technologies, if they can not be differentiated sufficiently from that approach.

Opportunistic Behaviour and Collusion

Findings

Interview excerpts such as the following point towards a dedicated, opportunistic renegotiation strategy as already mentioned above (see p. 135).

> ☐ (*N₅ line 103*) *[..] Construction service specifications are often incomplete. If you do this with a company such as [major supplier] they will definitely find the problem in the specification. And they will prepare the costly change order – which they plan to send later - right away along with their winning bid.*

Hence opportunism is not only a form of distrust, but subsumes a range of misbehaviour such as deception, cheating, sub-goal pursuit with many facets and levels (Jap 2003).

This unilateral renegotiation[54] strategy, which capitalises on information asymmetries, fundamentally changed the relationship between the two negotiating organisations – especially their power relationship. Similar settings were found repeatedly. Further, suppliers may strategically use social capital from horizontal relationships as pointed out in the following excerpt.

> ☐ (*N₇ line 6*) *Price coordination among certain suppliers is not infrequent – that's reality, whether there are laws or not. In that case you need people who really know what they are doing, who know the market, who have experience and the negotiation skills. A reverse auction that yields the same price over and over again does not get you any further.*

If the allocation is deterministic and bids are not sealed, an E-Auction platform can be used by suppliers as an efficient collusion coordination mechanism, because the suppliers can control their respective bids easily. On the other hand, the low media richness and lack of cues allows for so called phantom bids through buyers.

A working business relationship, i.e. a certain amount of social capital in the vertical relationships would reduce or prevent opportunistic behaviour. If however this relationship is threatened or explicitly declared to be irrelevant through the use of automation centric ENSs, this is no longer the case and opportunistic behaviour appears more likely on all sides.

(Hypothesis 28): The relationship threat role of ENSs yields collusion, if market liquidity allows for it.

In small markets we see the focal negotiator faced with the decision between competition, relationship investments and collusion (Bajari, Ye 2003).

Related Work

An international survey study indicated that suppliers participating in electronic auctions are compelled to retaliate (Emiliani, Stec 2004) with respect to pricing when the oppor-

---

54 See also p. 135 on renegotiations.

tunity arises. That study only provides ideas for the mechanisms that allow retaliation to actually take place such as spot buys and expedited orders etc.

Therefore, collusion and the use of other communication channels go hand in hand – secondary, private communication channels would circumvent this mechanism and allow for buyer-seller collusion, i.e. side bids. Note that, in line with a general networking trend, informal cooperative exchanges even between competing companies are found frequently in Germany (Sattler et al. 2003), which renders the idea of an ideal auction market without coalitions unlikely.

Drawing on the data collected, the application of auction technology is regularly perceived as an exercise of power. From the marketing channel literature we know that exercised power, in the sense of forcefully changing a channel members behaviour, (in contrast to un-exercised power) will decrease the satisfaction of that channel member and will increase intra-channel conflict (Gaski 1984) and opportunism.

Such settings negatively affect inter-organisational trust – probably the suspicion of such a setting may already yield such an effect (Carter, Kaufmann 2007). This can be seen by analysing the discussion in the industry concerning rules of conduct for reverse online auctions, which is very intensive and thus indicates a pressing issue in the mindset of the negotiators. The rules and norms surrounding this form of interaction are found to be fluid – they are shaping iteratively, as well as the relationships involved.

Dynamics of Relationship Shaping Moves

Findings

At this point it is evident that the relational impact of electronic auctions is of a dynamic, iterative and game-like character, wherein the negotiators try to shape their relationship strategically. The choice and appropriation of negotiation and auction technologies is of strategic concern while the idea that introducing electronic reverse auctions actively eliminates opportunities for strategic behaviour on either side (taking an isolated transaction as the unit of analysis) seems to be overestimating the regulatory power of such systems in their respective inter-organisational environment, considering interview excerpts such as the following one.

☐ *(S₄ line 22) [..], to use the [auction-based sourcing] technology appropriately, buying strategies became more, not less, important.*

☐ *(N₁₀ line 69) The gambler mentality is declining – that's no longer how it used to be. Here, the suppliers really learned their lessons well.*

An important aspect that needs to be pointed out is the dynamic development of the process, the strategies of application and their respective effects on the underlying business relationships, especially regarding power distributions. The power distribution in a particular relationship may change either through unilateral moves such as the introduction of electronic auctions into a market or learning and jointly coordinated moves such as strategic partnerships on the other hand.

Regarding electronic reverse auctions, the above interview excerpt on supplier price coordination (see p. 166) is a unilateral move of the supplier side into a dominant position. Any partner can quit the relationship and enter a state of independence, but a partner relationship can only be established through joint relationship-specific investments. Collusion strategies allow suppliers in illiquid markets to maintain a dominant state while competitive auctions allow buyers to maintain a dominant state as long as the market stays competitive, which is questionable in the long run. Markets may actually dry out in response to the increased competition and price focus of auction mechanism and consolidate over time. Mergers and acquisitions may then change the power relationship towards the supplier side in the long term (Jap 2003). The strategic decisions that constitute and run such a process are, therefore, path dependent – a sequence of ENS related decisions, actions and reactions occurs.

Trust and social capital are important factors to maintain states of cooperation – using deterministic negotiation tools low on media richness leads to the perception of a relationship threat, which in turn might yield two types of effects: maintenance actions such as the use of other communication media, open book policies or relationship changing strategies on the other hand. The following table (Table 16) lists examples of unilateral and jointly coordinated moves regarding a business relationship, and provides references to the according interview excerpts.

Move	Interview excerpts	Example
(a)	See p. 155.	Reverse auction with incongruent relationship framing.
(b)	See p. 140.	CEO communication commitment.
(c)	See p. 104.	Increased competition, bid compression.
(d)	See p. 8.	Heavily regulated E-Auction processes.
(e)	See p. 105.	Integration into buy-side procurement platform.
(f)	See p. 91.	Pruning strategy (Affects more than one relationships, some may maintain their state).
(g)	See p. 166, 136.	Bidder rings, change order strategy.
(h)	See N_1, $N_{1\ 0}$.	Open book policies (i.e. cost plus agreements can compensate information asymmetries)
(i)	See S_5.	Re-evaluation auctions with token bidding (Affects more than one relationships, some may maintain their state).

Table 16: Empirical evidence on relationship changing moves.

In consequence we arrive at the following hypothesis, which represents the environment wherein the other ENS effects identified can be located and framed.

(Hypothesis 29): The introduction and use of auction-based ENS lead organisations into an iterative dynamic, path-dependent game of both joint and unilateral relationship moves.

While this view seems overly simplistic and disregards the different types of business relationships that exist, it draws an accurate picture of the game-like iterative decision processes carried out in response to the introduction and application of electronic auctions.

Related Work

Observed through the lens of structuration (Giddens 1984), business relationships are structures, which are continuously reinforced or reinvented through individual actions or events, i.e. transaction processes in this case. Thereby a structure may change its character over time, strategically or unplanned. Poole and DeSanctis point out that a structuration view of Information Systems impacts must explain the workings of such systems and in particular must identify moves or activities, by which agents produce and reproduce structures. Further, a critical enquiry of power dynamics underlying the structuration processes and possible relations of dominance is required (Poole, DeSanctis 2004 p. 214, Giddens 1984).

It is precisely a set of such moves that emerge from the data analysis. This situation has changed in recent years, as it was reported earlier that suppliers participated in auction events frequently without a real strategy and without knowing what to expect (Carter et al. 2004). The conception of relationship moves by Dani et al. (2005), which builds on a socio-psychological view of business relationships, can be used to illustrate the present process of strategic interaction. The authors consider the framework to be in its infancy and in need of validation with further data, but it offers a useful frame for the impacts identified in the present study, as shown in Figure 12.

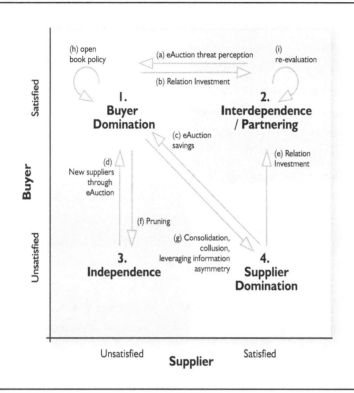

Figure 12: Iterative relationship development moves in response to Electronic Reverse Auctions (based on Dani et al. 2005).

Every entity involved is supposed to evaluate the position of their relationship to other entities involved in this simple schema, e.g. before and after an auction event.[55] In a next step, strategies are conceived in order to move to the desired quadrant, based on individual relationship goals – note that negotiation processes are often characterised by reciprocation moves. While some moves can be carried out unilaterally, others require joint action.

---

55 See also (Wolfe, McGinn 2005) on relative power as a perceived, relational construct.

This setting carries properties of a game. It is however not a traditional game theoretical one, but resembles Brams' seminal Theory of Moves (TOM, Brams 1994), which in contrast to game theory assumes that games do have a history that evolves from a given starting point in a pay-off matrix (that is, it allows for path-dependency), players make two-sided i.e. reflective decisions in a situation that may be characterised by information asymmetries as well as power asymmetries. Brams also emphasizes that decision makers plan (restricted by scarce cognitive resources) beyond a single move. They try to predict possible responsive actions to their own actions as well as the direction the iterative process is heading for in the long run.

Greenhalgh and Chapman (1995, p. 181) have a similar conception of relationships in non-electronic negotiations between individuals. Further, Ariño and la Torre (1998) find a similar iterative, event-driven process of relationship development and renegotiation in their longitudinal study of a joint venture and the according renegotiations. Dani et al. point out that a relationship may progress through a series of transitions quickly or may maintain a present status for years.

A follow-up question regarding the above set of moves is whether a relationship can move from independence (3) into partnering (2) by means of reverse auctions. This has not been the case in the dataset. While this is put forward by market makers, understanding short-term, cost cutting processes with negative feelings among incumbent suppliers as a prerequisite for developing a fruitful long-term relationship appears inconsistent (Giampietro, Emiliani 2007).

This game of iterative moves is clearly related to the electronic auction model of negotiation support and such cycles of moves could not be analysed regarding cooperative negotiation models, i.e. technologies that support integrative bargaining processes, or agent models respectively. NSSs that facilitate integrative bargaining may offer a (3)-(2) move.

4.5.4 A Contingency Model of Relational Impacts

The following illustration gives an overview of the business relationship threat role of ENS technology, its explanatory environment and iterative, recursive character. The impact model proposed here is iteratively dynamic, with the relationship threat perception in its centre.

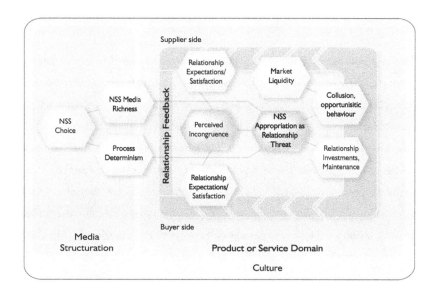

Figure 13: Overview of circular relationship effects.

Two distinct ENS properties trigger the threat perception of negotiators,[56] namely media richness (such as a reduction to the communication of prices) and process determinism. A low media richness raises the threat potential of a particular technology (see also Gelfand et al. 2006, p. 433) as well as a high degree of process determinism and automation.

---

56 In the illustration the common case of bilateral negotiation is assumed. The argumentation holds for multi-lateral negotiations as well. Note that the illustration excludes intra-organisational effects.

Both effects are mediated by social capital and rapport, in other words sufficient social capital (in the sense of trust, rapport and norms for informal problem resolution) may compensate them (see also Moore et al. 1999, Bazerman et al. 2000). The effects of these variables are hypothesised to be embedded both in (organisational or social) culture and the respective product or service domain. The latter is highly relevant for the relationship expectations of negotiators, which play a mediating role. Given congruent expectations (see also Gelfand et al. 2006), a low degree of communicative richness may not have negative effects. These effects can largely be compensated, if the negotiators are motivated to.

Given a threat perception, the focal negotiator chooses one of two (mutually exclusive) options, regularly in order to change the strategic position in the relationship satisfaction matrix (Dani et al. 2005). Consequently, either opportunistic behaviour, i.e. the focal negotiator tries to use the situation strategically (Bajari et al. 2001, Bajari et al. 2002), or relationship specific investments such as the (attempt of) use of further communication channels can be observed. Naturally, both affects the respective business relationship, the negotiators' perception thereof and supplier performance (Carter, Kaufmann 2007).

In consequence, and counterintuitively, under some circumstances the introduction of electronic auction technologies into a given business setting can actually yield a substantial reduction of process transparency, namely in case of opportunistic actions such as change order strategies and a lack of relational investments.

5. Discussion

This chapter will summarise and discuss the integrated findings, in order to assemble a theory of ENS use, grounded in the perceptions of buyers and sellers in B2B markets. Limitations of the present research are discussed. Further, research opportunities are derived and investigated in the light of the findings.

5.1 A Theory of ENS Use and Effects

First, we find that ENS effects and ENS use patterns strongly depend the on the role of the technologies at hand. Both depend on the meaning (or multiple meanings) business negotiators attach to them. There is a considerable breadth of meaning that different persons may attach to such technologies, even if they are similar or conceptually identical.

5.1.1 Hypotheses – An Overview

ENS use is a highly dynamic, reflective process, which is embedded into a set of discussions, wherein norms and rules of conduct are shaped iteratively. The multiple roles of the technologies are analysed in detail. Antecedents and consequences of the technologies' roles are identified. The following table collects all hypotheses derived during this analysis and thus comprises the Grounded Theory of communication related ENS impacts.

(Hypothesis 1):Electronic auction success, reliability of auction results and procurement process efficiencies are positively related to the descriptiveness of the goods and services to be transacted.

(Hypothesis 2):Supplier training is positively related to the process efficiency of ENS transactions.

(Hypothesis 3):Process transparency and supplier trust are positively related to process efficiency of ENS transactions.

(Hypothesis 4):ENS introduction offers an occasion for intra-organisational re-design in adjacent processes.

(Hypothesis 5):ENSs enable centralisation both in sourcing and supplying organisations.

(Hypothesis 6):ENS support in negotiated business sourcing events increases the internal, ex-post transparency of the process.

(Hypothesis 7):Regarding a single negotiated business sourcing event, auction-based negotiation support yields no decrease in buy-side negotiator workload compared to an unsupported process, which relies on electronic mail and/or traditional means of negotiation.

(Hypothesis 8):Regarding a single negotiated business sourcing event, auction-based ENS support yields an increase in supplier-side negotiator workload compared to an unsupported process, which relies on electronic mail and/or traditional means of negotiation.

(Hypothesis 9):ENS systems reinforce an artificial separation of professional lifeworlds.

(Hypothesis 10):Current ENS systems do not offer sufficient means for recovery from communicative breakdowns.

(Hypothesis 11):The use of electronic auction systems impedes the discursive making and questioning of validity claims in the negotiation process.

(Hypothesis 12):Present ENS technology in use does not provide sufficient actability to make credible commitments on allocation rules; credibility in this sense is instead largely a function of reputation.

(Hypothesis 13):The communication barrier perception is an emergent structure iteratively shaped by the communicative richness of technology, task-technology fit and negotiators' expectations.

(Hypothesis 14):Strict deadlines, over-formalisation and intra-organisational incentive structures contribute to the establishment of ENSs as communication barriers.

(Hypothesis 15):Communicative overconfidence in narrow, electronic channels facilitates the role of ENSs as communication barriers.

(Hypothesis 16):ENSs that are in a communication barrier role induce economic inefficiencies both in the societal and in the unilateral sense of unrealised gains.

(Hypothesis 17):ENSs that are in a communication barrier role induce an increased likelihood of renegotiations – both unplanned and for opportunistic purposes.

(Hypothesis 18):ENSs that are in a communication barrier role or integrate with product and service description standards decrease a sourcing organisations' capabilities for future innovations.

(Hypothesis 19):The prevalence of combination models in the industry is a consequence of the communication barrier role of ENSs.

(Hypothesis 20):The communication barrier role of ENSs decreases the role autonomy of business negotiators.

(Hypothesis 21):ENS technology is perceived as a threat to established business relationships.

(Hypothesis 22):Exclusive use of poor communication media in ENS scenarios induces a relationship threat perception.

(Hypothesis 23):Incongruence of expectations of the parties involved in ENS interaction determine, if ENS technology is perceived as a relationship threat.

(Hypothesis 24):Determinism of allocation mechanisms and intransparency in ENS enabled processes facilitate the relationship threat perception.

(Hypothesis 25):The relationship threat perception of ENSs is moderated by the cultural background of the focal negotiators.

(Hypothesis 26):The application of auction-based ENSs discounts the social capital of the negotiators involved.

(Hypothesis 27):Intra-organisationally, ENSs are perceived as devices for monitoring the performance of individual negotiators.

(Hypothesis 28):The relationship threat role of ENSs yields collusion, if market liquidity allows for it.

(Hypothesis 29):The introduction and use of auction-based ENS lead organisations into an iterative dynamic, path-dependent game of both joint and unilateral relationship moves.

Table 17 : List of all hypotheses generated from data analysis.

The present thesis has identified a broad set of hypotheses, which relate to a number of concepts regarding ENS use, mainly in the sense of reverse auctions. As described above, some of the findings replicate earlier findings made in the few empirical field studies available (such as Jap 2003, Carter et al. 2004, Emiliani, Stec 2004, Carter, Kaufmann 2007). The findings regarding communication aspects of the technology, on the other hand, are a novelty and are consequently embedded in the relevant literature mainly from Communication Theory and Social Psychology.

The value of the theory stems from the grounding in practitioners' reasoning and day to day behaviour, which can be seen as a trade off against the comprehensiveness and theoretical beauty of e.g. media richness theory (Daft, Lengel 1986). In this case, there is no monotonicity in media richness effects (Purdy et al. 2000). We find a lot of contingencies involved and, furthermore, there is no media choice in the strict sense for a business negotiation, but a choice of media sets over time, where effects depend on what the users of a technology make of it.

The following illustration (Figure 14) clusters the general structure of the above set of hypotheses into a more comprehensive contingency model, which takes the three core categories of ENS structure into account separately. It also provides references to the relevant chapters. Facets are arranged in a circle around the recursive structuration mechanism, which stresses the path dependency of the causal relationships identified (Giddens 1984, DeSanctis, Poole 1994, Poole, DeSanctis 2004).

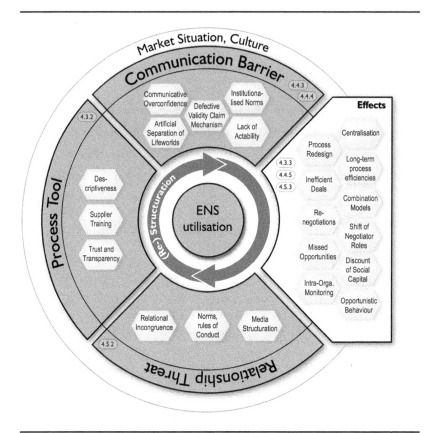

Figure 14: Summarised ENS technology appropriation and impact model.

The occurrence and relevance of the facets depends on contextual variables that are only partly under the control of the negotiators. The multi-faceted, socio-technical systems then potentially yield a set of effects listed on the right. From the theoretical point of view, the relational role and the communicative role of ENSs are more interrelated than the above model (rooted in negotiators' perceptions) suggests, because communication is always a relational activity (e.g. considering face-work, cf. Wilson 1992, Holtgraves 2002).

There are recursive dependencies (restructuration effects) in the model. Effects feed back into the perception of the technology and the behaviour of the negotiating parties. DeSanctis and Poole (1994) speak of emergent sources of structure. For example, a perception of unrealised gains will contribute to a communication barrier perception; a discount of social capital diminishes the potential gains from ENS in the role of process design tools, which depend on trust. Rules and norms of ENS application are evolving in a similar manner. Of course, these effects are embedded in and mediated by a certain market context, especially regarding the opportunities for action on the supplier side.

5.1.2 Revisiting the Research Questions

The main research question (see p. 55) of the study was decomposed into four sub-questions. Considering number 1), the structural features of the technologies, we find the technologies structured (DeSanctis, Poole 1994, Poole, DeSanctis 2004) as tools for process design, as communication barriers or business relationship threats. They may, but not necessarily do, have multiple roles for a single person.

Regarding question 2) of the thesis, namely appropriation of the technology in line with the Symbolic Interactionism school of thought (Mead 1934, Blumer 1969), the attached meanings are the basis for decision making and thus moderate or even invert any impact, which ENS technologies are considered to have (as artefacts). A number of reflective, compensation behaviours have been identified.

Consequently, questions 3) and 4) are targeted at the communicative and organisational effects of the appropriated technologies (Poole, DeSanctis 2004) respectively. As they are closely connected, we will answer them jointly. The major effects can be summarised as follows:

- In contrast to game theoretical predictions, auction-based ENSs are applied mainly as process tools, and with some success in the long run. Under suitable circumstances, they are tools for collaborative data handling and analysis, for centralisation and standardisation. Both fundamentally change the working environment of business negotiators and has spill-over effects in adjacent business process.

- Despite the availability of multiple means of communication, the use of especially auction type ENS constitutes a communication barrier. The interaction of buyers and suppliers systematically deviates from the Habermasian ideal in a way that frequently leads to inefficiencies, both in the direct monetary sense as well as in the sense of transaction costs for renegotiations or lost opportunities. E-Negotiators are aware of this and may find creative ways of compensation, such as combination models.

- Furthermore, the use of auction-type ENSs is a threat to business relationships and discounts social capital to a degree that is not justified by the goal of creating transparency and fair competition. Ironically, social capital is a precondition for effective computer-mediated collaboration and innovation. Communicative and relational effects together appear to impede innovation ability. Again in contrast to game theoretical predictions, the interaction is not strategy-proof, but regularly shifts the attention of strategic action to different means, such as change-order strategies or coopetition strategies.

Given these critical findings, the application and choice as well as the design of ENS technology are found to be of strategic relevance in itself; benefits and hidden costs of application need to be carefully evaluated. Given the diffusion of electronic communication and auction-based negotiation models in particular, these consequences deserve special attention. As Carr puts it, when a resource becomes essential to competition, but inconsequential to strategy, the risks it creates become more important than the advantages it provides (Carr 2003). After the opportunities of electronic auction strategies have been discussed, it may be time to consider the associated risks.

The above findings, in summary, suggest that electronic auctions carry the risk of decreasing the level of cooperation and coordination between businesses. While cooperation is not an economic goal in itself and decreasing it in favour of competition can in fact be desirable, cooperation is a precondition of potentially beneficial competition (Gambetta 2003). Coordination on the other hand is the essence of economic activity. Hence, the contribution made to the understanding of auction systems as a contingency of business coordination is highly relevant.

5.2 Critical Evaluation

The integration of the different research perspectives presented, access to and structuring of empirical data posed the major challenges of this research project. In the following paragraphs, the limits of the results as well as potential opportunities for further research will be evaluated.

5.2.1 Reliability and Validity

The study inherits some methodological limitations from the Grounded Theory approach: Quality assessment is always problematic in qualitative research. The Grounded Theory approach is inherently critical of its result – preliminary theory is repeatedly tested against newly collected data. Hence the reliability of the results, the consistency of measurement in the sense of repeatability, is a function of the careful execution of the research process in terms of documentation, replication and triangulation. The construction of the theory must be made traceable (Krotz 2005, p. 166). The present study achieves this goal by first explicating the author's pre-understanding, by carefully documenting findings and interpreting them before abstracting them into the threefold contingency model (this process is additionally documented chronologically).

Hence, within the limits of data confidentiality, the reader can follow the author's interpretation process and ensure its *fit* with the data (Glaser, Strauss 1967). This is also required in the set of seven principles for interpretative field research (marked as (1)-(7) subsequently) proposed by Klein and Myers (1999) already mentioned (cf. p. 71), notably in the principles of contextualisation (2) and the principle of multiple interpretations (6). The first principle, the principle of the hermeneutic circle (1), suggests that iterating between the interdependent parts and the whole that they form is required. This principle and the principle of abstraction and generalisation (4) are actually hard-wired into the Grounded Theory method. In this case they resulted in the observation of interrelations between codes that formed a *role*. The roles comprise an abstracted view of ENS technology, which in turn is embedded in an economic context.

The principle of dialogical reasoning (5) is related to the notion of theoretical sensitivity by Glaser and raises attention to possible contradictions between theoretical preconceptions guiding the research design and the *story* in the data. Such contradictions, such as the close association of eRfQs as single round auctions and competitive bidding in online auctions assumed in the theory as opposed to the complete separation of the concepts by practitioners, have been pointed out explicitly. Similarly, negotiation support system is a differentiated concept in academia, but it is subsumed with electronic auction approaches in practice.[57]

The principle of critical reflection of interaction between researchers and subjects (3) is taken up in different sections of the study. Mainly the explication of a theoretical starting point, the description of the initial interview blueprint and the description of the inquiry process serve to paint an adequate picture of the inference process and possible researcher-subject interactions.

Further, the validity or credibility in the words of Goulding (Goulding 2002, p. 89), is ensured through member checking as the prime strategy documented in the literature: interpretations and abstractions have been discussed with domain experts from industry and academia alike. The theory's pragmatic ability *to work* (Glaser, Strauss 1967), in the sense of providing an understanding of reverse e-auction appropriation and effects, is hence given. Furthermore, the final interviews clearly indicated saturation and enhanced many codes with further illustrative examples. In order to conform with Klein and Myers' (1999) final principle, i.e. the principle of suspicion (7), we will evaluate potential biases and distortions next.

5.2.2 Potential Biases in the Dataset

Due to the novelty of the topic and the current predominance of the auction paradigm in practice, the empirical part of the thesis is concentrated on that paradigm and the com-

---

57 We will revisit this issue in the chapter on implications.

municative environment applied around it. These tools have undergone evolutionary changes and do no longer resemble the archetypes of auction mechanisms; the border between ENS and auction tools is blurred. Argumentation on the technologies' features (such as determinism) may extend to the negotiation agent paradigm, but due to the lack of field data this is highly speculative. The application of this technology is mainly left open for future research.

Clearly, the present study does not suffer from student or laboratory biases and is rooted in the mindsets of business negotiators. The verifiability of interpretations made on interview statements is limited. Due to confidentiality reasons, some statements can not be presented at all or can not be presented in the full context of the interview process and the case at hand. As Poole and DeSanctis point out (Poole, DeSanctis 2004), the intensive nature of observational studies – which tends to make them intrusive – may result in selective sampling of cooperative sites or groups.

Further, both the Language Action Perspective with its references to the works of Habermas and the (adaptive) structuration ideas (see p. 30 and 23) are subject to criticism in IS research and elsewhere. This thesis is, however, not framed to make a major contribution to these discussions – both ideas are applied as starting points for the exploratory research and as illustrating reference points primarily for one reason: in the context of ENSs each explicitly draws attention to possible pitfalls, which need to be avoided, namely the narrow view of communication as an information transfer process and the illusion of an objective and static interpretation of a technology.

The resulting lens of analysis is doubtlessly not the only point of view that can be argued to be of relevance. Alternative lenses such as technology acceptance and technology diffusion approaches can possibly contribute to our understanding of ENS use in the field.

5.2.3 On the Generalisability of the Theory

While the non-diffusion of NSS type technologies such as those proposed in academia means that the focus of the data collected in the field is on auction type technologies, generalisability of the results to this class of systems is possible to a certain extent. NSSs are complex systems consisting of numerous features and approaches – directly comparing them is difficult and probably misleading.

The present thesis argues on negotiator perceptions or specific attributes of technologies. It abstracts from dedicated implementations. Thus, as far as negotiator perceptions apply or specific attributes are given in other systems, we should be able to learn about them from the present study. We do not directly learn about the appropriation effects of some specific NSS features such as optimisation of potential agreements towards the Pareto efficiency frontier (such as in Inspire) or semi-structured communication support (such as in Negoisst).

Further, the findings are considered to be applicable for German industry as a whole and thereby abstract from inter-industry differences and differences regarding product categories. The findings point out commonalities, which are grounded in the data from a broad set of industries. With respect to the codes and categories that emerged, these industries appear to be similar. Whether this similarity extends to other industry sectors needs to be carefully evaluated in a case by case analysis.

Generalisability is limited through the basic assumptions of Symbolic Interactionism in the sense of Blumer: the process character of meaning. While the result of the thesis may be valid according to accepted qualitative research standards, it can only offer an explanatory snapshot of a moving target. For example, the mentality of the actors changes over time. The subjective meaning of the technologies investigated as well as the underlying mechanisms of mediated social interaction may further change and thereby might invalidate that snapshot in the future. However, the interpretative flexibility of technologies is known to decrease over time.

5.3 Research Opportunities

This research points towards two types of research opportunities, those that extend the findings made and those that address the aforementioned limitations of the thesis. Many findings resemble a research position of critical social theory – they point out problems scholars might be able to solve, for example, through ENS designed for actability (Ågerfalk, 2003) or a better understanding of ENSs as socio-technical systems.

Evaluating this potential and offering guidance for the choice and application of negotiation technologies in a given inter-organisational business setting is the main research challenge this thesis contributes to. That discussion is, however, far from closed.

One finding calls for a larger quantification effort that can not be accomplished using the given research methodology and that is the momentum of the missed-opportunities effect measured in macro-economic, monetary terms. Our study points out the relevance of the effect, but can not offer estimations of its effect on societal allocation efficiency.

Beyond this large scale view, it is unknown how communicative action can be established and maintained in detail. Electronic business negotiations research shares some research questions with the international policy research community (Müller 2007):

- How do communicative actions and strategic actions interrelate (during electronic negotiations)?
- What counts as an argument in which context and what is the normative ground to refer to (in electronic business negotiations)?

An understanding of communication quality on this micro level of individual negotiation episodes would enable a far more sophisticated analysis as well as a dedicated negotiator training regarding these important aspects.

The thesis raises attention to the use and effects of negotiation model combinations and offers a first definition, but can not fully explore the issues and contingency factors surrounding the phenomenon. Given the prevalence of model combinations in practice and the little knowledge accumulated so far, this clearly constitutes a research opportunity. The same reasoning applies for the motivation to explore the design of low-formalisation level ENS technologies that integrate into standard communication tools such as electronic mail (see below).

Other research opportunities arise directly from the limitations of the present study. In order to complement the present thesis, the following points can be made:

- Replication of the study for the purpose of triangulation in different industries.

- Confirmatory research of the core hypotheses derived. For selected hypotheses, this might be possible in experiments using a different level of analysis such as an individual message (such as in the works of Köszegi et al. 2007) or an artificial electronic market (such as in the works of Weinhardt et al. - see e.g. Kolitz et al. 2007) that requires relationship building as well as successful communication beyond the exchange of bids.
- Empirical evaluation of the generalisability of the findings to NSSs and SRM technologies in general.
- Exploration of further lenses for enquiry, such as technology acceptance and diffusion theory.

Further, research on ENS impacts may benefit from interdisciplinary approaches that include, for example, approaches from Linguistics or Social Psychology.

6. Summary

Business negotiation processes are regularly conducted with electronic means, through online platforms, auctions and other dedicated technologies. The goal of the thesis, i.e. to gain an understanding of the use and effects of electronic reverse auction techniques is vital, due to the economic scale of such effects. While the thesis takes an integrative view of negotiation support technologies, the only technology that both qualifies as electronic negotiation in the strict sense (Ströbel, Weinhardt 2003) and has reached sufficient diffusion for a field study is the electronic reverse auction. This instrument is subject to extensive discussion in practice, however little empirical field research exists regarding key aspects.

A literature review has shown a lack of knowledge backed up by field studies, especially regarding organisational communication effects of negotiation support technologies. Different methods of theory generation have been evaluated and a Grounded Theory approach (Glaser, Strauss 1967) was selected. It has been further briefly introduced, along with the epistemological foundations of the thesis and the threefold technological foundations of negotiation support technology in general: online auctions, negotiation support systems and negotiation agents. In consequence, a theory of communicative electronic negotiation support impacts is derived, which mainly applies to reverse auction technology, but partly extends to the other two paradigms of electronic negotiation, which are so far mainly driven by academia. These approaches begin to blur and hybrid approaches can be observed. The theory is grounded in qualitative interview data, mainly collected in Germany for more than a year, as well as in secondary data. It, therefore, reflects the perceptions of actual system users, technology providers / developers and non-users.

The use of qualitative data from actual business settings is a novelty since this particular field of research was hitherto dominated by experimental and conceptual research methods. It allows to broaden the evaluation of electronic negotiations beyond the analysis of direct quantitative outcomes to the analysis of processes, relationships, commitments and understanding, because both are required properties of any useful business agreement. All findings are embedded in or contrasted with the relevant theory, such as decision theory, the theory of communicative action, media effects theory, the New Institutional Economics, Social Psychology and experimental ENS/NSS theory, where appropriate. The thesis draws heavily on the theory of communicative action by Habermas (1981, 2007) and posits it as a complementary, communicative analogon to Pareto efficiency, which is likewise an abstract reference point or ideal for the purpose of diagnosis of empirical negotiation data.

The first analysis of the dataset collected already indicated that electronic business negotiations are far more embedded in a context of previous negotiations and different technologies than E-Negotiation theory suggests. Further, a diverse set of operational goals was coded that shed light on what negotiators actually try to do in the process of interaction with a negotiation system. Communicative and relational aspects appear with approximately the same frequency as instrumental goals do, which confirms the relevance of the research question.

Although ENSs can yield process efficiencies, they also regularly get in the way of pursuing such goals. A detailed analysis explicates antecedents and consequences of these findings and thereby relates them to existing theory; including, but not limited to the literature reviewed earlier. While the data analysis supports the previous understanding on ideas such as for example:

- that negotiation support technologies work as and can be understood as process design tools, such as for centralisation purposes.
- the specifiability of goods for successful auctions as a key condition for successful electronic auctions.
- the role of electronic auctions as threats for established business relationships.

Further, a number of more surprising findings was made, which either extend or contradict existing theory. This category of findings includes for example:

- the finding that the language action (i.e. pragmatic) level of communication is insufficiently accomplished in present auction-based ENS technologies, which generates a number of pathologies such as misunderstandings and re-negotiations.

- the fact that E-Auction models are regularly applied in a way that does not decrease process costs directly if compared to the relevant benchmarks (RfQs conducted with a mixture of communication channels including electronic mail), but potentially in the long run.

- the role and prevalence of combination models and the compensatory rationale behind these models.

- the innovation-stifling role of the electronic auction approach, which is an innovative technology in itself. It acts as communication barrier for all aspects intangible or not part of established standards. Further, it diminishes the opportunities to build up and maintain informal social ties between the respective boundary spanning negotiators, which social capital theory (Ostrom, Ahn 2003) has identified as the main conduits for innovation.

In summary, it can be concluded that electronic auction models have significant communicative consequences. Further, electronic auction models do not reduce strategic behaviour in a way that could be expected according to traditional economic theory, but shift the attention of strategic behaviour to other aspects such as opportunities for renegotiation in a dynamic, long term game of relational development (Dani et al. 2005). All findings are integrated into an illustrative contingency model, which incorporates the emergent, recursive nature of the causal relationships identified (see p. 178). Drawing on this theory, we will investigate implications for research and practice below.

7. Implications

This chapter provides an evaluation of the implications of the findings made, both for ENS research and design, as well as for ENS choice and the organisational context of ENS application.

7.1 ENS Research Implications

The following chapters draw on the richness and embeddedness of the findings, in order to shed light on the contextuality of ENS use, to create a better understanding of the gap between academic and industrial technologies and finally, to propose directions on how to address the issue in future research.

7.1.1 Contextuality of ENS use - Does ENS Application Substitute Face-to-Face Interaction?

First of all, ENSs are usually not meant to substitute human interaction. The above question already falls short of the contextuality of electronic negotiations. As many business negotiations are conducted by electronic means such as electronic mail anyway, the question is how to do that effectively and efficiently. Auction applications regularly are complemented by face-to-face or telephone based interactions between the negotiators. However, present negotiation support systems are regularly conceptualised as isolated channels of interaction – this does not reflect the everyday work of business negotiators.

The interplay of interaction channels and the respective business context have considerable explanatory value: In N_7, the circle of expectations could be left only through a massive campaign including commitments from the CEO (see page 140). Such an action is, however, not only interesting as a communicative action per se, but also as an action that basically redefines the nature of a business relationship.

Although given the above analysis, flexible NSS systems would open an opportunity to leave the sketched strategic game and to generate efficiencies from information technology in negotiation processes, NSS systems proposed by academia and according experiments have potentially a common problem: It is claimed that current E-Negotiation studies do not capture and address the substantive problems of E-Negotiation service providers or users (Turel, Yuan 2006, p. 127) and that consequently technologies need to be explored in their intended context of use. The complexities identified regarding context and ENS effects in the present thesis justify this claim.

As we have learned from the present research, different aspects of context play a role in ENS introduction and use and need to be taken into account in empirical research on ENS effects and ENS choice.

- Historical context – a history of ENS enabled negotiations, or lack thereof, will likely influence future negotiation interactions. The technology structuration perspective (Giddens 1984, DeSanctis, Poole 1994, Orlikowski 2000) and the Symbolic Interactionism perspective (Mead 1934, Blumer 1969) proved valuable in this thesis. Both have this idea in their centre.

- Organisational context – involvement of different institutional levels or functional departments in an electronic negotiation can fundamentally change the negotiation process.

- Relational context – Present business relationships, relationships to third parties such as an incumbent supplier as well as intra-organisational relationships may change the character of the electronic negotiation game or represent primary goals on their own.

- Situational context – E-Negotiation work is potentially fragmented due to its asynchronous, dislocated setting. Negotiators conduct multiple negotiations in parallel, while they have the opportunity to refer to constituents or domain experts during a negotiation. These parameters constitute differences of traditional negotiations and the electronic case but have hardly been explored.

- Technological context – E-Negotiation is hardly a technologically isolated event, but has relations to e.g. enterprise resource planning and catalogue systems, contract management, SRM, CRM, as well as typical office and communication software. The interplay of these systems creates a major share of workload in E-Negotiations.

To conclude, there are certain contexts, in which E-Negotiation may substitute face-to-face interaction. But this is clearly the exception, as ENSs are applied in a socio-technical context as a non-exclusive communication medium and because ENSs sare less likely used in those settings, which are historically structured as to be addressed face-to-face. ENSs mainly substitute asynchronous, textual communication through other channels.

Some of these contextual aspects do lend themselves to experimentation, others do not. This underlines the need for qualitative field research and points ENS designers to critically evaluate system design decisions.

7.1.2 On the Technology Gap Between ENS Research and Practice

Recently, a special issue of the Journal of Group Decision and Negotiation was dedicated to a perceived gap between ENS research and practice. On the one hand researchers conceived systems and approaches for negotiation support since the 1980s and have shown their effectiveness in numerous experiments. On the other hand, the technology portfolio applied in practice is rather small. In practice, electronic mail is the dominant communication technology (see Schoop et al. 2006b), followed by and combined with well known auction platforms. Auction systems are the most widely diffused ENS technologies, but in recent years, the peak of electronic auction use seems to have passed, and there is a considerable gap between NSSs or advanced auction formats designed by the research community and those in use.

Can reasons for this gap be identified? Based on this study, multiple candidate explanations for the gap and the perception of a gap can be identified.

First of all, blurring concepts make it hard to differentiate innovative negotiation support technology both for researchers and for technology or service providers.

☐ (N_8 line 27) "[..] and if it is getting complicated or if I do not know exactly what I need, I let the guy visit us." If we talk about electronic negotiations the answer usually is something like "E-Negotiations? Sorry, we already have that [meaning an E-Auction or eRfQ system]."

Electronic auction platforms use the E-Negotiation term as well as a rich set of other newly introduced terms to describe a particular form of inter-organisational coordination. Further, e.g. multi-attribute auction methods blur the border between a negotiation mode of interaction in the sense of bargaining and that of auction procedures.

This confusion of terms is a potential reason for the non-dissemination of NSS ideas. The consequence seems to be a considerable confusion paired with non-interest, because all approaches appear to be similar in their nature. Negative connotations associated with (early) reverse auction practices thus carry over to other electronic negotiation technologies in the circle of re-structuration (Figure 14, p. 178) of a simple, dichotomous decision as analysed below (see p. 197).

This is a possible explanation for the (non-) adoption of ENS / NSS technologies so far, but what does that tell us about future ENS adoption in the industry? What we currently see evolving in the industry is an attempt to gradually change the nature of that game. Auction platforms are enriched with communication tools and document management facilities. Optimisation approaches, combination models and multi-attribute decision making gain attention. This is difficult and time-consuming however, because innovative approaches enter a context of existing behavioural structures that may contain perceptions of opportunism (Carter, Kaufmann 2007) or habituated communication barriers (p. 121).

7.1.3 Process Integration and Technology Integration

Considering the barriers of adoption for such (second generation) ENSs, interfacing other Information Systems from negotiation support systems is difficult and appears to be a major decision criterion in ENS investments.

In one of the interviews with technology providers, this was stated explicitly as follows:

> ☐ (N_8 *line 38*) *The core problem in practice is the interfaces: How do I get my data into Microsoft®-Word [58] or into the SAP® -system.[59]*

Obviously that problem depends on the degree of structuredness of the ENS considered (in terms of processes and data structures). Price-based auction systems can exchange data with an enterprise resource planning system more easily than a highly flexible system. Consequently, this may partly explain the dominance of highly formalised negotiation support technologies.

For the remaining gap, mainly a single aspect appears to be relevant on the level of analysis of an individual decision maker: the increasing formalisation of inter-organisational interaction and the decreasing role autonomy of negotiators (Goodhue 1995, Dennis et al. 2001). The informal *coffee-bar efficiency* that often seems to drive successful face-to-face negotiations is not sufficiently reflected in the negotiation technology available today. This means that ENSs should possibly shift away from a regulatory approach to an approach of process integrated support. Ostrom and Ahn make an important point of relevance here, while reviewing the social capital and social choice literature.

---

58 Registered trade-mark of Microsoft Corporation.
59 Registered trade-mark of SAP AG.

"Self-governing systems in any arena of social interaction tend to be more efficient and stable not because of any magical effects of grassroots participation itself, but because of the social capital in the form of effective working rules those systems are more likely to develop and preserve, the networks that participants have created, and the norms they have adopted."

(Ostrom, Ahn 2003, p. xxiii)

Consequently, ENS research should evaluate the potentials and risks of a bottom-up integration of ENS technology, i.e. to integrate ENS functionality with less formal day-to-day technologies such as electronic mail, as it is a vital part of common work practice both in ENS (combination models) and non-ENS environments.

It allows for some informal interaction on the one hand; on the other hand, it is used for tasks that require formality and traceability for auditing purposes, such as bargaining, making commitments and iteratively authoring and commenting a contract document. Therefore, it appears fruitful to facilitate an integration of dedicated negotiation support functions with the established infrastructure and habitus, in order experiment with different *tool sets* rather than with complex, monolithic systems. As we have seen, these tend to *get in the way* of efficient interaction in more than one way.

7.2 Management Implications

The grounding of the above theory allows to sketch some relevant implications for the management of electronic negotiation processes on the buy-side and on the sell-side, which both draw on the ideas and best practices of the interview partners, as well as on conclusions from the derived and theoretically embedded theory.

7.2.1 On the Business Value of Discursiveness in E-Negotiations

Does discursiveness in negotiation technology and in the respective business processes pay off? There is a trade-off to this question, which needs to be evaluated in context. To a certain extent it is a necessary requirement – a question of effectiveness not of efficiency and negotiators may actually be forced to act communicatively (Müller 2007). Beyond this kind of threshold, the optimal degree of discursiveness, in the sense of resources spent on enabling and pursuing a discursive mode of interaction, is not easily determined. The findings presented regarding the communicative and relational consequences of electronic auctions fundamentally question the explanatory sufficiency of economic efficiency (usually in the sense of total cost) as a static property of negotiated resource allocations. Efficiency in the lifeworlds of (e-) negotiators in practice is largely a dynamic and process oriented efficiency, probably more in the sense of Noteboom who argues for an extension of transaction cost economics in order to incorporate knowledge development and innovation (Nooteboom 1992), to include values in the evaluation and not only costs. This idea is partly immanent in the strategies of present negotiation support technology providers ("Sourcing for Best Value, Not Just Best Price", Emptoris Inc. 2005).

Consider the costs and benefits of a discursive style of electronic negotiation. Discursiveness *increases* bargaining costs to a certain extent. It may require multi-stage negotiations, the inclusion of further parties, which may be able to contribute and the process of interaction, can be expected to further lengthen the process. The ability to contribute is an important point, since it either requires negotiators to be both skilled in negotiation and the respective domain of discourse, or the negotiation specialists need to interact with the respective domain experts in their own organisation. Both are costly.

On the other hand, discursiveness *decreases* the cost variance (and uncertainty) caused by surprises of all kinds (renegotiations, litigation etc.) and also contributes to overall efficiency in the traditional sense. Only if the spirit of the deal can be communicated, can a contractor be expected to perform as required and to think ahead (Fortgang et al. 2003). In particular, high returns on discursiveness can be expected both in innovative environments and highly dynamic environments and further. In these environments, returns on information networks and social capital can be expected. While discursive modes of interactions allows buyers to benefit from suppliers expertise, a non discursive (price auction) model diminishes this possibility (Bajari et al. 2002).

It has been shown that negotiation support technologies cause considerable variance of efficiency in this *process sense*. This is not part of common, cost-driven business reporting and decision making today. The question whether discursiveness *pays* thus falls short. The return on discursiveness is difficult to quantify – its main benefit is the increased problem solving capability of an inter-organisational institution – and is hence a rich field for future research.

7.2.2 On Electronic Auctions and Relational Strategies

Given the prevalence of relational strategies and cooperations, the ultimate question is whether and how ENSs allow for relational marketing and sourcing strategies to succeed. For the auction case, the opportunities are limited, while some scholars see opportunities given appropriate guidelines (Daly, Nath 2005), which in turn are subject to criticism (Emiliani, Stec 2005, Daly, Nath 2005b). Others see the mode of offer exchange and the choice of a governance structure as independent decisions (Pearcy et al. 2007), which is questioned by the above findings. There appears to be a consensus that electronic reverse auctions offer a trade-off between rents from reduced prices and rents from relations (Daly, Nath 2005).

Having found aspects of both communicative and strategic action in electronic business negotiations, an analysis of incentives and decision alternatives on an organisational level can shed further light on the status quo and its developments, because a communication breakdown leaves the participating parties without real coordination and with their own strategies.[60] As we have seen, the model decision and its effects are not connected in a direct causal manner, but through an interactive process. With some simplifications, the situation as a game-like interaction lends itself to an analysis.

Given the *perceived* dichotomy of traditional (including electronic mail and other techno-logies) negotiation interaction on the one hand and the highly restrictive price-only reverse auction on the other hand and a certain fixed-pie bias in the discussion,[61] the

---

[60] Habermas notes that in the empirical analysis of negotiations the communicative rationalist may well rely on game-like strategic actions, if she finds the discursive approach unsuccessful (Habermas 2007).

[61] Neither of the three assumptions hold on closer inspection, but they occur as such in operative reason-ing. Hence, we use them to obtain a preference model.

present study provides information regarding a preference structure and the set of strategies of buyers and sellers.

While the model decision currently is clearly in the hand of buyers (except in the most unequal power distribution cases where open book policies can be enforced), the present study has shown that suppliers have a set of strategies to use in response to auction introduction, i.e. the inter-organisational interaction is not strategy-proof. Suppliers may retaliate in a number of ways (e.g. through change order strategies or collusion), which we will summarise as the set of non-relational strategies or opportunistic behaviours, opposed to the set of relational investments such as communication process compensations or dedicated cost cutting activities etc. In order to perform a game-theoretical analysis of this situation, we find the theory of moves (Brams 1994, see also p. 171) to be best suited, because it allows for an analysis of sequential game-play that is path-dependent, i.e. wherein history matters and players look ahead. Further, it depends on ordinal preference structures only. This makes it suitable for a broad and abstract situation, where cardinal preference structures can hardly be elicited nor generalised across a diverse set of organisations.

Regularly, collaboration in buyer-supplier relationships is worthwhile and allows for *pie-expansions* (Jap 1996, see also chapter 4.4). Claiming the rents from these is the most preferred alternative for either party. As we have seen, auction technologies require relationship specific investments as well as some relationship maintenance, i.e. a compensation effort, which makes highly restrictive negotiation technology costly for suppliers beyond price competition. This is, therefore the preferred alternative, for buyers and the least preferred alternative for suppliers. Consequently, the relational investments required are lower in the non restrictive interaction as well as the price competition, which makes this the preferred alternative for suppliers and less preferable for buyers.

If relational investment can not be enforced, suppliers can choose whether to invest or whether to follow a non-relational strategy as described above, which yields a buyer payoff that is independent of the interaction model decision. Further, non-relational collusion strategies are risky for suppliers and not to be achieved without investments as well. Suppliers therefore prefer the status-quo (of non restrictive interaction with moderate investments). Further, it has been observed that suppliers feel justified to use collusive strategies if buyers employ auction style interaction modes, i.e. their pay-off for such strategies is better than in the non restrictive interaction case. On the other hand, it is regularly claimed that auction protocols take the unpleasant part of negotiations out of the negotiator's hands. Therefore, it is reasonable to assume that, given comparable revenues and a non-relational strategy on the supplier side, buyers will prefer the auction state over the non-restrictive state.[62]

This situation is more abstractly represented in the following pay-off matrix (see Table 18), where (1) denotes the most preferred state for each party[63] on an ordinal scale; i.e. it marks the first choice. The starting state is state C and we assume the buyer to move first, i.e. to decide whether to introduce an online auction technology or not.

Buyer \ Supplier	Relational investment	Opportunism
Online Reverse Auction	A (1, 4)	B (3, 2)
Non restrictive interaction	C (2, 1)*	D (4, 3)

Table 18: Abstracted pay-off matrix regarding relational strategies and auctions.

Brams (1994) defines a non-myopic equilibrium as the stable outcome (given his assumptions there always is at least one) that is induced if players think ahead, i.e. they consider repeated games and their partner's reactions to their own actions etc. Such equilibria can be found by analysing game trees of consecutive choices and a process of backward induction to find out whether certain states either represent best (local) pay-offs or lead into cycles (i.e. additional transaction costs to no effect). In both cases it would be rational for a party not to move further from a state. If one termination rule holds for any party in a

---

62 Readers, who do not agree with this preference structure regarding a specific business relationship setting, find a comprehensive list of 2x2 games and their respective non-myopic equilibria in (Brams 1994).

63 Speaking of abstract parties, it is plausible to either think of the supplier as an individual organisation whose incentives for non-relational strategies increase if these are employed by other organisations or a potential cartel that may form, when collusion strategies are applied.

state, a non-myopic equilibrium is found (see Brams 1994). Thus we identify a single non-myopic equilibrium in state C. Given this plausible preference structure and a relational, strategic planning situation, it is rational for both parties to maintain state C as moving to A would further lead to state B, where both were worse off in the end.[64]

In order to capitalise on the potentials of electronic negotiation as well as on the competencies of suppliers, buyers need to define settings wherein rents from process efficiencies and a meaningful competition beyond prices can be extracted without forcing suppliers into the above decision, such as combination models or multi-attribute auctions (see also p. 205 on the idea of a Dialogue Sourcing strategy).

The challenge lies in the differentiation of the approaches, i.e. in the introduction of new columns and rows into the above decision model.

The present research contains two datasets of reverse, open-cry auction cases that were successfully approached with a relational sourcing strategy (N_9) and a relational, key-account based marketing strategy (C_3) respectively. Both cases are characterised by

- congruent relational expectations regarding large-volume, multi-year contracts,
- combination models where the auction event is the final part of a longer episode of negotiation exchanges
- as well as considerable relationship investments on either side.

Descriptively speaking, the answer to the above question therefore would be a conditional yes – though not frequently and only through considerable effort and deviation from the basic auction model.[65]

Prescriptively speaking, open-cry auction models are not suitable for relational strategies in a strict sense, while sealed bid RfQs are not raising similar relationship threat percep-

---

64 Other multi-round analysis techniques lead to a similar result through a process of learning and strategy adaptation. Note that the pay-off matrix contains a unique and pure Nash equilibrium (Nash 1950) in state B, which appears plausible, given a myopic setting of simultaneous choices without credible strategy coordination. However, this does not adequately reflect the interaction in business relationships which are inherently path dependent.

This may be a valid result for the less frequent cases of no previously existing relationships or those cases where relations are irrelevant.

65 In terms of the model based on Dani et al. 2005 (see Figure 12, p. 171), this would be rather a (3)-(1)-(2) move than a (3)-(2) move.

tions. Less deterministic and more communicatively oriented NSSs or combination models are probably better suited for this purpose, given that they can be differentiated accordingly.

7.2.3 Implications for the Supplier Side

Corporate Communication Management in Electronic Negotiation Settings

Bruhn proposes the following components of strategic communication (2004, see Figure 15, p. 202): corporate communication (to transport values/image/trust), traditional marketing communication (product and service information) and dialogue communication (personal interaction, relationships).

E-Negotiation settings driven by customers bring about an increased structuredness, formalisation and a concentration on content aspects. In terms of communication channels, this means that first all three channels become more narrow. They are not less important, but buyers and their technology guard these communication interfaces, which requires a careful re-consideration of corporate communication strategies on the sell-side. Second, the relative importance of the product and service related marketing communication is increasing. Negotiation as a communicative encounter is obviously highly relevant for all three goals.

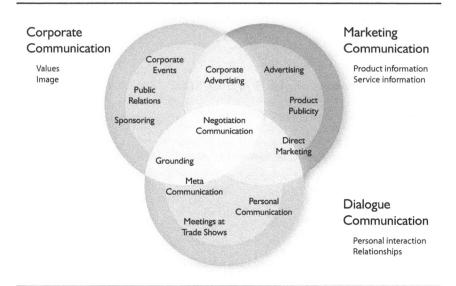

Figure 15: Marketing communication goals and interfaces narrow (adapted from Bruhn 2004, p. 710).

What does this mean for communication management in the sense of marketing strategy (Meffert 1998, p. 685)? First of all, the level of discursiveness needs to be assessed and taken into account as a key characteristic of individual customer relationships. Only when the discursive style of customers is known, they can be integrated into a communication and CRM strategy of adequate discursiveness (in N_2 this evaluation was of great concern). Such a strategy may be a selection or a combination of two options, namely taking the discursive style of a particular relationship as granted and treating it adequately (adapting to it) or strategically trying to adapt it.

The *first option* can be considered as an alignment of negotiation communication. Practically, this means that sales managers, for example, need to be prepared to communicate selling propositions (possibly including different configurations thereof) in a way suitable for competitive multi-attribute bidding, while controlling the according cost structures.

Whereas on the one hand, business relationships are perceived as being threatened, on the other hand direct interaction becomes more scarce and thus more critical. Two aspects will serve as examples: meta-communication, i.e. clarifying how to interact and transact with each other, and grounding – i.e. active topic management, the ability to react quickly and meaningfully with coherent communication acts. When the channels for corporate communication signals and traditional marketing communication become more narrow, such aspects of Corporate Identity (in the sense of a coordination of all channels of interaction with an organisation, see e.g. Meffert 1998, p. 686) gain importance proportionally as conduits for trust and values (trust as a prerequisite for successful E-Negotiation), as uncertainty increases in electronic interaction compared to the traditional face-to-face case. Such channels can easily transport relationship relevant corporate signals before and after a negotiation – especially in negative cases, e.g. when lacking preparation, attention, intra-company consensus or media competence. It may be useful to take these aspects into focus (e.g. N_9), whereas explicitly following a consequent price-only, non-discursive strategy in reaction to electronic auctions appears to be a risky strategy for suppliers (Emiliani, Stec 2004).

The *second option* is characterised by initiative action. It translates into the question of alternative relationship management strategies: How to maintain or establish business relationships under the given constraints? Marketing needs to establish business relationships creatively, for example by integrating products and service provision.[66] High quality services not only shift attention away from a price driven competition (such as in N_9), but naturally include some integration of and thus interaction with the external factor. It is an opportunity for relationship building and relationship maintenance. This strategy is successfully employed in the case N_6 by offering high quality training services beyond the product portfolio.

Either strategy decision may in consequence bind considerable resources prior to and during a negotiation. A structured account and evaluation of similar customers and processes can be of great value for this relational investment decision.

---

66 See e.g. www.sinprod.de, a research project wherein this approach is evaluated in detail for the construction industry.

Proactive Technology Use

So far, the development of negotiation support technologies is largely driven by buyers and their respective needs. We further need to consider opportunities of seller-driven system design in electronic negotiations.

First of all, given sufficient market power, seller consortia can take the initiative of interaction design, such as in the case of Supply-On in the automotive industry. Supply-On is governed by suppliers from the value chain and was established in reaction to the dominance of buyer based electronic trade platforms in a kind of coopetition scenario in this particular market. The software incorporates document management services as well as quality management services. Gradually, it progresses from a trade-platform to a collaboration platform. It is a rather successful negotiation support system, which takes sell-side requirements into account explicitly.

What else can be achieved for the sell-side by consistent system development for E-Negotiation interactions as a sales channel? To a certain extent, the potentials of sell-side E-Negotiation technologies have already been explored under the Mass Customisation label. Here, the increasing flexibility of production facilities and product modularity are leveraged by means of information technology, which literally turns customers into co-designers or prosumers (Toffler 1980). Web-based processes of product and service configuration can be seen as dialogues or negotiations. To an extent, the respective web interfaces, along with other points of contact, signal a suppliers willingness and ability for dialectic interaction (Totz 2005, p. 189). For example, American Power Conversion (APC) successfully applies such strategies in the electronics infrastructure business (Hvam 2006). In all cases, a buyer interacts with a software system that ensures that only technically viable meaningful designs are created. The underlying understanding of the coordination process between buyers and sellers in the case of Mass Customisation is similar to the understanding in the negotiation agent community, i.e. that of a joint search in a solution space (see p. 42). Similar approaches can possibly be transferred to the business negotiation domain in a more discursive NSS sense, where design options can actually be discussed and trade-offs can be found. In practice the application of Mass Customisation technologies implies an externalisation of both labour and responsibility from the supplier to the buyer, i.e. a self-service approach, while standardisation and auction-based coordination seem to imply the opposite.

Other opportunities for a pro-active application of negotiation support technology on the sell-side may exist, for example regarding preference modelling. While marketing literature and prescriptive negotiation literature both emphasise the importance of preference modelling, a dedicated tool support for the elicitation, documentation and analysis of customer preference models during a bilateral interaction is currently not given.

7.2.4 Implications for the Buyer Side - A Electronic Dialogue Sourcing Strategy

Drawing on the above empirical findings regarding possible problems and weaknesses of ENS application, a sourcing strategy can be derived that at least partly compensates for these weaknesses by taking the shared dialogue underlying business transactions into focus. While it may not be applicable for all product categories, it stresses that there is a trade-off regarding online reverse auction utilisation, which may yield savings on the one hand, and both non-cooperativeness (Pearcy et al. 2007) and inefficiencies due to communication frictions on the other hand. These may partly compensate or question those savings completely. The trade-off needs to be evaluated explicitly.

The Need for an Electronic Dialogue Sourcing Strategy

Dialogue Marketing or Interactive Marketing is a concept of increasing importance both in consumer markets and in industry settings. The impact of technology mediated interaction is also of concern in these communities[67] and leads to the proposition of dialogue-ability at the core of a web-aware, interaction oriented brand management strategy (Totz 2005). On the other hand, the idea of a dialogue focus is not yet of concern on the sourcing side. Supplier Relationship Management is an approach of actively taking supplier relationships and the respective information flows into focus. It stresses the importance of strategic

---

67 See for example Hermes (Hermes 2006) on the use of reverse online auctions in this field.

planning of relationships. It aims at integrating and inter-connecting sourcing relevant data electronically. Thereby it enables different sourcing strategies, but it is not a sourcing strategy in itself.

While supply chain integration also aims at a coordination of information flows in buyer-supplier relationships (and further), this information flow is designed to be a highly structured and efficient transfer of orders and related documents, such as demand forecasts or inventory data. Note that, for example, the Forrester Research Benchmark of eSourcing Suites (Forrester Research 2005) contains an integration criterion (weighted with five percent in that case), but does not analyse the suites' role as a communication platform at all.

Although this kind of integration can deliver substantial business value, it does not facilitate dialectic, flexible communication. The dialogue sourcing strategy proposed here is a relational governance structure that serves to draw attention to and compensate the communication and relationship barrier roles, which negotiation support technologies may carry with them unintendedly.

Components of an Electronic Dialogue Sourcing Strategy

Product and service flexibility are increasing continuously. Innovation is increasingly the result of networking activities, i.e. it happens mainly between different organisations or in groups of organisations. Both complexities are immanent in business negotiation processes. As Hauser and Clausing point out after introducing the well known House of Quality concept, it is not simple to develop an organisation capable of absorbing elegant ideas (Hauser, Clausing 1988).

This is precisely what the field study showed – electronic negotiation support systems can contribute to this problem, by acting as communication barriers and relationship threats. On the other hand, they may be of use in what can be considered to be a Dialogue Sourcing strategy, a term that is meant to draw attention to the fact that a positive return on communication may exist in procurement tasks, which can be realised through the application of information technology.

The idea is to establish an electronically supported, inter- as well as intra-organisational dialogue that is sufficiently discursive to carry the overall sourcing process, including interactions during requirements engineering, the conception of a specification and the after-sales phase of the transaction as well as the core negotiation phase, because all phases are potential cost drivers in case of a communication breakdown.

Different components are required to form a Dialogue Sourcing strategy, in order to bridge the communication barrier, as shown in Figure 16.

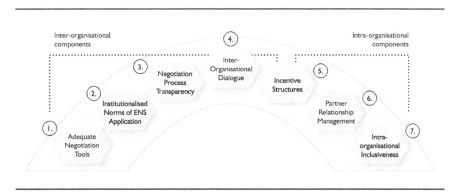

Figure 16: Components of a Dialogue Sourcing strategy; the dialogue bridge.

Below, we introduce the components and their interplay in detail, and take both communicative and relational aspects into account. Pointers to challenges, best practices and the role of negotiation support technology are provided.

(1.) **Adequate Negotiation Tools**

The potentials and promises of electronic sourcing and negotiation have led to the development of a large variety of e-sourcing and E-Negotiation tools of considerable power and complexity.

While formalisation of business communication has numerous benefits the present study points towards the dangers of over-formalisation, which have already been explored in early LAP research with The Coordinator (see e.g. Flores et al. 1988) – an office automation system. Informality may play a crucial, facilitating role (see p. 62) in business negotiations, especially when it comes to impasse situations or deadlocks.

Consequently, there is no monotonous relationship between the level of formality, the communicative restrictiveness enforced by an ENS, and negotiation effectiveness or efficiency. There is no all-purpose ENS technology, rather a composition of technologies and organisational rules that needs to be carefully and strategically chosen on a case by case basis. This makes the choice of (a mix of) appropriate technologies an important element of any electronic sourcing strategy (Beall et al. 2003), both in the sense of an investment and in the sense of shaping future interaction processes with suppliers.

From this point, it needs to be evaluated what requirements exist and what technologies exist to match the requirements. There is a large set of technologies to choose from in the high-formalisation sector (auction suites), whereas complementary moderate-formalisation technologies (e.g. Negoisst, Schoop et al. 2003) or low-formalisation technologies that are dedicated to negotiation support are scarce and largely open to future ENS research and development. For example electronic mail or instant messaging clients with integrated business negotiation specific functionality could be conceived.

An opportunity opened by ENS technologies is the idea of increasing flexibility, as a sourcing manager describes below.

☐ (*N₇ line 25*): *There is the idea of a more open competition (than in E-Auctions). In that case you only define some constraints such as there is so much room, this and that needs to happen in a [machinery component], but you don't specify how that is supposed to happen. This way new ideas come up and that is really interesting. In the dialogue with the suppliers it then turns out that one solution is more powerful while the other is less costly – it might cause more maintenance costs however. The final decision is then made separately.*

This resembles the idea of multi-attribute reverse auctions, where the utility model essentially replaces and aggregates a simulation model. Such a setting is, however, not supported through dedicated information technology yet, but can be facilitated by flexible computer-mediated communication tools such as electronic mail, which allow for a quick resolution of unclear aspects.

(2.) Institutionalised Norms of ENS Use

It has been shown that adequate institutionalised (i.e. lived) norms and rules of conduct can provide an environment that facilitates communicative (and strategic) rationality (see N_5) if they are used transparently and in a trustworthy manner. They can not only prevent negative effects as a relationship threat perception, they can be established as a strategic asset of social capital to draw on.

Although norm-guided behaviour is a borderline case of communicative action (Habermas 2007), it seems to offer the best opportunities for a strategic management of discursiveness. However, it needs to be stressed that this is an attempt to influence a reflective, emergent, inter-organisational system with different facets (see Figure 14, p. 178), i.e. it is a difficult task.

On the other hand, this aspect of the dialogue approach does not require total control but rather consciousness and the establishment and living of the respective norms. Dedicated activities such as an explicit commitment to value, rather than price, (as seen in N_9) can serve this purpose as well.

As already mentioned, the conception of norms, which can serve as a reference in discursive business interaction, is a challenge for future research and the operative discussion in practice.

(3.) Negotiation Process Transparency

In the interviews, the norm of transparency of negotiation processes was mentioned repeatedly as a success factor. Transparency means traceability of the decisions made for all process participants, especially for suppliers, with a twofold meaning. The decision made must be traceable ex post but also must the decision process be transparent ex ante – the (discursive) rules of interaction must be stable and explicit before they are in effect.

This is required to establish reputation and to avoid the perception of opportunism. The communication of motivations as well as auction rules play a key role. Here, misunderstandings would lead to dysfunctional conflict (Carter, Kaufmann 2007) and consequently to economic inefficiencies, both in the negotiation process and in the negotiated results.

(4.) Inter-organisational Dialogue

Persuasive argumentation lies at the heart of negotiation (Sycara 1990). Given the above components of the inter-organisational setting, the focal organisation can (in principle) enter a dialectic interaction as described above, which facilitates the communication of potential joint gains and innovations, while keeping opportunistic behaviour and transaction costs due to re-negotiations at a minimum.

There are three more components of the strategy, which describe whether discursive interaction can be and should be conducted and who should enter this dialogue.

(5.) Incentive Structures

In particular, it is necessary to provide dialogue-compatible incentives for all participants of the sourcing process, i.e. incentives that take the adapted role setting in the buying organisation into account. Instruments that may be of use for this purpose are multi-attribute quality metrics or $360°$ evaluations, which consider the fulfilment phase of a transaction, as well as other long-term quality metrics regarding negotiation processes. The use of electronic negotiation tools greatly improves the information level for a systematic controlling of negotiation processes and spend management. However, it carries the risks of over-simplification, for example regarding innovation ability and the risk that subsequent regulation actually diminishes negotiation efficiency – a process that largely lives from creativity and informality – since self-governed economic systems frequently outperform heavily regulated ones (Ostrom, Ahn 2003). On the other hand, open bargaining exchanges are more risky with respect to e.g. kick-back payments and the establishment of *old-boy* networks than more regulated, competitive bidding procedures (Milgrom 1989). Finding the right balance of regulatory controlling activity is the key challenge here.

The governance of the inter-organisational relationship is dialogue-compatible in case of cost-plus contracts, that is if multi-lateral negotiations address not total prices, but cost premiums in percent. This has been found to facilitate open information exchange (Bajari et al. 2002), but requires adequate means for cost-control.

(6.) Partner Relationship Management

Taking up for example the aspect of innovation ability in the supplier base, the idea of a knowledge oriented Supplier Relationship Management (Supplier Knowledge Management[68]) is a step into the right direction. On the other hand, the key question is to choose a set of discourse partners, which is a relational investment decision that should be backed up both by careful analysis and appropriate means, i.e. by some kind of a partner relationship management (Riemer 2004).

For example, the bonus-malus auction strategy which Griffith sketches from a practitioner's point of view in his paper "Trusting an auction" (Griffith 2003), is inherently both dialogue oriented and relationship oriented. It forces buyer and supplier to discuss their relationship openly and evaluate it. Further, it requires high standards of trust, reliability and transparency as prerequisites of a capitalisation on auction technologies.[69]

However, supplier relationships are interactive, i.e. communicative processes, which needs to be taken into account. Because the suppliers' willingness to engage into such interaction is a prerequisite, we find social capital to be of increased importance. Social, non-formalised links to suppliers, research and development partners lead to a faster dialogue and an improved quality of dialogue (Westlund 2006). The process described as token gesture bids (Griffith 2003), which is hardly contributing to the coordination task at hand, can be avoided, if a set of partners is either interacting in long-term relationships or if the value of relationships is adequately and transparently taken into account.

---

68 See http://www.localglobal.de/sixcms/detail.php?
id=751708&template_id=4240&_t=auto.world&_rubrik=Topics&_inhalt=German%20Suppliers
(last accessed 2007-27-06).

69 Griffith argues for bonus-malus auctions, i.e. single-attribute auctions where the buyer gives (and announces) a price premium in percent for an incumbent (or high reputation) supplier. Note that this implies the existence of a supplier evaluation system, which is able to quantify the value of the relationship reliably and transparently. A Dialogue Sourcing strategy in this sense thus depends on a broader SRM strategy.

(7.) **Intra-organisational Inclusiveness**

As we have seen, procurement management regularly has neither an incentive nor the resources (e.g. the expert domain knowledge necessary) to actually engage in dialectic exchanges, especially considering recent trends towards a more strategy-oriented and less category-oriented sourcing management. The organisation as a whole regularly has both resources. Thus it is beneficial to leverage the communicative features of ENSs in order to engage all relevant parties, i.e. in-house as well as external experts into the dialogue with certain suppliers directly.

The everyday coordinating boundary spanner role of departments beyond sourcing needs to be acknowledged and incorporated into the strategy, information and document management processes need to be aligned. The ENS then serves as a conduit to make sure the organisation speaks with one voice for example by providing hand-over mechanism for turn-taking as accomplished in N_5.

The strategy draws on some of the factors from an earlier study on selling partner relationships (Smith, Barclay 1997), which points out the role of trust and communicative openness for economic performance of the joint activities. The above strategy extends beyond such strategic partnerships and communicative openness, because it has been shown that considerable inefficiencies arise due to communicative pathologies in electronically mediated trade relationships. While communicative openness requires a sense of community and cooperation, discursive dialogue requires communicative rationality and a submission to the better argument (Habermas 1981).

7.3 Conclusion

The theory developed enables a better understanding of requirements for ENS design, and contributes to the informed choice of ENSs for specific purposes in specific business settings. Given the embeddedness and complexity of the E-Negotiation task and its connectedness to other tasks, the idea of developing interoperable tool sets, rather then monolithic tool suites is put forward.

Management implications are derived for both suppliers and buyers. For relational strategies, and many procurement and sales strategies are, a game-theoretical analysis based on the findings (such as a perceived dichotomy of auction- and non-auction approaches and a set of preferences for strategy combinations) finds it rational to avoid electronic reverse auctions, if decision makers plan ahead (see Brams 1994). However, opportunities to incorporate process efficiencies of E-Negotiation technology into relational strategies can be pointed out in selected best practice cases, which explicitly facilitate discursive communication. Consequently, a Dialogue Sourcing strategy is sketched. It draws attention to the shortcomings of the (socio-) technologies analysed and helps decision makers compensate or avoid these.

Appendix – Field Notes Example

Most of the interview data collected is confidential and is consequently subject to non-disclosure agreements. Because most interviews were narrative and fast-paced, but could
not be tape-recorded, the field notes only give an incomplete picture of the discussions
and the corroboration interview partners showed for the communication perspective on
electronic negotiations.

As an example this appendix contains the collected, anonymised and translated field
notes of case N_7, because the case is referred to regularly throughout the results section.
First contact with N_7 was established through a discussion with the IT department, where
an interesting business case was mentioned:

> *There was this just-in-time project – our service partner jumped in and helped to plan urgent*
> *changes. When it was clear that it can be done and the spec was written, the head of procure-*
> *ment insisted on running an E-Auction for the project.*

An informal face-to-face interview with a procurement manager followed shortly after
and the following notes were taken.[70]

> *Q: So do you have an example, a particularly successful or un-successful case to show when*
> *reverse auctions really work and when they don't?*
> *A: There are so many – soft factors that play a role, you can hardly get the picture of this. [..]*
> *There are online auctions were the winner does not get the deal. Maybe someone knows*
> *someone else and that person is told that well, if you go down 5000 [..] and then he is awarded*
> *the contract.*
> *Price coordination among certain suppliers is not infrequent – that's reality, whether there are*
> *laws or not. In that case you need people who really know what they are doing, who know the*

---

70 All questions asked by the interviewer are marked with 'Q:' and answers with 'A:' Because these are
translated field notes, the conversation may not be replicated precisely on the syntax level.

market, who have experience and the negotiation skills. A reverse auction that yields the same price over and over again does not get you any further.

[After an E-Auction initiated by upper management] we talked to the winning supplier and cut another 5% [laughs] - that was basically the point where it was finally decided to no longer really use reverse auctions. [..]

The Americans just love it [reverse E-Auctions]. [..] We were sceptical at first [..] but those in the states go through with it. Regardless of product quality.

Q: And regardless of business relationships?

A: Long-term relationships. Yes. You know, when I am visiting an exhibition, you have a contact person at almost every supplier. Actually, it is a small community. [..] If someone disappears from a suppliers payroll it does not take long – he reappears in a similar position with a competitor. They all know each other as well.

Q: Ok. You seem to have a negative conception of online auctions...

A: [...] There is the idea of a more open competition (than in E-Auctions). In that case you only define some constraints such as there is so much room, this and that needs to happen in a [machinery component], but you don't specify how that is supposed to happen. This way new ideas come up and that is really interesting. In the dialogue with the suppliers it then turns out that one solution is more powerful while the other is less costly – it might cause more maintenance costs however. The final decision is then made separately.

The procurement manager then referred the author to the head of indirect procurement since he accumulated the most direct experiences with electronic negotiations, mainly reverse auctions in this case. A telephone interview was scheduled and the following notes were taken.

Q: Regarding reverse auctions – when you read about them you usually read about savings in percent ranging from 5-30% and probably with an increasingly sceptical view...

A: [interrupts] I can not only report negative findings here. Those savings in X percent generated through E-Auctions [which you find in the press] - they are realistic from time to time. But let me first tell you something about the context. I am more or less the only person who does E-

Auctions here. We have a simple policy: For a volume of more then Y we are supposed to run an E-Auction – or apply an exception code for it [laughs]. That may happen quite often. But you always need to take your time and ask: Is it really worth the effort? [..].

Q: Which auction platform do you use?

A: It is an internally developed platform [..]. And there we are right at the point where it is getting problematic in Germany. The platform is completely in English – that is taken for granted. But we are talking about MRO and local suppliers here, which partly do not have personal e-mail addresses. Those are the info@something addresses, which are checked only from time to time., but we are talking about goods that do not become part of the procuct, though. If for example we want to pave the courtyard or something like that. The system sends notifications and invitations for newly created auctions in English automatically. [..] They [the system developers] did not show any sensitivity to these issues. I often prepare translations in advance and also have my own pamphlet as a specification. This is all quite problematic – not for me, but many smaller companies have a real problem with that.

Q: Do you remember any anecdotes that show in which situations the system works particularly well – or not at all?

A: Anecdotes – yes, I can tell you one. We set up an an online auction once; at nine o'clock – European Time [on an international procurement platform]. Consequently, invitations were sent out via email for a time X am., which the suppliers naturally interpreted in terms of local time. At nine, there was only one bidder and submitted a bid. Yes. A second one the latter called me and complained that he could not login for the auction and so on. Well, I also communicated that personally, but you can't do anything more. Who is reading that closely? It is always the same time zone, but [..] even for me this is error-prone.

Q: Yes – you are not used to it and then...

A: Yes. I had to call everyone and clarify that – quite uncomfortable. You prepare a schedule and allocate dedicated time slots to the events, you know... There was another incident where a supplier missed the auction. I called him and said "You missed a good deal today." And he just said: "Maybe next time". He had no idea what it was all about. The auction was about some security services – he might have made a really good deal with follow-up transactions and all. He really missed that point. The English language is really kind of getting in the way.

Q: And regarding the auction as a strategy?

A: We have to somehow live with it.

Q: I would be interested in the relationship with the supplier. Is there anything different in the online auction case?

A: Yes and no - I also care for things like cleaning staff and call centre services – there it (E-Auctions) is a commonality. They know it, they know the process. But I always try to do a review conversation with the supplier afterwards. There is for instance a price that was offered – I take the time to write a spec usually and that contains payment terms for example. Often questions arise like "Why discount? We have never been told about that." and I can just refer them to the specs.

Q: [Explains concept of strategic renegotiation in change requests] Have you made similar experiences?

A: We have not. Up to now it seemed to fit. But that does not mean much. This year we had... roughly 300 sourcing events of this kind – four of them E-Auctions. You really need to take your time and ask yourself: "Is the effort justified?"

Q: [Later after reviewing the platform] I have a question regarding the comment field in the auction form next to the field for the bid. Do suppliers use this field? And if yes – what do they use it for?

A: That is easily answered – that field has never been used, it lies idle completely.

References

Adler, P. S., Kwon, S. (2002) Social Capital: Prospects for a new Concept, in: Academy of Management Review, 27 (1), 17-40.

Ågerfalk, P. (2003) Nine Principles for Actable Systems Design, in: Proceedings of the 10th International Conference on Human-Computer Interaction, 1203-1207.

Ågerfalk, P. (2004) Investigating Actability Dimensions: A Language/Action Perspective on Criteria for Information Systems Evaluation, in: Interacting with Computers, 16 (5), 957-988.

Allan, G. (2003) A critique of using grounded theory as a research method, in: Electronic Journal of Business Research Methods, 2 (1), 1-10.

Allison, G. T. (1971) Essence of Decision: Explaining the Cuban Missile Crisis, Boston, Little, Brown and Co.

Ariño, A., de la Torre, J. (1998) Learning from Failure: Towards an Evolutionary Model of Collaborative Ventures, in: Organization Science, 9 (3), 306-325.

Auramäki, E., Lyytinen, K. (1996) On the Success of Speech Acts and Negotiating Commitments, in: Proceedings of the 1st International Workshop on Communication Modeling, Tilburg, Netherlands.

Bajari, P., McMillan, R., Tadelis, S. (2002) Auctions versus Negotiations in Procurement - An Empirical Analysis, NBER Working Paper Series, Cambridge.

Bajari, P., Tadelis, S. (2001) Incentive versus transaction costs: A theory of procurement contracts, in: Rand Journal of Economics, 32 (3), 387-407.

Bajari, P., Ye, L. (2003) Deciding between Competition and Collusion, in: Review of Economics and Statistics, 85 (4), 971-989.

Bakos, Y., Brynjolfsson, E. (1993) Information Technology, Incentives, and the Optimal Number of Suppliers, in: Journal of Management Information Systems, 10 (2), 37-53.

Bannister, F. (2002) The Dimension of Time: Histography in Information Systems Research, in: Electronic Journal of Business Research Methods, 1 (1), 1-10.

Barley, S. (1986) Technology as Occasions for Structuring: Evidence from Observation CT scanners and the Social Order of Radiology Departments, in: Administrative Science Quarterly, 31, 78-108.

Baskerville, R.L. (1999) Investigating Information Systems with Action Research, in: Communications of the Association for Information Systems, 2 (19), available online: http://www.cis.gsu.edu/~rbaskerv/CAIS_2_19/CAIS_2_19.html (2007-08-2).

Bazerman, M., Curhan, J., Moore, D., Valley, K. (2000) Negotiation, in: Annual Review of Psychology, 51, 279-314.

Bazerman, M.; Mannix, E.; Thompson, L. (1988) Groups as mixed-motive negotiations, in: Advances in Group Processes, 5, 195-216.

Beall, S., Carter, C., Carter, P. L., Germer, T., Hendrick, T., Jap, S., Kaufmann, L., Maciejewski, D., Monczka, R., Petersen, K. (2003) The Role of Reverse Auctions in Strategic Sourcing, CAPS Research Paper, available online: http://www.capsresearch.org/publications/pdfs-public/beall2003es.pdf (2007-08-02).

Beuquelsdijk, S., de Groot, H. L. F., van Schaik, A.B.T.M. (2004) Trust and economic growth: A robustness analysis, in: Oxford Economic Papers, 56 (1), 118-134.

Bichler, M. (1999) Decision Analysis - A Critical Enabler for Multi-attribute Auctions, in: Proceedings of the 12th International Bled Electronic Commerce Conference, Bled, Slovenia, 123-137.

Bichler, M. (2001a) BidTaker - An Application of Multi-Attribute Auction Markets in Tourism, in: Proceedings of Wirtschaftsinformatik 2001, Augsburg, Germany, 533-546.

Bichler, M. (2001b) The future of e-Markets: Multidimensional Market Mechanisms, Cambridge University Press.

Bichler, M. (2003) Trading Financial Derivatives on the Web - An Approach towards Automating Negotiations on OTC Markets, in: Electronic Commerce: Integration of Web Technologies with Business Models, Kluwer, 401-414.

Bichler, M., Kersten, G., Strecker, S. (2003) Towards a Structured Design of Electronic Negotiations, in: Group Decision and Negotiation, 12 (4), 311-335.

Bijker, W., Law, J. (1992) Shaping Technology/Building Society: Studies in Sociotechnical Change, MIT Press.

Blumer, H. (1969) Symbolic Interactionism: Perspective and Method, CA: University of California Press.

Brams, S. J. (1994) Theory of Moves, Cambridge University Press.

Bruhn, M. (2004) Kommunikationspolitik für Industriegüter, in: Handbuch Industriegütermarketing, 699-721.

Bryant, A. (2002) Re-grounding grounded theory, in: Journal of Information Technology Theory and Application, 4 (1), 25-42.

Bryant, A. (2003) A Constructive/ist Repsonse to Glaser, in: Forum: Qualitative Social Research, 4 (1), available online: www.qualitative-research.net/fqs-texte/1-03/1-03bryant-e.htm (2007-08-2).

Burt, R. S. (1992) Structural Holes, Harvard University Press.

Carr, N. G. (2003) IT Doesn't Matter, in: Harvard Business Review, 81 (5), 41-49.

Carter, C., Kaufmann, L. (2003) Deciding on the mode of Negotiation - To Auction or not to Auction Electronically, in: Proceedings of the North American Research Symposium on Purchasing and Supply Managment, 191-226.

Carter, C., Kaufmann, L. (2007) The impact of electronic reverse auctions on supplier performance: The mediating role of relationship variables, in: Journal of Supply Chain Management, 43 (1), 16-26.

Carter, C., Kaufmann, L., Beall, S., Carter, P. L., Hendrick, T. E., Petersen, K. J. (2004) Reverse auctions - grounded theory from the buyer and supplier perspective, in: Transportation Research, Part E, 40, 229-254.

Charmaz, K., Mitchell, R. (1996) The myth of silent authorship: Self, substance, and style in ethnographic writing, in: Symbolic Interaction, 19 (4), 285-302.

Charon, J. (1979) Symbolic Interactionism, Prentice-Hall.

Chen, E., Weber, I. (2006) Assessment of an Electronic Auction System: Beliefs about Usage, System and Institutions on Intention to Use, in: Proceedings of Group Decision and Negotiation, 106-107.

Chin, W. W., Gopal, A., Salisbury, W.D. (1997) Advancing the Theory of Adaptive Structuration: The Development of a Scale to Measure Faithfulness of Appropriation, in: Information Systems Research, 8 (4), 229-254.

Cicourel, A. V. (1973) Cognitive sociology: language and meaning in social interaction, Penguin Books.

Clark, H. H. (1996), Using Language, CUP.

Clemons, E. K., Reddi, S. P., Row, M. C. (1993) The Impact of Infosymbolic interactionismrmation Technology on the Organization of Economic Activity: The "Move to the Middle" Hypothesis, in: Journal of Management Information Systems, 10 (2), 9-35.

Clopton, C. W. (1984) Seller and buying firm factors affecting buyers negotiation behavior and outcomes, in: Journal of Marketing Research, 21 (1), 39-53.

Clyman, D., Tripp, T. (2000) Discrepant Values and Measures of Negotiator Performance, in: Group Decision and Negotiation, 9 (4), 251-274.

Coase, R. (1937) The Nature of the Firm, in: Economica, 4 (16), 386-405.

Coleman, J. S. (1984) Introducing Social Trust into Economic Analysis, in: American Economic Review, 74 (2), 84-88.

Contractor, N. S., Seibold, D. R. (1993) Theoretical Frameworks for the Study of Structuring Processes in Group Decision Support Systems - Adaptive Structuration Theory and Self-Organizing Systems Theory, in: Human Communication Research, 19 (4), 528-563.

Cornelius, C., Boos, M. (2003) Enhancing Mutual Understanding in Synchronous Computer-Mediated Communication by Training, in: Communication Research, 30 (2), 147-177.

Culnan, M. J., Markus, M. L. (1987) Information technologies, in: Handbook of organizational communication: An interdisciplinary perspective, Sage, 420-443.

Curhan, J., Xu, H., Elfenbein, H. (2006) What do People Value When They Negotiate? in: Journal of Personality and Social Psychology, 91 (3), 493-512.

Daft, R. L. (1986) A proposed integration among organizational information requirements, media richness, and structural design, in: Management Science, 32, 554-571.

Daly, S., Nath, P. (2005) Reverse Auctions and buyer-seller relationships: A rejoinder to Emiliani and Stec's commentary, in: Journal of Industrial Marketing Management, 34 (2), 173-176.

Daly, S., Nath, P. (2005) Reverse Auctions for Relationship Marketers, in: Journal of Industrial Marketing Management, 34 (2), 157-166.

Dani, S., Burns, N. D., Backhouse, C. J. (2005) Buyer-supplier behaviour in electronic reverse auctions: a relationship perspective, in: International Journal of Services and Operations Management, 1 (1), 22-34.

Dasgupta, P. (2000) Economic Progress and the Idea of Social Capital, in: Dasgupta, Social Capital: A Multifaceted Perspective, The World Bank, Washington DC, 325-424.

David, N., Bewernick, B., Cohen, M., Newmen, A., Lux, S., Fink, G. R., Shah, N.J., Vogeley, K. (2006) Neural Representations of Self versus Other: Visual-Spatial Perspective Taking and Agency in a Virtual Ball-tossing Game, in: Journal of Cognitive Neuroscience, 18 (6), 898-910.

Davis, R., Smith, R. G. (1983) Negotiations as a Metaphor for Distributed Problem Solving, in: Artifical Intelligence, 20 (1), 63-109.

De Moor, A., Aakhus, M. (2006) Argumentation support: from technologies to tools, in: Communications of the ACM, 49 (3), 93-98.

Delaney, M. M., Foroughi, A., Perkins, W. C. (1997) An empirical Study of the Efficiency of a Computerized Negotiation Support System (NSS), in: Decision Support Systems, 20, 185-197.

Dennis, A. R., Garfield, M. J. (2003) The Adoption and Use of GSS in Project Teams: Toward More Participative Processes and Outcomes, in: Management Information Systems Quarterly, 27 (2), 289-323.

Dennis, A., Wixom, B., Vandenberg, R. (2001) Understanding Fit and Appropriation Effects in Group Support Systems via Meta-Analysis, in: MIS Quarterly, 25 (2), 167-193.

Denzin, N., Lincoln, Y. (1994) Handbook of qualitative research, Sage.

DeSanctis, G., Gallupe, R. B. (1987) A Foundation for the Study of Group Decision Support Systems, in: Management Science, in: Management Science, 33 (5), 589-609.

DeSanctis, G., Poole, M. (1994) Capturing the Complexity in Advanced Technology Use: Adaptive Structuration Theory, in: Organizational Science, 5, 121-147.

Dignum, F., Cortes, U. (2001) Agent-Mediated Electronic Commerce III, Springer.

Döring, N. (2003) Sozialpsychologie des Internet - Die Bedeutung des Internet für Kommunikationsprozess, Identitäten, soziale Beziehungen und Gruppen, Hogrefe.

Dumas, M., Governatori, G., ter Hofstede, A. H. M., Oaks, P. (2002) A formal approach to negotiating agents development, in: Electronic Commerce Research and Applications, 1 (2), 193-207.

Eisenhardt, K. (1989) Building Theories from Case Study Research, in: Academy of Management Review, 14 (4), 532-550.

Emiliani, M. L. (2004) Sourcing in the global aerospace supply chain using online reverse auctions, in: Journal of Industrial Marketing Management, 33, 65-72.

Emiliani, M. L., Stec, D. J. (2002) Realizing savings from online reverse auctions, in: Supply Chain Management, 7 (1), 12-23.

Emiliani, M. L., Stec, D. J. (2004) Aerospace parts suppliers' reaction to online reverse auctions, in: Supply Chain Management, 9 (2), 139-153.

Emiliani, M. L., Stec, D. J. (2005) Commentary on "Reverse auctions for relationship marketers" by Daly and Nath, in: Journal of Industrial Marketing Management, 34 (2), 167-171.

Emptoris Inc. (2005) Moving Beyond Reverse Auctions for Scalable, Sustainable Value, available online: http://www.emptoris.com/solutions/strategic_sourcing_solutions.asp (2008-08-02).

Epley, N., Caruso, E.M., Bazerman, M. (2006) When Perspective Taking Increases Taking: Reactive Egoism in Social Interaction, in: Journal of Personality and Social Psychology, 91 (5), 872-889.

Filzmoser, M., Vetschera, R. (2006) The Influence of Bargaining Steps on the Process and Outcome of Online Negotiations, in: Proceedings of Group Decision and Negotiation, 224-227.

Finch, J. (2002) The role of grounded theory in developing economic theory, in: Journal of Economic Methodology, 9 (2), 213-234.

Fisher, R., Ury, W., Patton, B. (2004) Das Harvard-Konzept - Der Klassiker der Verhandlungstechnik, Campus.

Fitzgerald, B., Howcroft, D. (1998) Towards Dissolution of the IS Research Debate: From Polarisation to Polarity, in: Journal of Information Technology, 13 (4), 313-326.

Flores, F., Graves, M., Hartfield, B., Winograd, T. (1988) Computer systems and the design of organizational interaction, in: ACM transactions on office Information Systems, 6 (2), 153-172.

Foroughi, A., Perkins, W. C., Jelassi, M. T. (1995) An Empirical Study of an Interactive, Session-Oriented Computerized Negotiation Support System (NSS), in: Group Decision and Negotiation, 4 (6), 485-512.

Forrester Research Inc. (2005) eSourcing Vendor Scores - Fall 2005, available online: www.forrester.com (2007-08-02).

Forschauer, U., Lueger, M. (2003) Das qualitative Interview, Facultas, Vienna.

Fortgang, R. S., Lax, D. A., Sebenius, J. K. (2003) Negotiating the Spirit of the Deal, in: Harvard Business Review, 81 (2), 66-75.

Fulk, J. (1993) Social Construction of Communication Technology, in: Academy of Management Journal, 36 (5), 921-950.

Fulk, J., Schmitz, J., Steinfield, C. W. (1990) A Social Influence Model of Technology Use, in: Fulk, Organizations and Communication Technology, Sage, 117-140.

Fundenberg, D., Tirole, J. (1990) Moral Hazard and Renegotiation in Agency Contracts, in: Econometrica, 58 (6), 1279-1319.

Fussel, S. R., Krauss, R. M. (1992) Coordination of knowledge in communication: effects of speakers' assumptions about what others know, in: Journal of Personality and Social Psychology, 62 (3), 378-391.

Gambetta, D. (2003) Can We Trust Trust? in: Foundations of Social Capital, 274-290.

Gaski, J. F. (1984) The Theory of Power and Conflict in Channels of Distribution, in: Journal of Marketing, 48, 9-29.

Gasson, S. (2004) Rigor in Grounded Theory Research: An Interpretative Perspective on Generating Theory from Qualitative Field Studies, in: The Handbook of Information Systems Research, 79-102.

Gattiker, T. F., Huang, X., Schwarz, J. (2007) Negotiation, email, and Internet reverse auctions: How sourcing mechanisms deployed by buyers affect suppliers' trust, Journal of Operations Management, 25 (1), 184-202.

Gelfand, M., Smith Major, V., Raver, J., Nishi L., O'Brien, K. (2006) Negotiating Relationally: The Dynamics of Relational Self in Negotiations, in: Academy of Management Review, 31 (2), 427-451.

Giampietro, C., Emiliani, M.L. (2007) Coercion and reverse auctions, in: Supply Chain Management, 12 (2), 75-84.

Giddens, A. (1984) The Constitution of Society, Polity Press, Cambridge.

Glaser, B. (1978) Theoretical Sensitivity, CA: Sociology Press.

Glaser, B. (1992) Emergence vs. Forcing: Basics of Grounded Theory, CA: Sociology Press.

Glaser, B. (2002) Constructivist Grounded Theory, in: Forum: Qualitative Social Research, 3 (3), available online: http://www.qualitative-research.net/fqs-texte/3-02/3-02glaser-e.htm (2007-08-02).

Glaser, B., Strauss, A. (1967) The discovery of Grounded Theory: Strategies for qualitative Research, Aldine, Chicago.

Goh, K. Y., Hock-Hai, T., Haixin, W., Kwok-Kee, W. (2000) Computer-supported negotiations: an experimental study of bargaining in electronic commerce, in: Proceedings of ICIS 2000, 104-116.

Goodhue, D.L. (1995) Understanding User Evaluation of Information Systems, in: Management Science, 41 (12), 1827-1844.

Ghoshal, G., Moran, P. (1996) Bad for Practice: A Critique of the Transaction Cost Theory, in: Academy of Management Review, 21(1), 13-47.

Goudling, C. (2002) Grounded Theory - A practical Guide for Management, Business and Market Researchers, Sage.

Goulding, C. (1999) Consumer research, qualitative paradigms, and methodological ambiguities, in: European Journal of Marketing, 33 (9/10), 859-873.

Graf, A., Köszegi, S., Pesendorfer, E.M., Srnka, K. (2006) Intercultural Negotiation Patterns: An International Study of Computer-Mediated Negotiations, in: Proceedings of Group Decision and Negotiation, 177-180.

Granovetter, M. S. (1973) The Strength of Weak Ties, in: American Journal of Sociology, 78 (6), 1360-1380.

Greenhalgh, L., Chapman, D. (1995) Joint Decision Making - The Inseparability of Relationships and Negotiation, in: Negotiation as a Social Process, Sage, 166-185.

Grice, H. P. (1975) Logic and conversation, in: Syntax and Semantics 3: Speech acts, Academic Press, 41-58.

Griffith, A. (2003) Trusting an Auction, Supply Chain Management, 8 (3), 190-194.

Güth, W., Ivanova-Stenzel, R., Königstein, M., Ströbel, M. (2002) Bid Functions in Auctions and Fair Division Games: Experimental Evidence, in: German Economic Review, 3 (4), 461-484.

Habermas, J. (1970) Toward a Rational Society, Beacon Press.

Habermas, J. (1981) Theorie des kommunikativen Handelns, Suhrkamp, 2 volumes.

Habermas, J. (2005) Zwischen Naturalismus und Religion, Suhrkamp.

Habermas, J. (2007) Kommunikative Rationalität und grenzüberschreitende Politik: eine Replik, in: Anarchie der Kommunikativen Freiheit - Jürgen Habermas und die Theorie der Internationalen Politik, 406-459.

Hammersley, M. (2002) Ethnography and Realism, in: The Qualitative Researchers Companion, Sage, 65-80.

Hanna, A. S., Camlic, R., Peterson, P. A., Nordheim, E. V. (2002) Quantitative Definition of Projects Impacted by Change Orders, in: Journal of Construction Engineering and Management, January-February, 57-64.

Hannon, D. (2003) Purchasing survey shows e-sourcing adoption stalls, in: Purchasing, 132 (12), 49-50.

Haribi, N. (1998) Innovation through vertical relations between firms, suppliers and customers: A study of German firms, in: Industry and Innovation, 5 (2), 175-179.

Hart, O., Moore, J. (1988) Incomplete Contracts and renegotiation, in: Econometrica, 56, 755-785.

Hauser, J. R., Clausing, D. (1988), The House of Quality, Harvard Business Review, May-June, 63-73.

Heng, M. S. H., de Moor, A. (2003) From Habermas's communicative theory to practice on the internet, in: Information Systems Journal, 13, 331-352.

Henke, J. W. (2000) E-Commerce: Commentary; The Price is Wrong, in: Ward's Auto World, April 2000.

Hermes, V. (2006) Auftragsvergabe per Auktion - Bittere Pille für Kommunikationsdienstleister?, in: Direkt Marketing, 10, 13-26.

Hesse, H. J. (2001) Theorie der Symbolischen Interaktion - Ein Beitrag zum Verstehenden Ansatz in Soziologie und Sozialpsychologie, Teubner.

Hirsch, P. M., Levin, D. Z. (1999) Umbrella advocates versus validity police: A life-cycle model, in: Organization Science, 10, 199-212.

Hirschheim, R., Klein, H., Lyytinen, K. (1995) Information Systems Development and Data Modeling, Conceptual and Philosophical Considerations, Cambridge University Press.

Holtgraves, T. M. (2002) Language as Social Action - Social Psychology and Language Use, Erlbaum.

Holzinger, K. (2001) Verhandeln statt Argumentieren oder Verhandeln durch Argumentieren? Eine empirische Analyse auf Basis der Sprechakttheorie, in: Politische Vierteljahresschrift, 42, 414-446.

Hopmann, P. T. (2002) Negotiating Data: Reflections on the Qualitative and Quantitative Analysis of Negotiation Processes, in: Journal of International Negotiation, 7, 67-85.

Horton, W. S., Keysar, B. (1996) When do speakers take into account common ground? in: Cognition, 59, 91-117.

Hvam, L. (2006) Mass customisation in the electronics industry: based on modular products and product configuration, Journal of Mass Customisation, 1 (4), 410-426.

IBM Corp. (2006) Global CEO Study - Expanding the Innovation Horizon, available online: http://www-935.ibm.com/services/us/gbs/bus/html/bcs_ceostudy2006.html (2007-08-02).

Iivari, J. (1991) A paradigmatic analysis of contemporary schools of IS development, in: European Journal of Information Systems, 1 (4), 249-272.

Jap, S. (1999) Pie-expansion efforts: Collaboration processes in buyer-supplier relationships, in: Journal of Marketing Research, 36 (4), 461-475.

Jap, S. (2003) An Exploratory Study on the Introduction of Online Reverse Auctions, in: Journal of Marketing, 67, 96-107.

Jarke, M. (1986) Knowledge Sharing and Negotiation Support in Multiperson Decision Support Systems, in: Decision Support Systems, 2, 93-102.

Jarke, M., Jelassi, M. T., Shakun, M. F. (1987) MEDIATOR: Towards a Negotiation Support System, in: European Journal of Operational Research, 31, 314-334.

Jelassi, T., Foroughi, A. (1989) Negotiation support systems: an overview of design issues and existing software, in: Decision Support Systems, 5 (2), 167-181.

Jennings, N. R.; Wooldridge, M. J. (1998) Applications of Intelligent Agents, in: Agent Technology: Foundations, Applications, and Markets, Springer, 3-28.

Johns, G. (2006) The Essential Impact of Context on Organizational Behavior, in: Academy of Management Review, 31 (2), 386-408.

Kahneman, D., Tversky, A. (1984) Choices, Values, and Frames, in: American Psychologist, 39, 341-350.

Kakas, A., Moraitis, P. (2006) Adaptive agent negotiation via argumentation, in: Proceedings of the 5th International Conference on Autonomous Agents, 384-391.

Kalai, E., Smorodinsky, M. (1975) Other Solutions to the Nash's Bargaining Problem, in: Econometrica, 43 (3), 513-518.

Kaufmann, L., Carter, C. R. (2004) Deciding on the Mode of Negotiation: To Auction or Not to Auction Electronically, in: Journal of Supply Chain Management, 40, 15-26.

Kellogg, K., Orlikowski, W., Yates, J. (2006) Life in the Trading Zone: Structuring Coordination Across Boundaries in Postbureaucratic Organizations, in: Organization Science, 17 (1), 22-44.

Kenny, D. A. (1995) The effect of nonindependence on significance testing in dyadic research, in: Personal Relationships, 2 (1), 67-75.

Kersten, G. (1985) NEGO - Group Decision Support System, in: Information and Management, 8 (5), 237-246.

Kersten, G., Lo, G. (2003) Aspire: an integrated negotiation support system and software agents for e-business negotiation, in: International Journal of Internet and Enterprise Management, 1 (3), 293-315.

Kersten, G., Michaelowski, W., Szpakowicz, S., Koperczak, Z. (1991) Restructurable representations of negotiation, in: Management Science, 37 (10), 1269-1290.

Kersten, G., Noronha, S. (1997) Negotiation Via the World Wide Web: A Cross-Cultural Study of Decision Making, IIASA Interim Report IR-97-21997, available online: www.iiasa.ac.at/Publications/Documents/IR-97-052.pdf (2007-08-02).

Kersten, G., Noronha, S., Teich, J. (2000) Are all e-commerce negotiations auctions? in: Proceedings of the 4th International Conference on the Design of Cooperative Systems.

Kieser, A., Walgenbach, P. (2003), Organisation, Schäffer-Poeschel.

Kießling, B. (1988) Kritik der Giddenschen Sozialtheorie, Lang, Frankfurt.

Klein, H., Myers, M. (1999) A Set of Principles for Conducting and Evaluating Interpretative Field Studies in Information Systems, in: Management Information Systems Quarterly, 23 (1), 57-93.

Klein, S., O'Keefe, R. (1999) The impact of the web on auctions: Some empirical evidence and theoretical considerations, in: International Journal of Electronic Commerce, 3 (3), 7-20.

Knack, S., Keefer, P. (1997) Does social capital have an economic payoff? A cross-country investigation, in: Quarterly Journal of Economics, 112 (4), 1251-1288.

Köhne, F., Schoop, M., Staskiewicz, D. (2004) A Communication Perspective on Electronic Negotiation Support Systems: Impacts, Challenges, and Solutions, in: Proceedings of the 7th International Conference on Business Information Systems, 530-541.

Köhne, F., Schoop, M., Staskiewicz, D. (2004) Decision Support in Electronic Negotiations - State-of-the-Art and new Challenges, in: Proceedings of the DSS 2004 Conference.

Köhne, F., Schoop, M., Staskiewicz, D. (2005) Use Patterns in Different Negotiation Media, in: Proceedings of the Conference on Group Decision and Negotiation 2005, Vienna.

Kolitz, K., Block, C., Weinhardt, C. (2007) meet2trade: An Electronic Market Platform and Experiment System, Proceedings of Group Decision and Negotiation, 169-184.

Kools, S., McCarty, M., Durham, R., Robrecht, L. (1996) Dimensional Analysis: broadening the conception of grounded theory, in: Qualitative Health Research, 6 (3), 312-330.

Köszegi, S., Pesendorfer, E.-M., Vetschera, R. (2007) Data-driven Episodic Phase Analysis of E-Negotiations, in: Proceedings of Group Decision and Negotiation, 113-130.

Köszegi, S., Srnka, K. J., Pesendorfer, E.-M. (2004) Comparing Web-Based Negotiation Processes: A Combined Qualitative-Quantitative Approach, Working Paper OP 2004-02, University of Vienna.

Kraatz, M. S. (1998) Learning by association? Interorganizational networks and adaptation to environmental change, in: Academy of Management Journal, 41, 621-643.

Krishna, V. (2002) Auction Theory, Academic Press.

Krotz, F. (2005) Neue Theorien Entdecken - Eine Einführung in die Grounded Theory, die Heuristische Sozialforschung und die Ethnographie anhand von Beispielen aus der Kommunikationsforschung, Herbert von Halem Verlag, Cologne.

Kruger, J., Epley, N. (2005) Egocentrism Over E-Mail: Can We Communicate as Well as We Think? in: Journal of Personality and Social Psychology, 89 (6), 925-936.

Kubicek, L. (1975), Informationstechnologie und organisatorische Regelungen, Duncker & Humblot, Berlin.

Leavitt, H., Whisler, T. (1958) Management in the 1980's - New information flows cut new organizational channels, in: Harvard Business Review, 36 (6), 41-48.

Leuthesser, L., Kohli, A. K. (1995) Relational Behavior in Business Markets, in: Journal of Business Research, 34, 221-233.

Li, P. P. (2007) Social tie, social capital, and social behavior: Toward an integrativ model of informal exchange, in: Asia Pacific Journal of Management, 24 (2), 227-246.

Lim, J., Gan, B., Ting-Ting, C. (2002) A Survey on NSS Adoption Intention, in: Proceedings of HICSS 2002, 26c.

Lim, L., Benbasat, I. (1993) A Theoretical Perspective of Negotiation Support Systems, in: Journal of Management Information Systems, 9 (3), 27-44.

Lyotard, J. F. (1984) The postmodern Condition, University of Minnesota Press.

Lyotard, J. F. (1989) Der Widerstreit (Le differend), Fink.

Macredie, R. D. (1998) Mediating Buyer-Seller Interactions: The Role of Agents in Web Commerce, in: Electronic Markets, 8 (3), 40-43.

Maes, P., Guttman, R. H., Moukas, A. G. (1999) Agents that Buy and Sell, in: Communications of the ACM, 42 (3), 81-91.

Malone, T., Yates, J., Benjamin, R. (1987) Electronic Markets and Electronic Hierarchies, in: Communications of the ACM, 30 (6), 484-497.

Markus, L., Robey, D. (1988) Information Technology and Organizational Change: Causal Structure in Theory and Research, in: Management Science, 34 (5), 583-598.

Markus, M. L. (1999) Finding a Happy Medium: Explaining the Negative Effects of Electronic Communication on Social Life at Work, in: ACM Transactions on Information Systems, 12 (2), 119-149.

McAfee, R. P.; McMillan, J. (1996) Game Theory and Competition, in: Journal of Marketing Research, 33, 263-267.

McGinn, K. L. (2004) For Better of Worse: How Relationships Affect Negotiations, in: Negotiation, November, 3-5.

Mead, G. H. (1934) Mind, self and society, University of Chicago Press.

Meffert, H. (1998) Marketing - Grundlagen marktorientierter Unternehmensführung, Gabler.

Milgrom, P. (1989) Auctions and Bidding: A Primer, in: Journal of Economic Perspectives, 3 (3), p. 3-22.

Mintzberg, H. (1973) The nature of managerial work, Harper and Row.

Mir, R., Watson, A. (2000) Strategic Management and the Philosophy of Science: The Case for a Constructivist Methodology, in: Strategic Management Journal, 21, 941-953.

Moore, D. A., Kurtzberg, T. R., Thompson, L. L., Morris, M. W. (1999) Long and Short Routes to Success in Electronically Mediated Negotiations: Group Affiliations and Good Vibrations, in: Organizational Behavior and Human Decision Processes, 77 (1), 22-43.

Müller-Lankenau, C., Klein, S. (2003) Analyzing the Business Model of a Corporate Procurement Platform: The Case of Siemens click2procure, in: Proceedings of RSEEM 2003, 159-167.

Müller, H. (2004) Arguing, Bargaining and All That: Communicative Action, Rationalist Theory and the Logic of Appropriateness in International Relations, in: Journal of International Relations, 10 (3), 395-435.

Müller, H. (2007) Internationale Verhandlung, Argumente und Verständigungshandeln, in: Anarchie der kommunikativen Freiheit - Jürgen Habermas und die Theorie der internationalen Politik, 199-223.

Nahapiet, J., Goshal, S. (1998) Social capital, intellectual capital, and the organizational advantage, in: Academy of Management Review, 23 (2), 242-266.

Nash, J. (1950) Non-cooperative games, PhD Thesis, Princeton University.

Neale, M. A., Bazerman, M. H. (1985) The Effects of Framing and Negotiator Overconfidence on Bargaining Behaviors and Outcomes, in: Academy of Management Journal, 28 (1), 34-49.

Newton, L. (1990) Overconfidence in the communication of intent: Heard and unheard melodies. PhD Thesis, Stanford University.

Ngwenyama, O. K., Lee, A. S. (1997) Communication Richness in Electronic Mail: Critical Social Theory and the Contextuality of Meaning, in: Management Information Systems Quarterly, 21 (2), 145-167.

Nooteboom, B. (1992) Towards a dynamic theory of transactions, in: Journal of Evolutionary Economics, 2 (4), 281-299.

Nunamaker, J. F., Dennis, A. R., Valacich, J. S., Vogel, D. R. (1991) Information Technology for Negotiating Groups: Generating Options for Mutual Gain, in: Management Science, 37 (10), 1325-1346.

O'Donnell, D., Henriksen, L. (2002) Philosophical foundations for a critical evaluation of the social impact of ICT, in: Journal of Information Technology, 17 (2), 89-99.

Oliver, J. R. (2005) On Learning Negotiation Strategies by Artificial Adaptive Agents in Environments of Incomplete Information, in: Formal Modelling in Electronic Commerce, Springer, 445-461.

Orlikowski, W. J. (1992) The Duality of Technology: Rethinking the Concept of Technology in Organizations, in: Organization Science, 3 (3), 398-427.

Orlikowski, W. J. (1993) CASE tools are Organisational Change, in: Management Information Systems Quarterly, 17 (3), 309-340.

Orlikowski, W. J. (2000) Using technology and constituting structures: A practice lens for studying technology in organisations, in: Organization Science, 11 (4), 404-428.

Orlikowski, W. J., Gash, D. (1994) Technological frames: making sense of information technology in organizations, in: ACM Transactions on Information Systems, 12 (2), 174-207.

Ostrom, E., Ahn, T. K. (2003) Foundations of Social Capital, Edward Elgar Publishing.

Pearcy, D., Giunipero, L., Wilson, A. (2007) A Model of Relational Governance in Reverse Auctions, in: Journal of Supply Chain Management, Winter 2007, 4-15.

Perrone, V., Zaheer, A., McEvily, B. (2003) Free to Be Trusted? Organisational Constraints on Trust in Boundary Spanners, in: Organization Science, 14 (4), 422-439.

Pervan, G. (1998) A review of research in Group Support Systems: leaders, approaches and directions, in: Decision Support Systems, 23 (2), 149-159.

Peters, R. (2000) Elektronische Märkte und automatisierte Verhandlungen, in: Wirtschaftsinformatik, 42 (5), 413-421.

Picot A., Dietl H., Franck E. (2005) Organisation – Eine ökonomische Perspektive, 4th Ed., Schäffer, Poeschl.

Pinker, E., Seidmann, A., Vakrat, Y. (2003) Managing Online Auctions: Current Business and Research Issues, in: Management Science, 49 (11), 1457-1484.

Poole, M. S., DeSanctis, G. (2004) Structuration Theory in Information Systems Research: Current Status and Future Directions, in: The Handbook of Information Systems Research, 206-249.

Poole, M. S., Shannon, S. L., DeSanctis, G. (1992) Communication Media and Negotiation Processes, in: Putnam, Roloff: Communication and Negotiation, Sage, 46-66.

Poster, M. (1995) CyberDemocracy: Internet and the Public Sphere, available online: http://www.h-net.uci.edu/mposter/writings/democ.htm (2007-08-02).

Purdy, N., Nye, P., Balakrishna, P. V. (2000) The impact of Communication Media on Negotiation Outcomes, in: International Journal of Conflict Management, 11 (2), 162-187.

Putnam, L. L. (1985) Bargaining as task and process: Multiple functions of interaction sequences, in: Sequences and pattern in communication behavior, Edward Arnold, 225-242.

Putnam, L. L., Roloff, M. E. (1992), Communication and Negotiation, Sage.

Putnam, R. D. (1993) The Prosperous Community: Social Capital and Public Life, in: The American Prospect, 4 (13), 11-18.

Rahwan, L., Sonenberg, L., Jennings, N. R., McBurney, P. (2007) STRATUM: A methodology for designing heutristic agent negotiation strategies, in: Applied Artificial Intelligence, 21 (10).

Raiffa, H. (1982) The Art and Science of Negotiation, Harvard University Press, Cambridge.

Raiffa, H., Richardson, J., Metcalfe, D. (2002) Negotiation Analysis - The Science and Art of Collaborative Decision Making, Belknap Press.

Rangaswamy, A., Shell, G.R. (1997) sing Computers to Realize Joint Gains in Negotiations: Toward an "Electronic Bargaining Table", in: Management Science, 43 (8), 1147-1163.

Raulet, G. (1987) Die neue Utopie. Die soziologische und philosophische Bedeutung der neuen Kommunikationstechnologien, in: Die Frage nach dem Subjekt, Suhrkamp, 283-316.

Rebstock, M., Thun, P. (2003) Interactive Multi-Attribute Electronic Negotiations in the Supply Chain: Design Issues and an Application Prototype, in: Proceedings of HICSS, 79.2.

Reimers, K. (2002) The Unit of Analysis in E-Commerce Studies, Discussion Paper, Tsinghua University, Beijing, available online: http://www.kai-raimers.net/Unit_of_Analysis.pdf (2007-08-02).

Reiser, A., Schoop, M. (2007) Analysing Strategy Patterns of Offer Communication in Electronic Negotiations, in: Proceedings of Group Decision and Negotiation, 279-292.

Reyes-Moro, A., Rodriguez-Aguilar, J. A., Lopez-Sanchez, M., Cerquides, J., Gutierrez-Magallanes, D. (2003) Embedding Decision Support in E-Sourcing Tools: Quotes, A Case Study, in: Group Decision and Negotiation, 12 (4), 347-355.

Riemer, K. (2004) Partner-Relationship-Management - Zur Rolle von Sozialkapital im Management zwischenbetrieblicher Kooperationen, PhD Thesis, University of Münster.

Risse, T. (2000) "Let's Argue!": Communicative Action in World Politics, in: International Organization, 54 (1), 1-39.

Riva, G., Galimberti, C. (1998) Computer-mediated communication: identity and social interaction in an electronic environment, in: Journal of Genetic, Social and General Psychology Monographs, 124, 434-464.

Robert, L., Dennis, A. R. (2005) Paradox of Richness - A Cognitive Model of Media Choice, in: IEEE Transactions on Professional Communication, 48, 10-21.

Rubin, H. J., Rubin, I. S. (1995) Qualitative Interviewing - The Art Of Hearing Data, Sage.

Salacuse, J. (2001) Renegotiating Existing Agreements: How to deal with Life Struggeling Against Form, in: Negotiation Journal, October.

Salacuse, J. W. (1998) Ten ways that culture affects negotiation style: Some survey results, in: Negotiation Journal, 14 (3), 221-240.

Sandholm, T. (1999) Automated Negotiation. The Best for All Concerned, in: Communications of the ACM, 42 (3), 84-85.

Sattler, H., Schrader, S., Luthje, C. (2003) Informal Cooperation in the US and Germany: Cooperative managerial capitalism vs. competitive managerial capitalism in interfirm information trading, in: International Business Review, 12 (3), 273-295.

Schatzman, L. (1991) Dimensional Analysis: Notes on an alternative approach to the grounding of theory in qualitative research, in: Social organization and social process, Aldine De Gruyter, 303-314.

Schoop M., Köhne, F., Staskiewicz, D., Ostertag, K., Kügler, J., von Vangerow, A., Weber, S. (2006a) Communication Quality in Electronic Negotiations, in: Proceedings of Group Decision and Negotiation.

Schoop, M. (2001) An Introduction to the Language-Action Perspective, in: ACM SIGGROUP Bulletin, 22, 3-8.

Schoop, M. (2002) Electronic Markets for Architects-The Architecture of Electronic Markets, in: Information Systems Frontiers, 4 (3), 285-302.

Schoop, M., Becks, A., Quix, C., Burwick, T., Engels, C., Jarke, M. (2002) Enhancing Decision and Negotiation Support in Enterprise Networks Through Semantic Web Technologies, in: Proceedings of XSW-2002, 161-167.

Schoop, M., Jertila, A., List, T. (2003) Negoisst: A Negotiation Support System for Electronic Business-to-Business Negotiations in E-Commerce, in: Data and Knowledge Engineering, 47 (3), 371-401.

Schoop, M., Köhne, F., Staskiewicz, D. (2006b) An Empirical Study on the Use of Communication Media in Electronic Negotiations, in: Proceedings of Group Decision and Negotiation.

Schoop, M., Köhne, F., Staskiewicz, D., Voeth, M., Herbst, U. (2007a) The antecedents of renegotiations in practice - an exploratory analysis, in: Journal of Group Decision and Negotiation, to appear, available online: http://www.springerlink.com/content/v750x67052q330u4/ (2007-08-02).

Schoop, M., Köszegi, S., Köhne, F., Ostertag, K. (2007b) Process Visualisation in electronic negotiations - an experimental exploration, in: Proceedings of Group Decision and Negotiation, 128-130.

Schoop, M., Quix, C. (2001) DOC.COM: Combining Document and Communication Management for Negotiation Support in Business-to-Business Electronic Commerce, in: Proceedings of HICSS.

Schreyögg, G. (2003) Organisation, Grundlagen moderner Organisationsgestaltung, 4th ed., Gabler.

Schülein, J.A., Reitze, S. (2002) Wissenschaftstheorie für Einsteiger, Facultas, Vienna.

Schütze, F. (1976) zur Hervorlockung und Analyse von Erzählungen thematisch relevanter Geschichten im Rahmen soziologischer Feldforschung, in: Kommunikative Sozialforschung, Fink, Munich, 159-260.

Schwab, A. (2003) Elektronische Verhandlungen in der Beschaffung, PhD Thesis, University of St. Gallen.

Searle, J. (1969) Speech Acts: An Essay in the Philosophy of Language, Cambridge University Press.

Sears, D. O. (1986) College Sophomores in the Laboratory: Influence of a Narrow Data Base on Social Psychology's View of Human Nature, in: Journal of Personality and Social Psychology, 51 (3), 515-530.

Shakun, M. (2005) Multi-bilateral Multi-issue E-Negotiation in E-commerce with a Tit-for-Tat Computer Agent, in: Journal of Group Decision and Negotiation, 14 (5), 383-392.

Shannon, E., Weaver, W. (1949) The mathematical theory of communication, University of Illinois Press.

Sheth, J. N., Sharma, A. (2004) Behavioral Approaches to Industrial Marketing, in: Handbuch Industriegütermarketing, 147-173.

Simon, H. (1957) Administrative Behavior - A Study of Decision-Making Processes in Administrative Organisation, Macmillan.

Smeltzer, L. R., Carr, A. S. (2003) Electronic reverse auctions - Promises, risks and conditions for success, in: Industrial Marketing Management, 32 (6), 481-488.

Smith, J. B., Barclay D. W. (1997) The Effects of Organizational Differences and Trust on the Effectiveness of Selling Partner Relationships, in: Journal of Marketing, 61, 3-21.

Stein, A., Hawking, P., Wyld, D. C. (2003) The 20% Solution?: A Case Study on the Efficacy of Reverse Auctions, in: Management Research News, 26 (5), 1-20.

Stern, L.W., El-Ansary, A. (1977) Marketing Channels, Prentice-Hall.

Strauss, A. (1959) Mirrors and Masks. The Search for Identity, Free Press of Glencoe.

Strauss, A. (1979) Negotiations: Varieties, Contexts, Processes and Social Order, Jossey Bass, San Francisco.

Strauss, A., Corbin J. (1990) Basics of Qualitative Research: Grounded Theory Procedures and Techniques, Sage.

Strauß, R. E. (2006) Strategischer Sparring-Partner versus Preisfokus!, in: Direkt Marketing, 10, 28.

Strecker, S., Seifert, S. (2004) Electronic Sourcing with multi-attribute auctions, in: Proceedings of HICCS 2004.

Ströbel, M. (2000a) Effects of Electronic Markets on Negotiation Processes, in: Proceedings of ECIS 2000, 445-452.

Ströbel, M. (2000b) On Auctions as the Negotiation Paradigm of Electronic Markets, in: Electronic Markets, 10 (1), 39-44.

Ströbel, M., Weinhardt, C. (2003) The Montreal Taxonomy for Electronic Negotiations, in: Group Decision and Negotiation, 12 (2), 143-164.

Subramanian, G., Zeckhauser, R. (2005) "Negotiauctions": Taking a Hybrid Approach to the Sale of High-Value Assets, in: Negotiation, February.

Suchman, L. (1987) Plans and Situated Actions, Cambridge University Press.

Swaab, R., Medvec, V. H., Diermeier, D. (2006) Communication Media and Negotiation Meta-Analysis: Meta-Analyzing Effects on Outcomes, Information Sharing, and Relationships, Working Paper, available online: http://www.kellogg.northwestern.edu/research/fordcenter/documents/research063006.pdf (2007-08-02).

Sycara, K. P. (1990) Persuasive Argumentation in Negotiation, in: Theory and Decision, 28 (3), 203-243.

Thiessen, E., Soberg, A. (2003) SmartSettle Described with the Montreal Taxonomy, in: Group Decision and Negotiation, 12, 165-170.

Thompson, L. (1990) Negotiation behavior and outcomes: Empirical evidence and theoretical issues, in: Psychological Bulletin, 108 (3), 515-532.

Thompson, L., Nadler, J. (2002) Negotiating Via Information Technology: Theory and Application, in: Journal of Social Issues, 58 (1), 109-124.

Toffler, A. (1980) Die Zukunftschance (Orig: The Third Wave), Bertelsmann Verlag.

Totz, C. (2005) Interaktionsorientierte Markenführung - Bedeutung internetbasierter Formen der Kundeninteraktion für die Markenführung, PhD Thesis, University of Münster.

Truschkat, I.; Kaiser, M.; Reinartz, V. (2005) Forschen nach Rezept? Anregungen zum praktischen Umgang mit der Grounded Theory in Qualifikationsarbeiten, in: Forum: Qualitative Social Research, May, 6 (2), available online: http://www.qualitative-research.net/fqs/ (2007-08-02).

Turel, O. (2006) Actor-partner Effects in E-Negotiation: Extending the Assessment Model of Internet Systems, in: Proceedings of Group Decision and Negotiation.

Turel, O., Yuan, Y. (2006) Trajectories for Driving the Diffusion of E-Negotiation Service Providers in Supply Chains: An Action Research Approach, in: Journal of Internet Commerce, 5 (4), 125-149.

Turner, D. B. (1992) Negotiator-Constituent Relationships, in: Communication and Negotiation, Sage, 233-249.

Turoff, M. (2006) Keynote Presentation - Future Opportunities for Group Decisions and Negotiations, in: Proceedings of Group Decision and Negotiation.

Uzzi, B. (1997) Social structure and competition in interfirm networks: The paradox of embeddedness, in: Administrative Scince Quarterly, 41, 35-67.

Valley, K. L., Thompson, L., Gibbons, R., Bazerman, M. H. (2002) How Communication Improves Efficiency in Bargaining Games, in: Games and Economic Behavior, 38, 127-155.

Van Boven, L., Thompson, L. (2003) A Look into the Mind of the Negotiator: Mental Models in Negotiation, in: Group Process and Intergroup Relations, 6 (4), 387-404.

Van Heck, E., Ribbers, P. (1998) Introducing electronic auction systems in the dutch flower industry - a comparison of two initiatives, in: Wirtschaftsinformatik, 40 (3), 223-231.

Vetschera, R., Kersten, G., Köszegi, S. (2003) User Assessment of Internet-Based Negotiation Support Systems: An Exploratory Study, available online: http://www.interneg.org/interneg/research/papers/2003/04 (2007-08-02).

Vickrey, W. (1961) Counterspeculation, auctions, and competitive sealed tenders, in: Journal of Finance, 16 (1), 8-37.

Voeth, M., Rabe, C. (2004) Preisverhandlungen, in: Backhaus, Voeth: Handbuch Industriegütermarketing, 1017-1037.

von Neumann, J., Morgenstern, O. (1944) Theory of games and economic behavior, Princeton University Press.

Walther, J. B. (1992) Interpersonal Effects in Computer-Mediated Interaction: A Relational Perspective, in: Communication Research, 19, 52-90.

Walther, J. B.; Bunz, U. (2005) The rules of Virtual Groups: Trust, Liking, and Performance in Computer-Mediated Communication, in: Journal of Communication, 55 (4), 828-846.

Wannenwetsch, H. (2006), Erfolgreiche Verhandlungsführung in Einkauf und Logistik, Springer.

Webster, F. E., Wind, Y. (1972) Organizational Buying Behaviour, Englewood Cliffs.

Weigand, H., Schoop, M., De Moor, A., Dignum, F. (2003) B2B Negotiation Support: The Need for a Communication Perspective, in: Group Decision and Negotiation, 12 (1), 3-29.

Weigand, J., TWS Partners (2004) Innovative Vergabeformen im strategischen Einkauf, Research Report, available online: http://www.tws-system.com/deutsch/konzepteundideen/publikationen/img/BA%20Innovative%20Vergabeformen.pdf (2007-08-02).

Westlund, H. (2006) Social Capital in the Knowledge Economy – Theory and Empirics, Springer.

Williamson, O. (1975) Markets and Hierarchies, Macmillan.

Williamson, Oliver (1985) The Economic Institutions of Capitalism, Macmillan.

Williamson, O. (2000) The New Institutional Economics: Taking Stock, Looking Ahead, in: Journal of Economic Literature, XXXVIII, 595-613.

Wilson, S. R. (1992) Face and Facework in Negotiation, in: Communication and Negotiation, 176-205.

Wilson, S. R., Putnam, L. L. (1990) Interaction goals in negotiation, in: Communication yearbook 13, 374-406.

Wolfe, R. J.; McGinn, K. L. (2005) Perceived Relative Power and its Influence on Negotiations, in: Journal of Group Decision and Negotiation, 14, 3-20.

Yates, J., Orlikowski, W. (1992) Genres of organizational communication: A structurational approach to studying communication and media, in: Academy of Management Review, 17, 299-326.

Yin, R. K. (1994) Case Study Research, Sage.

Yuan, Y., Rose, J. B., Archer, N. P. (1998) A Web-Based Negotiation Support System, in: Electronic Markets, 8 (3), 13-17.

Zhang, X., Lesser, V., Wagner, T. (2006) Integrative negotiation among agents situated in organizations, in: IEEE Transactions on Systems, Man and Cybernetics Part C, 36 (1), 19-30.

Zhao, R. R. (2006) Renegotiation-proof contract in repeated agency, in: Journal of Economic Theory, 131 (1), 263-281.

Zumpe, S., van der Heijden, H. (2006) Integrating variable user goals into user acceptance models, in: Proceedings of RSEEM, 78-84.

Abbreviation Reference

AI	Artificial Intelligence
ASP	Application Service Provider
AST	Adaptive Structuration Theory; see Poole and DeSanctis.
B2B	Business to Business Commerce
BME	Bundesverband Materialwirtschaft, Einkauf und Logistik e. V.
CMC	Computer Mediated Communication
CRM	Customer Relationship Management
CSCW	Computer Supported Cooperative Work
E-DIN	Group of official standards, Deutsches Institut für Normung e. V.
ENS	Electronic Negotiation Support, the set of E-Auction, negotiation agent and NSS approaches
eRfQ	Electronic Request for Quotation
FOTE	Fully Open Truthful Exchange; see Raiffa.
GAEB	Gemeinsamer Ausschuss Elektronik im Bauwesen
GDSS	Group Decision Support System
GSS	Group Support System
IS	Information System(s); also used to describe the respective research discipline.
IT	Information Technology
LAP	Language Action Perspective
MAS	Multi-Agent System
MRO	Maintenance, Repair and Operations
NIE	New Institutional Economics
NSS	Negotiation Support System, a special class of ENS system
ODR	online Dispute Resolution
OWL	Web Ontology Language; a W3C driven standard
POTE	Partially Open Truthful Exchange; see Raiffa.
PRM	Partner Relationship Management; see Riemer.
RfQ	Request for Quotation
SCM	Supply Chain Management
SOX	Sarbane Oxley Act
SRM	Supplier Relationship Management
TOM	Theory of Moves; see Brams.
VOB	Vergabe und Vertragsordnung für Bauleistungen
XML	Extensible Markup Language

Index of Data Excerpts and Data References

Index of Illustrations

Index of Tables

www.ingramcontent.com/pod-product-compliance
Lightning Source LLC
LaVergne TN
LVHW022306060326
832902LV00020B/3306